Critical Acclaim for
THE HEALING POWER OF FAITH

"Inspiring and rewarding... one of the most complete, impartial accounts of healing through faith ever written."
—Springfield (MO) *Sunday News and Leader*

"Marvelous... a gold mine of information and evidence."
—*The Pensacola News-Journal*

"Authentic, objective, timely, and interesting... a 'must' volume of any year."
—Daniel A. Poling, *Christian Herald*

"Most readers will find Will Oursler's facts as well as his faith in healing highly persuasive."
—*Saturday Review Syndicate*

"Wonderful evidence of faith at work in the life of man."
—Dr. Marcus Bach, Professor, School of Religion, University of Iowa

D1475418

ABOUT THE AUTHOR

Will Oursler was a versatile and prolific writer and has been called a renaissance man.

He started his writing career at Harvard as student correspondent for the Hearst papers in Boston. He graduated from Harvard *cum laude* in 1937. His first book was published by Simon and Schuster in 1941.

His literary career was interrupted by World War II. He went to the Pacific for three years, where he represented Fawcett Publications with a monthly column and articles in *True*, *Mechanix Illustrated* and *Motion Pictures*. He received commendations for meritorious service in the Southwest Pacific from General Douglas MacArthur and Secretary of the Navy James Forrestal.

After the war he served as vice-president of the Mystery Writers of America and later as president of the Overseas Press Club of America.

Among Will Oursler's books are *Father Flanagan of Boy's Town*, 1942, Doubleday (later the screenplay for the beloved film starring Spencer Tracy); *The Boy Scout Story*, 1955, Hawthorn Books; *The Road to Faith*, 1960, Rinehart; *Family Story*, 1963, Funk & Wagnalls; *The Atheist*, 1965, Paul S. Eriksson Inc.; *Hemingway and Jake* (with Jake Klime), 1972, Doubleday; *Explore Your Psychic World*, 1970, Harper & Row; *Lives Unlimited, Reincarnation East and West* (with Banerjee), 1974, Doubleday, and several popular mystery novels under the pseudonyms Gale Gallagher and Nick Marine.

The Will Oursler Manuscript Collection was established in the 1950s at Syracuse University and the remainder of his writings and memorabilia was donated to the collection in 1989.

Will Oursler died in 1985 after a long and distinguished career.

THE HEALING POWER OF FAITH

WILL OURSLER

BERKLEY BOOKS, NEW YORK

This Berkley Book contains the complete text of the original edition.
It has been completely reset in a typeface designed for easy reading
and was printed from new film.

THE HEALING POWER OF FAITH

A Berkley Book / published by arrangement with Westwood Publishing

PRINTING HISTORY
Hawthorn edition published 1957
Westwood edition published 1989
Berkley edition/August 1991

All rights reserved.
Copyright © 1989 by Westwood Publishing Company, Inc.
Original © 1957 by Hawthorn Books, Inc.
This book may not be reproduced in whole or in part, by mimeograph
or any other means, without permission. For information address:
Westwood Publishing Company, Inc.,
312 Riverdale Drive, Glendale, California 91204.

ISBN: 0-425-12854-7

A BERKLEY BOOK® TM 757,375
Berkley Books are published by The Berkley Publishing Group,
200 Madison Avenue, New York, New York 10016.
The name ''Berkley'' and the ''B'' logo are trademarks belonging to
Berkley Publishing Corporation.

*Introduction**
by Gil Boyne

Throughout America groups of people are meeting on a regular basis for the purpose of initiating healing! Millions across the nation view nonmedical healing as part of their lives. Some seek healing in churches and prayer meetings, while others take classes to learn spiritual healing methods.

Many middle-class Americans now adhere to a wide range of beliefs and practices not sanctioned by traditional medicine. These approaches include faith healing, Christian Science, psychic healing, meditation systems, American Indian healing and many others. Most adherents of spiritual healing use conventional health care as well, but they have very different ideas of what illness and healing really are. The values and theories of traditional medicine must now compete with many other concepts of illness, its causes and treatment.

Most adherents of spiritual healing are attracted by a larger belief system which provides an alternative explanation of the origins of illness and a theory of healing power.

Spiritual healing addresses the problem of suffering by placing the sick person's experience within a transcendental order. They make no distinctions between physical, emotional, social or spiritual troubles—all are relevant. The person's condition is transformed through prayer and ritual actions. This transformation involves creating a new meaning from the situation that caused the suffering. People who experience successful healing often report a sense of being enlarged and strengthened by the process.

*This is the Introduction to the Westwood Publishing Edition published in 1989.

Suffering is resolved or reduced by taking control in the face of problems, gaining insight into how change can occur and experiencing the support of empathic others and discovering how their lives and suffering are linked with something larger—variously interpreted as God, cosmic energy or Universal Mind.

Most groups spiritualize rather than medicalize the issue. In so doing, they challenge the medical model of healing by redefining the sources of illness and individual responsibility for it.

Spiritual healing systems stand in contrast to mainstream medicine and challenge it. They also propose new ways of experiencing the world and offer extensive transformations of physical and emotional life.

In all of the groups, healing rituals are prominent, and members engage in these rituals collectively yet also seek privately expressed ways to personal transformation. Health to them is the "idealized self" and "healing" is growth toward that ideal.

Healing is also aimed at restoring wholeness in the face of the fragmentation of everyday life in a highly specialized world.

"Health" is linked with a greater awareness of a core self with a powerful sense of connection to others and with the natural environment.

Such a transformation of self could have far-reaching consequences for the cultural, political and economic spheres in modern society. Spiritual health systems—and the new kinds of individualism they promote—undoubtedly are symptoms and symbols of profound changes in our society and in ourselves.

Will Oursler's survey of alternative treatment modalities remains a timely and powerful testament to modern America's embrace of The Healing Power of Faith.

To my mother
Rose Oursler
with gratitude and love

Contents

BOOK THREE: HEALING THE SOUL

APPENDICES

Preface

The exploring and writing of the material for this book has been a tremendous personal adventure.

I have written ten books under my own name—and many magazine articles. I have gathered material for stories in many parts of the world. Nothing that I have attempted before, however, has affected me as profoundly as this present work.

Covering wars and battles, the underworld, the international conspiracies of the world of narcotics—all of these, for me, pale in power and significance beside the unpredictable excitement of religion in action as I have had the opportunity of observing it at first hand.

Yet, as a reporter on the front lines tries to maintain objectivity in the midst of combat, I have tried also to hold the reporter's point of view through these investigations.

I have been permitted, as a journalist, to enter the laboratory of faith and to observe its mechanism in operation in moments of triumph and tragedy, tensions and perils, sudden death and sudden new-found life.

I have relied in most instances upon personal investigation and interviews and upon documented facts, the sources of which I have tried to indicate wherever possible. In cases where the evidence is weak or sketchy, I have pointed out that fact also.

If it is objected that, as a Christian who believes in God and prayer, I cannot be entirely unbiased, I can only answer that there are many Christians who believe in God and prayer but who do not believe in spiritual healing, or modern healing miracles of any kind.

If it is objected that I am opposed to doctors, I can only state that this is not true and that, with the exception of Christian Science, few religious healing movements oppose medicine in any way.

If it be argued that in citing this evidence I am giving people

1

false hope, I can only answer as a Christian Scientist practitioner said to a man who declared, "If you save my wife I will become a Christian Scientist."

The practitioner's reply was: "If Christian Science is not the truth, you do not want it, even if it heals her. If it is the truth, you want it, even if she is not healed."

For nearly two and a half years, I have delved into an enormous mass of material on this subject, extending back—it seems—to the dawn of time itself, and to every race and creed on earth.

Although not unaware of the many reported healing miracles in religions beyond the scope of this book, I have deliberately limited this work to investigation of healing falling within what is called the Christian-Judaic tradition.

In gathering the material I have interviewed scores of individuals and read hundreds of individual reports. I have talked to people who claimed to have been miraculously healed at the point of death—and to others who claim that such things are impossible. I have examined and studied reports for and against, weighed and analyzed and compared, questioned and cross-questioned.

Many of those to whom I talked did not wish their names used. Doctors practicing spiritual healing techniques prefer to do so without publicity. (I know of no physician, however, who employs these techniques without doing so in conjunction with full medical techniques.)

I am indebted to many sources. Above all, I wish to thank Weyman C. Huckabee and Wainwright House for their aid and cooperation; Rev. Mr. Mark Shedron, of the Department of Pastoral Services of the National Council of Churches; Rev. Dr. Otis Rice, and the Rev. Dr. John Ellis Large; the Religious News Service; the Rev. William Walsh, S.J., of the parish library of the Roman Catholic St. Ignatius Church in New York City; and the many other Protestant clergymen, Roman Catholic priests, and Jewish rabbis who gave time, effort and profound patience to help a layman understand.

I am indebted to many friends who helped, particularly to Kenneth Giniger, who aided both in suggestions and research, and to Spencer Valmy who also helped in gathering the mass of material and who was close to this book from its inception.

There are other individuals whom I would like to thank personally, but space does not permit. I know they are aware that my deepest appreciation goes to all who aided my efforts in drawing together the facts of this story.

—WILL OURSLER

BOOK ONE

Healing the Body

1

The Unknown Force

When the National Council of Churches a few years ago sent out a questionnaire on spiritual healing to a cross-section of clergymen in the United States, a number of replies contained a contradiction in terms: a pastor would assert that he had little or nothing to do with such cures—but would then describe seemingly miraculous healings within his own experience.

One response along these lines came from a Lutheran minister of a large eastern city:

"I cannot say that I have at any time *directly* resorted to spiritual healing except in the sense of directing the sick person's attention to the fact of God, and the relationship of man to Him in the way of faith. I want to cite two instances out of many in my experience where the fact of spiritual healing was a factor.

"I got a call from these folks asking me to visit their father, who had become very ill and very little hope was given of survival. I made the visit and followed the usual procedure of getting acquainted; learning the nature of his illness, having him express his feelings, etc., etc., then some quotations from the Word of God . . .

"In pronouncing the benediction, I always place my hand on the patient's head, always with the knowledge that it is not my blessing, but God's. I should mention that before the benediction I ask the patient to join me in praying the Lord's Prayer. During this prayer I hold the patient's hand in mine. Two days later the patient was well."

The pastor then went on to explain that six months later he received another call from the same people. "Their little girl was at the City Hospital Contagion Ward," he reported. "She had spinal meningitis. I was told that the doctors held very little hope for her recovery.

"I felt rather bewildered as I thought of ministering to a child of five. In speaking with the child I got no response. I took it that her throat was inflamed and so she found it difficult to speak. Try as I might, I got no response to my questions. I asked her to repeat 'Now I lay me down to sleep,' but no response.

"I became embarrassed as she may never have been taught the prayer. I tried to help her sense the presence of Jesus, the Friend of children. Then followed a simple prayer, the Lord's Prayer, and the Benediction. How relieved I was when I had said goodbye to hear the little girl recite the whole prayer, 'Now I lay me . . .'

"At our morning worship the next day I prayed a special prayer for her and asked my congregation to remember her in their daily prayers. The next day I was informed that the little girl would get well. A month later the parents came with their girl to a special service at which time they had the girl present a thank offering to one of our institutions.

"The father stated so many times to me after that, 'You worked a miracle.' I told him it was no miracle on my part, but the power of God."

What happened in these two cases, particularly that of the little girl with the often fatal disease of spinal meningitis? Was it a miracle, achieved through the power of God, as the minister stated?

Was it mere coincidence that in these two cases the patients happened to get well where others with similar illnesses died? Were the doctors wrong in their prognoses? Or was it the power of suggestion, hysteria, the will power of the patient or the drive to live that saved them?

There is no agreement in the answers to these questions. Able and well-informed leaders of religion, psychiatry, medicine and science, as well as experts in related fields, respond with different and conflicting replies.

There are doctors who say it was the work of God, and cite similar cases out of their own medical experience, where prayer and not medicine did the job.

Other doctors cite a variety of physical explanations, none of which include Divine intervention, and any one of which might—or might not—have been responsible.

There are ministers of all faiths, Roman Catholic and Protestant alike, who regard cases like that of the little girl as the direct intervention of God. Further, they insist that it is typical of what happens constantly in their own experience.

There are other ministers who state their belief that God works solely through His doctors and surgeons and psychiatrists and that most, if not all, "miraculous healings" in modern times have at their core mundane mechanisms associated with the human mind and human emotions.

Laymen likewise differ in their ideas about spiritual healing. There are believers and skeptics, and there are those who consider the whole thing a terrible deception and a fraud upon credulous and suffering people.

All informed persons in these groups would agree on one fact: since the end of the Second World War there has been a steadily increasing interest in religious healing, not only in Roman Catholic shrines and Christian Science, but also in all major Protestant faiths.

There are differences of opinion, however, as to precisely what we mean by spiritual healing. Professor Cyril Richardson of Union Theological Seminary defines it as "healing within a religious context, without medical, surgical, or psychiatric methods, and by means of spiritual disciplines."[1] Others state that it may occur along with medicine and surgery and psychiatry.

There is, in any event, evidence that the question of where and under what circumstances divine intervention occurs in healing may become one of the most significant scientific issues of our age.

Scientific postulates and time-tested theories are shifting their ground to meet new discoveries. Especially is this true in medicine. Psychosomatic medicine dealing with illnesses produced by the mind and emotions is still an infant science; one day it may sweep before it half of medicine as we know it. In her book *Mind and Body*, Dr. Flanders Dunbar asserts: "A physician with a scientific understanding of the psychosomatic approach can effect cures by medical methods which would have been considered miracles a generation ago."[2]

The effect of the emotions on sickness is a new and ever enlarging field involving both medicine and psychiatry. The strange

[1] Third Spiritual Healing Seminar, Rye, N. Y., Wainwright House Publications, 1955. p. 4.
[2] Dr. Flanders Dunbar, Mind and Body, Psychosomatic Medicine. New York: Random House, 1947. p. 95.

history of the ulcer is a good example. At the turn of the century, ulcers of the stomach were treated as organic—requiring chemical or surgical treatment, with some dietary ramifications. By mid-century, however, the ulcer had become a symbol: doctors and psychiatrists began to probe for its root causes not in the tissues but in mortgages and bills, business or personal ambitions and frustrations, wives and sweethearts, divorces and remarriages and alimony. The treatment for ulcers became more and more the treatment of ulcerating tensions in the patient's mind and psyche.

The discoveries of science, instead of leading man to ever-increasing reliance on materiality, actually seemed to be doing the reverse. So much so, that a book called *What Prayer Can Do*, prepared by the editors of *Guideposts*, points out a startling example of change in scientific theory. "Years ago, all sorts of smart people laughed . . . at the statement of Mrs. Mary Baker Eddy that matter did not exist: that it was an error of mortal mind. But only a few yesterdays ago man split the atom and discovered, indeed, that there is no such thing as matter; that energy is all."[3]

One may wonder if scientists in the future may also have to redefine their concept of energy and its attributes and effects.

The scientific attitude has never permitted medicine to deny that there was such a thing as "faith healing" nor the role of faith in all cures. "Faith is indeed one of the miracles of human nature which science is as ready to accept as it is to study its marvelous effects," the noted physician Sir William Osler wrote in an article on the power of faith, published in the *British Medical Journal* in 1910.[4] ". . . Faith has always been an essential factor in the practice of medicine. My experience has been that of the unconscious rather than the deliberate faith healer."

Sir William's article was written as a result of the unrest among many doctors of that day because of the growth of Christian Science and other paranormal healing groups. Sir William certainly did not accept Christian Science—in fact he called that religion's denial of the reality of disease and pain "a bit comic." But he did assent to the worth and importance of what he called in his article "mental healing," which he described "as a measure to be carefully and scientifically applied in suitable cases."

[3]The Editors of *Guideposts*, What Prayer Can Do, New York: Doubleday & Co., p. 18.

[4]Sir William Osler, "The Faith That Heals," *British Medical Journal*, Vol. 1, June 18, 1910. pp. 1470-1472.

Like many other physicians, then and later, Sir William was disturbed by the idea of supernatural healing. Yet he was too much a scientist to deny the reality of many cures in Christian Science and other religious movements of that day, particularly the Emmanuel healing movement in Boston, started by a group which included a doctor who was one of Sir William's good friends and former pupils.

The power of faith to heal he recognized in the great Roman Catholic shrines, the ancient healing temples and techniques of suggestion, the healing work of modern movements and new religious movements then developing in both Britain and America. "This is the status of the faith problem today," he said. "Not as a psychologist, but as an ordinary clinical physician concerned in making strong the weak in mind and body, the whole subject is of intense interest to me. A group of active, earnest, capable young men are at work on the problem, which is of their generation and for them to solve. The angel of Bethesda is at the pool—it behooves us to jump in!"[5]

Many doctors followed Sir William's advice. Some have come to employ prayer and religious healing as a part of their practice. To others the concept of God actively intervening to effect a healing is a disrupting idea which must be rejected, even after every other possible physical reason for the healing has been eliminated. Faced with evidence of cures of diseases through prayer and faith—healings of cancer, healings of tuberculosis, healings of broken limbs—these doctors cite the following possibilities: The diagnosis may have been wrong. Or the patient was really recovering when the doctors thought he was dying. The disease may not be cured but merely alleviated and will return. It may have been a spontaneous remission, as happens in many cases, particularly in cancer. Or possibly it was a spontaneous cure, effected by causes which cannot be isolated but which do not necessarily imply that "spiritual ministrations" or prayer were responsible. If healing is achieved through a combination of prayer plus medical prescriptions, some doctors believe it would be "dangerous" to give spiritual healing even partial credit.

Yet there is, at the same time, awareness by all men of medicine that the evidence must be examined with scientific objectivity. Some healings are too obviously valid and lasting to be cast aside.

---

[5] A pool in Jerusalem where the angel troubled the waters and healing was said to occur. (See John, V:2-4)

There have been too many reported, from too many ministers of too many denominations, to disregard the whole pattern. Moreover, some cures are of organic as well as functional illness. And some happen instantaneously, in mere minutes or hours. Records are available in many cases, with X-rays, statements of witnesses and hospital reports. Dismissing all of it as medical error, hypnotic suggestion or hysteria which will wear off, does not meet a scientific standard of objectivity. Psychosomatic medicine can explain some of the cures but not all.

In spite of areas of opposition, revival of interest in spiritual healing in our churches has, in fact, brought the two disciplines of medicine and religion closer together in many ways. One pastor who conducts weekly healing services attended by hundreds, many of whom claim extraordinary healings, told me: "I do not accept patients who refuse to go to the doctor. Medicine is an instrument of God and we must use it to its fullest measure. Prayer and the laying on of hands are instruments through which He also channels healing. And pastoral counseling is a healing method of God, too, helping to rid the patient of negative emotions, hate, resentment, envy, fear and guilt. All three forces together—medicine, pastoral counseling and prayer—is the way we work for healing of the whole individual, physical, mental and spiritual."

One expert, the Rev. Dr. Otis Rice, for years religious director of St. Luke's Hospital in New York City, told me that his experience indicates that there are various levels of healings: the purely physical healing of a physical ailment; the healing of a psychosomatic illness with medicine plus psychiatric and religious counseling; the healing of a functional disease by prayer where it is possible the prayer had a psychological and therapeutic effect of itself; and finally the miraculous healing, the rare case in which no other explanation can fit all the facts logically and honestly except the intervention of a superior force—the force we call God.

But Dr. Rice does not intend to use these distinctions as a roundabout route back to materiality. "The healing ministry is of no less importance than the spreading of the evangel," he wrote in a magazine article. "Salvation and health go hand in hand. Indeed, the root meaning of the two words is the same: the achieving of wholeness . . .

"All truth is from God. We therefore see His grace and His love in the therapies of the internist, the surgeon, or the psychiatrist, as well as in the ministrations of the faith healer or the sacred minister in their use of charisma[6] or sacraments for healing. . . .

"However, a too facile explanation of spiritual healing on the basis of psychosomatic medicine or psychological suggestion would seriously violate the truth and the experience of many centuries of healing which cannot be analyzed or justified on these grounds alone. There is in some persons and in some sacraments and sacramentals a power beyond the usual *modus operandi* of medicine and psychiatry which makes for healing."[7]

Louis Pasteur stated that "a little science estranges men from God; much science leads them back to Him." A modern corollary might be: A little religion widens the chasm between faith and science; much faith brings them together.

Before an assembly of the American Association for the Advancement of Science, a distinguished neurochemist, Dr. Albert H. Page, warned the scientists not to overlook the soul of man and its power as the guiding force in man's life and health and happiness.

"For the small part we play in the shaping of things to come," he said, "the neurochemist will pursue his science to the utmost, never forgetting that the dualism of body and soul may not be solved in material terms only, and that on its solution hangs the fate of society."

At every advance, pushing to new borders of knowledge, man seems to run into questions of the soul, of God and of forces not understandable in terms of present scientific information. It may well be that at some of these frontiers man can advance scientifically only with a complete revision of what we mean by scientific method. Deity may not lend Himself to outmoded laboratory techniques.

As a first step, what appears essential is an objective examination of what actually is happening in the field of religious healing, in the various denominations and creeds. The *why* may be a matter of surmise and belief and debate: the *what* is a matter of record. In some cases it is a record with full documentation; in others it is only an unsupported assertion.

There are many kinds of so-called religious healings, and many kinds of healers. There is healing through the ancient practice of

[6]Charisma refers to "special gifts" of a healer.
[7]Dr. Otis Rice, The Church and Spiritual Healing, *Pastoral Psychology*, Vol. 5, No. 44, May, 1954. p. 7.

the laying on of hands, through prayer and affirmation, through confession and communion, through the sacraments of all types. There are gifted individuals—the "charismatic healers"—who seem to have a special power to make men well; people said to be used by God as channels of healing. There are different methods of approach; some ministers prefer to work in private counseling sessions, others in public meetings.

One of the most difficult questions involves these individuals who seemingly have special gifts of healing in their touch or their words. I have interviewed a number of such persons and studied their case records with care. Some of their "cures" are of functional ailments, others of organic diseases. Some healings appear complete, others partial. Some are accomplished in conjunction with medical treatment, others without medical treatment of any type. Some insist they can take no profit for this work. Others take only enough to support themselves.

There does not appear to be any serious suggestion, from any quarter, that all of these healers and their claims are frauds. Attacks are leveled primarily at the kinds of illnesses healed and the *modus operandi* of the healing. There is general agreement among those who have investigated this question that some persons are more gifted in effecting cures than others. The "healing gift" is well known not only in terms of metaphysical healing, but equally among doctors, nurses and others concerned with the treatment of the sick.

Is it merely suggestion, or is there a force of healing? In my investigation, I talked with a man who claimed to have been cured of a usually fatal disease by a famous evangelist-healer whose touch, the man said, "was like an electric shock that went through my whole body."

It is important in understanding religious healing to explore the nature of this gift which some healers appear to have.

It is important to learn how and under what conditions healing occurs through the sacraments, through prayer, through unction, through the laying on of hands, through Novenas and Roman Catholic shrines—at Lourdes, St. Anne de Beaupré, St. Joseph's Oratory and others.

The kinds of cures claimed are not new. Similar cases have been reported across the centuries—back to the healing temples of an age long before the birth of Christ.

The trouble has been that healings in too many instances have been clouded in the fog of superstition and paganism, in sorcery and fakery. They have been clouded, too, in the battles between the church and medicine. Anesthesia, for example, was for a long time considered sinful and outrageous by religious leaders, as thwarting "God's will" that man should suffer the pain of the knife. This theological misinterpretation was recognized as an error and corrected by later church leaders. But the feuds between science and faith created rival camps, each claiming to hold the keys to the future, to truth and to healing, each setting forth its own results as proof of its efficacy.

In such an atmosphere and under such conditions of competition, the truth about spiritual healing became hard to find.

But science no longer is fighting for its life against the theologians, and religion has reached a state of co-existence with science. Religion is stronger than ever in the midst of modern scientific investigation openly able to probe, question and contest at any point.

In the crucible of today, old and new forces are combining to produce what may be an entirely different attitude and approach to the total healing of mind, body and soul. Yet it is only by understanding the old that we may recognize the new.

2

The Blind Who See

A city in the Middle East was the scene of a healing that aroused wide public discussion.

A healer assertedly had cured a man who had been blind from birth, one of the beggars of the streets. Some of the community insisted that the man had been born sightless because of some secret crime of his parents or grandparents—the sins of the fathers visited upon the offspring. According to reports, this healer placed spittle and clay on the blind man's eyes and told him to go wash it off. When he did this, the story went, he was suddenly able to see.

Rumors spread rapidly. According to one, when the healer passed the man, some of his followers had asked, "Who sinned in this instance, the blind man or his parents?" The healer replied that neither had sinned; the man was blind in order "that the works of God might be manifest in him." It was then that he began to mix the clay and spittle.

The cure produced prompt reaction from agnostics and atheists as well as from religious leaders. Some said this couldn't be the same man who once had been blind; others said it was the same one, but that he was lying about how he gained his sight.

A delegation of citizens went to the man's parents to question them. The parents somewhat reluctantly admitted that their son had been cured of blindness but beyond that they had no more information than anyone else.

Determined to pin down the facts, the delegation questioned the former beggar himself. They hinted that he must have been cured by someone working with dark forces. The beggar shook his head incredulously. He did not know who the healer was, or where he came from, yet the man had opened his eyes. Such a cure, he argued, was too miraculous to be the work of a man

15

alone; it had to be from God. "If this man were not of God," he declared, "he could do nothing."

Unable to shake the story, the frustrated investigators denounced him as a creature born "absolutely in sin" and ordered him banished from their sight.

Such are the recorded details of a spiritual cure that happened twenty centuries ago. The unknown healer was Jesus of Nazareth.

In Philadelphia, Pennsylvania, two thousand years after this incident, a group of thirty-five men and women knelt at a white marble altar in St. Stephen's Episcopal Church, a house of worship, built around 1800, on the spot where—tradition has it—Benjamin Franklin flew his kite to prove that lightning was electricity.

Like those at the altar, other men and women in the old-fashioned, square-box pews bowed their heads in silent prayer. Within the railing the towering figure of the minister in his white vestments moved from one kneeling figure to the next, placing his hands upon the head of each, praying to God to cure this man or woman or child, through the healing love of Jesus Christ.

A stark simplicity characterized the service. There was no music, no choir, no repetition of prayers. Each prayer offered by the minister for each individual at the altar was spontaneous and different from the others; each was an invocation for divine aid and an expression of gratitude for God's help.

The people and the service were like a group apart, cut off from the world just outside the doors—the trucks, taxis, shoppers and workers in the heart of Philadelphia's downtown business district, the men and women hurrying to homes and families in the late afternoon rush.

Among those at the altar was a young woman who had come into the church while on her way to a hospital. The business firm for which she worked in Watertown, Mass., had sent her to Philadelphia on a special assignment. While in Philadelphia she had been incapacitated by a fungus infection that developed in one leg, spreading from her ankle to her knee. The leg had become a mass of running sores. Her physician informed her that gangrene had developed. Consultation with other doctors confirmed the diagnosis. The condition required immediate treatment; amputation appeared almost certain.

"Alone in the city and panic-stricken," she later wrote to the Reverend Alfred Price of St. Stephen's, "I happened to see the sign in front of your church calling attention to the healing services. I was on my way at the time to Jefferson Hospital where the doctor had engaged a room for me.

"It was close to 5:30 P.M. And I entered St. Stephen's. I listened to your address on healing. Your words seemed to reach my inner consciousness and lead me to come forward in faith with the others to receive the laying on of hands. I cannot describe the feeling that came over me. I seemed to receive immediate healing. I walked away without the help of my cane. I continued my journey to the hospital and the next morning when the bandages were removed the surgeon noted with amazement the improved condition. In two days I was discharged from the hospital as completely cured."

In these two cases, separated by centuries, there are contrasts and similarities. There is the contrast of ancient and modern eras, the age of camel caravans and that of turbine jets; there is the contrast of medical and surgical knowledge then and now.[1] There is the similarity of the miraculous in each case, as reported; the apparent intervention of forces beyond the individuals involved, producing almost instantaneous change in the condition of each. There is the similarity also of skeptics and disbelievers and of honest questioners, on guard against charlatans and quackery.

Perhaps the most significant fact about the two cases is the persistence of spiritual healing itself, from the time of Christ and before, to our own day. That God does hear individual prayers, that His power can be brought into our personal lives to cure us of ailments, physical, mental, emotional, whatever they might be—the belief persists, as strongly in the present century as at any time in the past, accepted by many millions throughout the world, of many different faiths.

Belief in the miraculous, in the face of the advances of science and medicine, of exploded myths and superstitions, and the exposure of the many fraudulent healers who prey upon the credulity of misery, is in itself almost a miracle.

What is the substance of this faith? Is it only another aspect of superstition and wish fulfillment? Are the "facts" on which it rests a rubble of coincidence and half truths plus the wrong di-

---

[1] Spittle and clay were used frequently by physicians of ancient days in treatment of the eyes. Spittle was believed to have healing properties. Jesus, employing this method in a metaphysical cure, was making an obvious gesture of goodwill toward doctors.

agnosis, spontaneous remission, exaggeration and fraud?

Or are we drawing on healing forces beyond the borders of our material universe?

Belief in supernatural causes and cures for every evil has been a trait of mankind from his earliest groping for understanding. Primitive man finds his gods and devils in every facet of nature—in thunder and lightning, winds and waves and rocks and trees. In primitive societies, medicine and religion are almost inextricably combined in the awesome mask of the witch doctor, his herbs and his incantations.

Metaphysical healing in primitive culture consisted chiefly in tricks for getting rid of the devils. In one tribe, a devil-dancer was called in when someone was dangerously ill. By his dancing he was supposed to draw unto himself the demons of sickness, and then slip off somewhere and pretend to die. The demons, thus fooled, would leave, and the devil-dancer would go back and claim his fee—if the patient happened to live. "Transference" of an evil or a demon from an individual to some other individual, or to an animal or object or tree, was regarded, and still is in many tribes, as a standard aspect of medical treatment. To protect himself from demons of sickness, man wore special charms, bracelets and amulets. When he suffered misfortune or became seriously ill, he tried to see on whom or what he could shift his trouble.

Some of these ancient supernatural "remedies" persist down to modern times. Frazer, in *The Golden Bough*, tells of a Flemish method of curing the ague, in which the afflicted individual goes out in the early morning to an old willow tree, ties one of its branches in three knots and says, "Good-morrow, Old One, I give thee the cold; good-morrow, Old One."[2] Then he must turn and run off without looking back.

In the advance of civilization from primitive ideas, two divergent lines developed in supernaturalism. On one side was the purely magical; sorcerers, astrologers, diviners, readers of palms and animal-livers. On the other was a developing religious awareness concerned with the individual and his relationship to a single divine force called God.

Most early civilizations explained disease, pain and trouble in terms of many gods; some brought disease and some took it away.

[2]Sir James George Frazer, The Golden Bough. New York: The Macmillan Company, 1940. p. 546.

The Egyptians had a whole gallery of deities. One was a cat-headed goddess named Bubastic who, when properly propitiated, gave fertility to women. Another was Ibis to whom one prayed when suffering from indigestion. Babylonians had Uragal, Namtor and Nergal, gods of pestilence; but they had also the powerful Marduk, who took away sickness. In the religion of Zoroastrianism of ancient Persia, all illness, like all other evil, was believed to have come from the god of darkness, Ahriman, and healing could be achieved only through a caste of sacred magicians that sprang up in one of the Median tribes and became tremendously powerful. Only a few were allowed into this caste, but once initiated, the priest-magician—Magus—became a "Conqueror of Evil," authorized to practice medicine and perform the mysterious rites by which disease and pain were banished.[3]

Priest-physicians in neighboring Babylonia employed a technique of incanting the names of the demons to a patient until he came to one which obviously agitated the patient; the priest then concentrated his efforts on driving out this particular devil.

Out of this melange of superstition, magic, fantasy and fraud, and a growing religious understanding, came both the dawn of medicine and the beginning of a more spiritual approach to metaphysical healing in the pagan world. The outstanding example of this "spiritual paganism" is found in the great Hellenic god of healing, Asklepios, also known as Aesculapius, whose followers and temples of healing of the pre-Christian era were found throughout the Mediterranean world of the pre-Christian era. In many of the temples were tablets telling the stories of healings which had occurred after prayers to this powerful god of health.

The legends which sprang up around this god also reflected the ambivalent attitude of the people of that time, the mixture of folklore and faith. Asklepios was considered both human and divine. As a human he was called a man of science, with a vast knowledge of herbs and healing; as a god he was reported to have restored to life Greek heroes slain in battle. According to earliest legends, this healing deity was the son of Apollo and Coronis, a lovely goddess who resided in northern Greece and whose name meant "The Crow Woman." After her affair with Apollo, Coronis married a man named Iachys, and Apollo became so angry when he heard about the wedding that he sent his twin sister, Artemis,

[3]From them developed the generic use of the word "Magi" for "wise men."

to slay Coronis with her arrows. However, Apollo grew remorseful about his son Asklepios, rescued him and brought him to a centaur named Chiron who reared the young god and taught him to heal the sick and injured.

Later, this mythology underwent changes; it was said that Coronis came to Epidaurus—where afterwards a great temple was erected to the god—and left her new-born son on the side of a mountain where he was found and reared by a goat herdsman. Because of a radiance around the child, people said that when this boy grew up he would have great powers.

The roots of such legends reach far back into prehistory in Asia Minor, although some authorities believe that the Hellenic god of healing originated in a magician named Imhotep, a conjurer who performed for the Egyptian Pharaohs three thousand years before Christ. Whatever strands of magic and myth and religion merged in Asklepios, his influence reached spectacular heights in the centuries preceding the Christian era. Hundreds of temples were built in his honor. The greatest of these, at Epidaurus, dates back to before the fifth century, B.C., was rebuilt in the fourth century, B.C., and was famed for its miraculous cures. On the walls of this beautiful temple, excavated in 1881, the names of men and women who came here and were cured by the god are inscribed on clay tablets, with details of the diseases from which they suffered.

In the healing rituals at Epidaurus and other temples of Asklepios, the practice of "incubation" was followed, in which the patient remained overnight or longer in the temple; it was thought that the god came to the afflicted in visions and dreams during the night and cured them. That persons actually were healed can hardly be doubted in view of the many detailed inscriptions of gratitude found in temples to this deity. That a large part of the healing was due to the great faith people of that day put in this god cannot be questioned. Much of it also may have been due to the tradition of healing which developed around the temples and the name of Asklepios. Some of the healing was due to the use of primitive medicine by temple priests, to hypnotic suggestion, and even to elemental forms of psychotherapy. Some historians refer to the temples as the first examples of what we know today as a general hospital.

The patient who came to Epidaurus, however, went through a remarkable "intake" procedure. He was first given a summary of people who had been healed of diseases similar to his own. Then he was given a conducted tour of the temple—the miraculous cures which had occurred in this corner or that were described and the tablets on the wall were read and explained, all in a hushed aura of mystery and sanctity.

As night spread over the Grecian skies, the patient was dressed in fresh white robes and placed on a couch in the temple. He was told by the priest that the god would come while the patient slept and would heal. As darkness came the priests extinguished the lamps. In the quiet of night, in this temple set in the midst of Hellenic hills, the priest offered up prayers. In the morning, as the sun spilled through the columns of the temple, the priest loosed harmless yellow snakes to glide across the patient; the spirit of the god was said to live in these snakes. The priests also talked with the patient, and suggested medicines and herbs. In many instances, particularly in cases of the blind, the patients were anointed with sacred ointment.

The records tell us nothing about the percentage of failures, the permanency of cures, or the psychological effect upon those who remained uncured at these temples. Those who were healed, however, were said to have been filled with religious joy and to have left offerings to Asklepios, frequently in the gifts of money for the upkeep of the temple.

Asklepios—called Aesculapius in Latin—was brought to Rome in 296 B.C., at the urging of the sacred oracles, to eradicate a terrible pestilence. According to tradition, a messenger was sent to bring back one of the sacred serpents from Greece. As the vessel with the snake came up the Tiber, the serpent slithered off the boat and onto an island in the river. A temple to the god was built on this island. Many inscriptions and gifts of gratitude have been found here. One included a silver model of a tumor below which was the inscription, "To Aesculapius, the great god, the savior and benefactor, saved by thy hands from a tumor of the spleen . . ." It was signed "Neochares Iulianus, Freedman of the Imperial Household."[4]

Temples and altars to this god of healing have been found throughout the Roman empire, even in Britain where a carved altar to Aesculapius, and his daughter Hygia, was found in Chester.

But dedication of the river island—Isola Tiberina—to the healing of the sick has persisted throughout the Christian era, even to

[4]Walter Addison Jayne, The Healing Gods of Ancient Civilizations, New Haven: Yale University Press, 1925. p. 470.

our own day. In the year 1000 A.D., on the site of the temple ruins, a hospital was built. This hospital—now called San Bartolomeo—has continued to operate for nearly one thousand years.

While the popularity of Asklepios spread in the pagan world, among the Hebrews a different attitude—one involving their basic monotheistic morality—was in process of unfoldment.

Although miracles and miracle-workers are recorded throughout the Old Testament, there are few actual spiritual healings. One of the most important recorded is that of the Syrian military chieftain, Naaman, a victim of leprosy, healed by Elisha, who told him to go and wash seven times in the Jordan "and thy flesh shall come again to thee, and thou shall be clean." Naaman was at first angered at this suggested method of cure, demanding to know why the Jordan had any more curative power than the rivers in his own country, Syria. He did as Elisha commanded, however, and he was cured. Filled with gratitude he offered riches to the prophet. Elisha refused any payment.

Elisha's servant Gehazi ran after Naaman and received from him two talents and expensive raiment, but when he returned, Elisha angrily asked, "Is it a time to receive money, and to receive garments, and oliveyards, and vineyards, and sheep, and oxen and manservants and maidservants?"

The prophet then declared, "The leprosy therefore of Naaman shall cleave unto thee, and unto thy seed . . ."[5]

For the average man in normal circumstances, emerging Judaic thought took a rather practical position in regard to sickness and suffering. Job was the average good man and his suffering, as his comforter says, must come from hidden evils and sins. Health was a favor from God, sickness a result of man's sin. But man could pray, and God could hear his prayer, the more progressive leaders agreed.

Even before the Grecian Hippocrates launched medicine as a pure science divorced from religion, in the fifth century before Christ, many among the Hebrews held physicians in high honor. Since healing of any kind came only from God, they said, the earthly physician was doing the work of the Lord and must therefore be greatly esteemed. The Lord made medicines and sweet waters and apothecaries that man might be healed.

"My son, in thy sickness be not negligent, but pray unto the

[5]II Kings V:1-27.

Lord, and He will make thee whole," declares the practical philosopher-teacher of Ecclesiasticus. "Leave off from sin, and order thine hands aright, and cleanse thy heart from all wickedness."[6] A few verses later, comes the second half of the prescription: "Then give place to the physician, for the Lord had created him: let him not go from thee for thou hast need of him. There is a time when in their hands is good success. For they shall also pray unto the Lord, that he would prosper that which they give for ease and remedy to prolong life." But the next verse adds, with what appears to be a touch of ancient humor, "He that sinneth before His Maker, let him fall into the hands of the physician."[7]

Among a minority of the rigidly orthodox rabbinate, particularly in the era of the earlier prophets, even this middle-of-the-road position regarding medicine was apparently untenable. Since disease was God's will, the extremists held, any act of healing was impiety, whether by rabbi or physician.

At the same time, the Mosaic laws—as revealed in the Torah and the oral tradition—contained many regulations regarding health and hygiene and disease prevention.

It was in this land of confused and contradictory ideas, while Pharisees and Sadducees debated their interpretation of the laws and Roman occupation forces patrolled Palestinian towns, that an obscure but momentous event occurred: an infant was born in a stable.

Among the gifts Christ brought to man is the concept of God in terms of divine, compassionate love—a love that can have no part of sickness or pain. Jesus declared that he came not only to forgive sin but to heal the sick, to cleanse lepers, to alleviate suffering. It was—and remains—a dazzling new outlook.

Ancient concepts of a God of vengeance and punishment and pain are swept aside; the good news Jesus brings is a message of joy; illness and suffering are part of the progeny of sin, they are not from God. The illogicality of a God who punishes the individual by making him sick, but allows him to engage a physician to make him well, thereby thwarting the punishment, finds no place in the new religion.

The healing miracles of Christ's ministry bear out this message. He does not heal merely the pious, the rich, the poor, the good

[6]Ecclesiasticus XXXVIII:9-10.
[7]*Ibid*. XXXVIII:15.

or the bad. He heals all types of men, in all conditions—the centurion's son, the maniac of Gerasene, the woman bound by her infirmity for eighteen years, the possessed, the innocent, the epileptic. He does not chide or scold, refuse or demand; He heals.

"And the people, when they knew it, followed him," declares St. Luke. "And he received them, and spake unto them of the kingdom of God, and healed them that had need of healing."[8]

The scope of the healings of Jesus is one of the most significant facts of the gospel record. He healed all kinds of people, at all hours of the day, on weekdays and the Sabbath. In His healings, He employed a variety of methods: He healed by touch; by anoint-ment; with mud and spittle; by casting out devils; by a suggestion or word, or by simple command, as when he ordered the paralytic of Capernaum, "Arise; and take up thy bed, and go thy way unto thine house";[9] by prayers; and by the faith of the individual.

"Go thy way," He says. "Thy faith had made thee whole."[10]

He states repeatedly that he has come not to violate but to uphold the laws of God. In proof of this he cites two laws from the ancient Hebraic code as revealed in the work of Deuteronomy: "Thou shalt love the Lord thy God with all thy heart, and with all thy soul, and with all thy mind. This is the first and great command-ment. And the second is like unto it, Thou shalt love thy neighbor as thyself. On these two commandments hang all the law and all the prophets."[11]

He makes unequivocally clear that the kingdom of God of which He speaks is a kingdom of law, and at the heart of that law is love, the love of the individual for God and his fellow-man, the love of God for His children. The healing of the sick, the de-mented, the pain-ridden, the so-called incurable—even the raising of the dead—does not involve the abrogation of the rules but rather the application of this higher law. In God's love, as revealed through His Son, all things are possible.

This is the message Jesus brought. And He told His apostles to do likewise. He commanded them to go forth and heal the sick, cleanse the lepers, and preach the kingdom of God, in the light of His teachings and demonstrations.

Belief in the miraculous healings of Jesus Christ, in His teach-

---

[8]Luke IX:11.
[9]Mark II:11.
[10]Mark X:52.
[11]Matthew XXII:37-40.

ings regarding the healing power of faith, lies at the core of the creed adhered to by tens of millions of human beings throughout the modern Christian world.

Through the centuries, however, the emphasis in Christianity shifted from healing to other aspects of Christian faith. While spiritual healing did go on—and there were shrines and sacred places and relics with assertedly curative powers—much of this was mixed with superstition, exaggerated stories and pagan ideas grafted into Christian practice. Sacred methods of healing that continued included prayer and Holy Communion, anointing with oil and with water, and the touching of a sacred object, the bone of a saint, a piece of clothing from the catacombs.

There were in the early church a number of healers of apparent great power, among them St. Francis of Assisi and St. John of Neverly, who lived around 700 A.D. There was St. Martin, Bishop of Tours in the fourth century, and Gregory, who became Bishop of Tours two centuries later and devoted his life to healing the sick at the shrine of St. Martin. Wrote Gregory of one healing, "A certain man named Theodomundus, whose organs of speech and hearing were blocked, came to the sacred basilica and came back every day to bow himself in prayer. But he only moved his lips, for he was unable to produce a word of sense, since he was bereft of the use of his voice. He was seen to pray so fervently that often men saw him weep amid his unspoken words. If anyone for the sake of profit had given him alms, he immediately passed them on to beggars like himself, and asking by a nod for coins from others, he gave money to the needy. And when he stayed in this holy place for a space of three years with such devotion, on a certain day he was warned by divine piety and came before the sacred altar. As he stood with his eyes and hands raised to Heaven there burst from his mouth a stream of blood and corruption. And spewing on the ground, he began to groan heavily and to cough up matter mixed with blood in such a way that it might be thought that somebody was cutting his throat with a knife.

"The corruption hung from his mouth like a bloody thread. Then with the bonds of his ears and his jaw broken, he raised himself up and again lifting his eyes and hands to Heaven, he poured forth from his bloody mouth these first words, 'I return great thanks to you, blessed master, Martin, because opening my mouth you have caused me after so long a time to offer words in your praise.' Then all the people in wonder and amazement at such a great miracle asked him if he had recovered his hearing likewise. He replied before all the people that he heard everything freely . . ."[12]

Along with shrines and relics and prayers of the devout seeking healing from God, there was also widespread ignorance, belief in magic and elves and fairies, soothsayers, astrology and other pseudosciences throughout the Middle Ages. Medicine was practiced largely by monks who usually combined medicine and prayer, and often left records of extraordinary healings. Secular physicians existed, but lived in constant peril in an age of absolute power and ruthlessness; the surgeon was held personally responsible if the patient died. For failing to effect a cure, doctors and surgeons in several recorded instances paid with their own lives at the hands of outraged local rulers. Monks, however, backed by the authority of the church, could not be tried in secular courts and therefore could carry on healing without fear of being tortured to death if their patients succumbed.

In this bewildered medievalism, devout religious faith, pagan superstition and the practice of medicine became inextricably intertwined. Curative powers were attributed by learned and ignorant alike to gold and silver and precious stones, to human feces, urine, menstrual blood, powders ground from human bones. Elaborate rituals for exorcising devils were practiced, particularly as a means of stopping hemorrhages. The prayers of the exorcism were said to be most effective when written on bits of paper or carved on precious stones and worn or carried on the person as an amulet. The wearing of "healing rings"—also called "cramp rings"—was widespread. Nuns in some instances were not permitted to wear rings set with precious stones, except in cases of illness.

During the early centuries of the Middle Ages, the practice of "church sleep" developed—a form of incubation taken over from the pagan practice of sleeping in the temples of Asklepios. Churches were equipped with couches and mattresses, often placed between the altar and the grave of the saint of that particular church. Priests were constantly on duty with the patients. After prolonged prayers the patient slept and either thought or dreamed that the saint touched him, or informed him of what medicine would make him well. Legends arose concerning miraculous healings achieved during "church sleep."

[12]Gregory of Tours, *Selections from the Minor Works*, trans. by William C. McDermott, Philadelphia: University of Pennsylvania Press, 1949. p. 39.

Hundreds of afflicted came to the healing shrines for this practice, and buildings had to be erected beside the shrines and churches to provide shelter for pilgrims. Many who received cures found that only when they remained at or near the shrine did the cures remain permanent.

With the Renaissance and the Reformation came the fresh winds of new ideas, new knowledge, new approaches. Galileo, Copernicus and other men of science were making important discoveries about the universe, in spite of the disapproval their findings aroused in official church circles. Luther and Calvin and their followers denounced the worship of saints and insisted that spiritual healing could be found not in relics but in prayer to God and through Holy Scripture. At least one healing by prayer is ascribed to Luther: when his associate Melanchthon lay ill and close to death, Luther, after prayer, enjoined him, "Give no place to the spirit of sorrow, and be not your own murderer, but trust in the Lord..." Melanchthon reportedly recovered within the next forty-eight hours.

Luther believed and taught that many illnesses are caused by negative forces emanating from anxiety, sorrow, guilt, fear, hate and lust, while therapeutic value is found in the positive spiritual force of love and forgiveness.

Across the centuries, new ideas warred with old: science with religion; superstition with fact; medicine with magic; new discoveries, explorations and inventions with tattered myths.

There were still healers and shrines, in both Roman Catholic and Protestant churches, and in secular circles the "faith healer" could also be found. There were always those who appeared to be "gifted" with the healing touch, often against their own desires.

At the same time, the schism between intellectuals and religionists widened, and nowhere more than in the area of healing. At the start of the nineteenth century, rationalism and the scientific approach centered on so-called "natural" man and appeals to the "supernatural" became in disrepute among most of the intellectual leaders of the age. A surging, unleashed naturalism roared its way into twentieth century materialistic cant, into the cynicism of the 1920s with its lack of faith either in its religion, its vices, or in life itself.

Except at some of the Roman Catholic shrines, and in certain Protestant faiths such as Christian Science, concern with the subject of supernatural healing had faded.

We sloughed ahead through turmoil and violence and terror and death. The bombs became bigger and the toll mounted. Then came the super-killer, the megaton atom bomb. Mankind had not only unleashed a new killer, he had crossed a new frontier.

It is significant that the return of interest in spiritual healing began in the years immediately after this discovery. In the dawn of this new day, we turned to a reawakened concern not with mass murder but with how to make men whole.

After Christ had healed the blind man with spittle and clay, He spoke with a group of Pharisees gathered around Him. "For judgment I am come into this world, that they which see not might see; and that they which see might be made blind."

The Pharisees, greatly puzzled, demanded, "Are we blind also?"

Aware how a Pharisee liked to split the hairs of meaning, He answered, "If ye were blind, you should have no sin; but now ye say, We see; therefore your sin remaineth."[13]

His words have meaning for today. But they must be examined closely and understood, in the light of our own times.

[13]John IX:39-41.

3

Many Mansions

Spiritual healing is not and has never been a technique reserved exclusively to the temple, the church or the sacred shrine. It is primarily a relationship between the individual and God as that individual is able to perceive and accept Him. Religious healing practice goes on in many places and under conditions about which the public may hear little.

An eight-year-old little child lay close to death, in a modern hospital. The youngster was unconscious, paralyzed from the neck down, the brain struck by a deadly infection. In the fourth day of high fever, the child was having frequent convulsions. Four pediatricians concurred with staff physicians at the hospital: medically they could do no more. The chances of survival were infinitesimal; if the child lived, they asserted, it would be completely paralyzed and in all likelihood imbecilic.

The mother asked her minister in the local Presbyterian church to pray. She asked Roman Catholic sisters to pray, and personal friends also. She talked with the hospital chaplain, and together they prayed. There was no improvement in the condition of the child.

The hospital chaplain had heard of a woman who reportedly had achieved some remarkable results through spiritual healing. She was Mrs. Agnes Sanford, the wife of an Episcopalian minister, the Reverend Edgar Sanford. In Whitinsville, Massachusetts, Mrs. Sanford and her husband have established a research and educational center for spiritual healing, with the full approval of the Episcopal diocese of Western Massachusetts. Clergymen from all parts of the United States and Canada come here to study techniques employed in religious cures.

The chaplain reached Mrs. Sanford by long-distance telephone and told her the situation. Mrs. Sanford agreed to employ intercessionary prayer for this child, but said also: "You have a man who knows much about spiritual healing right in your own town. He is also a medical physician. Why don't you call him, too?"

She gave the physician's name. A doctor of high standing, he is also a man with deep religious convictions and belief in religiously oriented techniques. In response to the chaplain's call, he agreed to come at once to the hospital. When he arrived the child was having a convulsion. The doctor told the nurse he was there at the request of the mother, and that she needn't pay attention to anything he did, but just to go ahead with her orders as she had them; that he was doing something entirely different.

The physician placed his hands upon the patient and began to pray. The child went to sleep. The convulsions stopped.

The physician remained at the bedside with his hands upon the child for another ten minutes. Relaxed and even breathing continued as in normal sleep. There were no further convulsions.

The youngster was still sleeping peacefully when the physician left the hospital some minutes later. The following morning, while consciousness had not returned, there were signs of movement. The doctor continued the laying on of hands and prayer.

Step by step as he prayed, recovery continued. Within three weeks the patient was allowed to go to his home for convalescent care.

Periodically attacks of agitation returned and the physician would come, use prayer techniques, and the agitation would pass.

By Christmas the child was completely recovered, had all his mental faculties and complete use of limbs and body and no residual disabilities. Ten years later the physician was able to report that there were no recurring symptoms of this nearly fatal case of what doctors had called encephalomyelitis.

The healing of this little child might be explained in many ways. It could be called coincidence; the patient was going to get better anyway, with or without the physician and his prayers. Or the other doctors were merely wrong or overly pessimistic in stating that the child had little chance to live, or would be paralyzed and imbecilic if by any chance the illness did not prove fatal.

Objectively, one of the most significant aspects of the case is the fact that it is typical of literally thousands reported from all parts of America and the world. A youth is cured of cancer by a prayer group in San Francisco, when the doctors had given him a month to live. A woman called an incurable cripple claims to be healed instantly at Brother André's St. Joseph's Oratory, a Roman Catholic healing shrine in Montreal. A child with arthritis is cured in a regular healing service at the Church of the Heavenly Rest on New York's Fifth Avenue.

One interesting part of this mid-century revival of the healing ministry is that most leading figures in the revival are realistic, responsible men and women of integrity, intellect, and faith. There are doctors, psychiatrists and physicists. Others are pastors and priests. Others are laymen seemingly gifted with special power and using it in the service of God.

The causes of the revival are complex. The world had come through an era of storm and shifting ideas. In the midst of his own home-spun evils, man groped for God. Churches long empty began suddenly to fill. Bibles were opened. The message of Christ ceased to be something vaguely recalled and began to take on immediate meaning.

Along with this were important developments in psychosomatic medicine, the treatment of illness traceable directly to the mind, illness brought on by the unconscious as a solution to environmental or personal problems, or because with sickness the patient obtained attention not otherwise possible, or because persons had to punish themselves for imaginary or real guilt. The power of the mind to produce symptoms and chemical changes, even to the point of manufacturing welts and bruises, began to be recognized by physicians. They were learning now to ferret out and remove deep-rooted causes for symptoms which a century before were inexplicable to the physician and two centuries earlier would probably have been called the mark of the devil.

New concepts and discoveries regarding the mind's influence on illness and physical symptoms severely jolted traditional medicine. Physicians had made unprecedented advances in the chemistry of healing; miracle drugs, serums and antibiotics had outmoded old techniques. Medicine was triumphant as never before. But the psychiatrists, the doctors, and the public were learning that chemistry was not the whole story.

In one of its greatest periods of triumph, medicine found itself also in a time of great uncertainty. In spite of all the "wonder drugs" at the doctors' command, healing could no longer be discussed entirely in terms of what was written on a prescription pad. It concerned not merely body or mind or emotions, but the total individual, his relationship to himself, his environment, his universe.

At a time when medical science appeared in complete ascendancy, millions of human beings, particularly those for whom medicine had failed, were turning to healing through faith.

The religions to which they turned, and the gifted charismatic healers, presented a divergence in patterns of belief and procedures and claims.

Some of what was happening in the various denominations reached back over centuries; some of it was as new as the latest findings of pyschiatry.

In Roman Catholicism, religious healing had been practiced from earliest times. In modern years the fame of Catholic shrines—in France and Portugal and Canada particularly—had become worldwide. Pilgrims to Lourdes, to the Shrine of Our Lady of Fatima, to St. Anne de Beaupré in Canada, and others, come from every nation and every faith—Catholic and Protestant and Jew, Hindu and Buddhist, agnostic and atheist.

But in contrast to the long-discarded idea of some early church zealots who denounced all medicine—and who in some cases had closed down medical schools and denounced surgery and the study of anatomy—modern Roman Catholicism holds that the individual must first exhaust whatever medical aid is available to him before he seeks the intercession of the saints.

To Lourdes many physicians have gone to examine and study the case records carefully kept there by the board of medical doctors, to talk to the patients, to witness the baths in the pool—and the results. One American physician, who has made a number of visits to this shrine, told me that it was the "atmosphere of love" which drew him back, an atmosphere like nothing he had ever experienced before.

"There is a medicine of love at work in that place," this doctor said. "The love of priests who pray, of nurses who come with the sick and dying, of the healed who voluntarily stay in gratitude to work with the sick. And it is true that even where the waters of Lourdes may not result in physical healing, they do work upon the mind and the spirit. And this is another kind of miracle we must learn to understand."

What do men mean when they speak of a "healing miracle"? There is no single answer. At Lourdes, the strictest rules of science apply. Doctors in the *Bureau des Constatations Medicales,* which tests all claims of cures, refuse to certify anything as a miracle except a cure of an organic disease. The organic nature of the illness must be established by irrefutable and documented medical proof. The cure must continue for at least a year without regression, and it must be inexplicable *by any other means except divine intercession*. The result of this strict interpretation is that actual "accepted" miracles at Lourdes number far less than one-tenth of one per cent of those supplicants who come to bathe in its icy waters.

Not all Roman Catholic shrines exert the same care as Lourdes in "checking" on healings. But the evidence available of cures is extensive. Whether these are "divine miracles" or not is another question.

Healings are said to occur at Lourdes and other shrines that do not fit the "miracle" category technically but cannot be disregarded as meaningless in the story of spiritual healing. To grasp what spiritual healing implies at these shrines, we must examine the full scope of healing claims. Only then can any acceptable pattern begin to be clear.

Part of the problem of piecing together this pattern arises from the need of examining healings not in one church or shrine or faith but in many churches and shrines, and many faiths. The reporter can show no special favor, however. We examine first, in ensuing chapters, the healings at Roman Catholic shrines, because Roman Catholicism has had shrines and the healing tradition during many centuries, and has carried this tradition across the medieval era into the religious currents of modern times.

Equally significant in this pattern, however, and equally to be examined in fullest detail is the story of healing within Protestant churches of all denominations.

Although they are all part of the same emerging pattern, each church and faith presents its individual motif in the design.

Our theologies and beliefs and modes of reaching out to Infinite Love are a many-colored cloak.

At the Church of the Heavenly Rest in New York City, a new minister was appointed in 1952, the Rev. Dr. John Ellis Large. He was one of those who approached spiritual healing with some distrust. To this preacher, it smacked of superstition and the wishful building of false hopes at best, and charlatanism and destruction of faith at worst. He did not believe that the sawdust trail had a place in the Episcopal approach to religious life.

But his new parish had held healing services once a week under the former minister, and had a tradition of healing for nearly a

quarter of a century. When Dr. Large blandly announced that
healing services would be discontinued because he himself was
in no sense a healer, he had not anticipated a revolt of the faithful.
There were telephone calls and postcards of protest, and personal
visits from parishioners. Vestrymen reported that the church was
in a state of turmoil and something would have to be done quickly.
"You have no right to halt these services," the pastor was told
by one thoroughly outraged member of his flock. "It is *our* service.
You are here to conduct it for us; not to throw it away."

"But I do not heal."

"Neither did the last minister. He never said he did. He said
God healed."

Dr. Large was greatly disturbed. He was too honest to dismiss
his own doubts and too sincerely religious not to be aware also
that healing was a vital part of the Christian message. He asked
his congregation for a little time.

He used this reprieve to examine the problem carefully. Out of
a mass of material which he covered, he came to a solution:
whether he was or was not gifted with a power did not matter.
Some are born with a healing gift, he decided, some achieve it,
and some have it thrust upon them. Healing was possible and often
obtained, according to the records and information of his own and
other churches, through the sacraments, Communion, anointing,
and the laying on of hands.

A few weeks after his arrival, the new pastor announced from
the pulpit that the following Thursday healing services would be
reinstated, employing the sacramental approach.

As the sick and the troubled came to the altar, he had no idea
what might result. All he knew was that he was turning it over to
God.

To his surprise, cures began to be reported almost from the first
service. "I felt a power that came to me, from the congregation
itself," Dr. Large told me. "It seemed to me that it flowed to me
from them and back from me to them. And that was when I began
to get reports that people had been healed. The letters continue to
come in. There are all kinds of cases, the crippled, the chronically
ill, the arthritic, the mentally lost."

What happened in this church was in a measure what has been
happening throughout the Protestant Church itself in the period
following World War II. Throughout all the major Protestant
faiths, particularly in England and the United States, a resurgence
of the "ministry of healing," often with parishioners themselves

taking the lead, was building spiritual fires under a hesitant and over-cautious Protestant priesthood.

One contribution in the Protestant revival is the concept of healing as a total thing employing all available instruments of healing provided—minister, doctor, psychiatrist, and psychologist. Writing in the *Manchester Guardian* in August, 1955, Anglican Canon Roger Lloyd declared that the healing ministry had been "doubly reborn" in the past half-century.

"It has come again through the new medical knowledge of drugs and right treatment, and this is no doubt one part of the truth into which the Holy Spirit promised to lead us. But it has come more directly than that through the constant intervention of God to make whole so many of those whose state of disease had defeated every measure of medical science. The weight of evidence is quite overwhelming. . . ."

The clergyman's role, the Canon pointed out, is often that of a "creative synthesis" holding together various agencies taking part in the healing—doctors, nurses, relatives and friends who are praying. "It is when they work together to dispense their different forms of the healing of God that miracles start taking place . . ."

Throughout the Episcopal church in America, and the Church of England, healing returned; similarly in the Methodist Church, the Congregationalist and the Presbyterian—particularly, in the latter case, in Scotland. Ministers who once had scoffed at the idea were now returning to reexamine and reappraise the Church's role in this field. The National Council of Churches sent out its questionnaires to Protestant ministers; replies indicated that thousands of clergymen could cite cures of diseases both functional and organic in character. In California, the Fellowship of St. Luke, a national Protestant healing order of ministers and laymen, was helping to effect the "restoration of the Apostolic Practice of Healing as taught and demonstrated by the Lord Jesus."

The growth of Christian Science, and of other healing movements, continued to accelerate in the United States. Christian Science, in less than a century, had grown from an obscure cult of individuals looked upon as crackpots into a world religion with hundreds of thousands of adherents.

There were many who gave Christian Science the credit for having launched the healing revival. Declared one Baptist minister: "We may not go along with all of their ideas, but who can deny that they blazed the trail in our own time—back to what Christ was preaching?"

Churches of all kinds, and their ministers and priests, have accepted the new challenge of spiritual healing with mixed feelings and attitudes.

A return to one of the most vital actions of the early Christian church—healing—presented a provocative vista which lay before the entire Christian world.

Writing in *Presbyterian Life* in December, 1955, the Reverend W. Paul Monteath, Church of Scotland minister of Glasgow, told the story of a lady whom he called Miss Ann, a member of his congregation who had been in critical condition with what physicians called pleurisy. She was healed, the pastor reported, after he prayed with her at her bedside.

Until this healing case, the minister had never thought of himself in the role of healer. Following that experience, he began to search for answers to a series of questions. "Had I, by means of an impulsive action, touched some spring in Miss Ann's mind? Had her prayers really been answered? Would it not be more reasonable to give the credit of recovery entirely to the doctor's treatment? On second thought I wondered whether all these factors might be necessary and complementary to ensure Miss Ann's restoration to health."

Such an introduction to the subject of spiritual healing, the Scottish pastor added in his report, "must be typical of the experience of many ministers in the Church of Scotland today. Up and down the land a surprising number of men are quietly and unobtrusively but actively engaged in investigating healing through prayer, with or without the laying on of hands. Others are giving intense study to the subject but have not yet begun to practice. Still others are making an approach through psychology, emphasizing the spiritual factor in therapy and its relation to psychosomatic medicine, a field which modern doctors are exploring."

The Church of Scotland began, in 1954, an official study of spiritual healing, with a commission of clergymen and laymen and physicians participating. A similar study was conducted by the Church of England.

In 1956 in Holland, one spiritual healer rose to such heights that she shook the stability of the Dutch throne. Margaretha Greet Hofmans—a gray-haired woman whom many consider a truly gifted, even saintly, creature—was denounced because of her influence over Queen Juliana of the Netherlands.

Greet Hofmans, after achieving a reputation as a healer throughout Holland, came into the royal circle because the Queen's fourth child, her daughter Marijke, was born blind in one eye, said to have been caused by a case of measles the Queen suffered during pregnancy.

For almost a decade, beginning in 1948, the healer had a strong effect on the royal family. Prince Bernhard, at first not unfriendly, became convinced that she had built a clique of her own in the palace. Their daughter was no better. But the Queen seemed to listen to the white-haired woman even more than she did to her most reliable ministers.

The story eventually was reported in the press and became a worldwide *cause célèbre*. Juliana reluctantly surrendered to pressure and dismissed the healer from the court itself, along with several of the Queen's own inner circle who had become too close to the healer who had almost toppled a crown. Even so, she lived close to the court and there were reports that the Queen continued to visit her.

In the United States, a series of seminars on spiritual healing— with leaders from the medical profession, psychiatry and psychology, nursing, the ministry and the lay public participating— was held at Wainwright House in Rye, New York. Participating were men and women of many fields—healers, doctors, psychiatrists, nurses and laymen.

American Lutheran magazine, speaking for millions of Lutheran faith, revealed the ambivalent point of view held by many church authorities. In its September, 1955, issue, one article declared: "It is noteworthy that, when the Church is most active in the healing ministry, its Gospel message has the greatest vitality, and, when the Church loses interest in the health of its members, its message loses much of its interest too. Right now, it may be said, the Church stands at a most important cross-road, and will have to make some far-reaching decisions in these matters in the near future."[1]

But editorially, in the same issue, the magazine declared, "Lutherans acknowledge and worship the Spirit who bestows gifts of

---

[1] Lee G. Egloff, "Faith and Healing," *American Lutheran*, Vol. XXXVIII, No. 9, September, 1955. p. 15.

healing upon His own. They also remember the injunction of St. John, 'Beloved, believe not every spirit, but try the spirits whether they are of God: because many false prophets are gone out into the world.' "[2]

[2] I John IV:1.

4

A Man Without Faith

In the summer of 1956, a man who did not believe in God at all went to the shrine at Lourdes to seek healing for a paralytic condition in his right side, the result of a fall from a ladder.

At Lourdes he encountered a ten-year-old blind boy who had great faith in God.

One was cured, according to the facts available, and the other was not.

The dramatic case of Louis Olivari, former French Communist leader of a Red cell in Nice, involved a cast of three main characters: the Communist Olivari; his wife, who was a Roman Catholic; and the boy who was blind.

Olivari did not believe in Lourdes, or the Catholic Church, or in miracles, or the intercession of saints. He was a Marxist. Religion was a narcotic for subjugating the masses; belief in the supernatural was superstition.

When his wife first urged him to go to Lourdes, he thought she was joking. When she kept at him and he saw that she was in earnest he told her, "Why should I waste my time going there? The doctors have done all they could." He could still work as an electrician. She could be grateful for that much.

But his wife refused to be quiet. Her nagging at last reached a point where the half-paralyzed husband cried out, as other husbands have before, "All right—if only to keep you silent—I'll go there."

At Lourdes, like thousands of petitioners, he allowed himself to be taken to the grotto where Bernadette Soubrious saw her vision of The Lady of Lourdes, and he bathed in the icy mountain waters. Even at this usually traumatic moment, his belief was so slight that he did not bother to pray, but rather was curious about what was going on around him, with an objective, reportorial interest.

Beside him was the ten-year-old boy who was blind. The boy was making his fifth pilgrimage to the grotto. As the Communist started to plunge into the water, the boy, hearing the splash, said, "Pray." And the boy's own lips began to move in prayer.

Seeing and hearing this boy, Olivari was deeply moved. As the icy water went over him, he cried out, "God, if You exist, cure this boy who deserves it more than I do."

As he uttered these words, Olivari said afterwards, he felt faint. He had to be dragged from the water. When he was placed on the ground he stood shivering for an instant. Then he moved his right leg. He could walk.

The *Bureau des Constatations Medicales* at Lourdes did not certify it as a miracle. It had to be determined first that this paralysis was caused by a proven organic injury and not a neuro-muscular disorder. It had to be established also that the cure was permanent and not due to hysteria. The processing of a miracle at Lourdes is long and painstakingly thorough.

But to Olivari the miracle was real and neither the rigorous requirements of the Lourdes medical board nor the glib derision of his political associates could change his mind. In the light of his spiritual awakening, he announced that he was abandoning Communism for the warmer road of faith in God. He announced also that he would never forget that this new insight had been brought to him by the blind boy who told him to pray.

While not a confirmed miracle by the Lourdes rules, this case attracted world attention because it involved a figure of a political movement whose fundamental principles denied God's power.

Why was the non-believing Communist cured—and the boy of faith overlooked?

All of our sentiment would be with the child. But it is clear, too, that spiritual truth and power, while built out of the mortar of love, is by no means of a sentimental nature; it is a vigorous and overpowering force.

Some Catholic authorities believe that Olivari, in his moment of being born again, when he made his prayer of intercession on behalf of the boy, attained a spiritual power capable of achieving the healing; while the boy, for reasons we do not comprehend, still groped for this spiritual force.

Perhaps. But none can say with any positiveness why cures occur at Lourdes, or fail to occur. There are cures without faith, and thousands with seemingly deep faith go home unhealed.

Yet the miracles that do occur—the certified miracles which have withstood stringent tests of validity—are among the most impressive phenomena of supernatural cures.

A man named John Traynor, a native of Liverpool, England, and a Roman Catholic, was wounded in World War I. In combat as part of the Naval Brigade of the Royal British Marines, he was struck in the head by shrapnel in the Antwerp expedition in 1914. He was unconscious for three weeks in the hospital but recovered. Later he fought in the Dardenelles, and was wounded by machine-gun bullets in the head and chest. One bullet lodged under the collar bone, paralyzing his right arm. The muscles of this arm eventually atrophied. His legs were also paralyzed. He developed epileptic fits.

In 1916, he underwent four operations in an effort to connect the severed arteries of his arm. All were unsuccessful. In 1920, in an effort to relieve the epileptic seizures, he underwent a brain operation to remove the shrapnel. This also failed to improve his condition.

In 1922, he learned that the Liverpool diocese of the Roman Catholic Church was organizing a pilgrimage to Lourdes. Traynor decided to go along. A physician informed him that the trip would be "suicide." His friends entreated him not to go. Only his wife encouraged him. To help meet expenses of the journey she sold pieces of her jewelry.

Three times the directors of the pilgrimage were so concerned over Traynor's condition that they urged him to leave the train and go to a hospital. Traynor refused. At Lourdes, he was taken at once to Asile, the hospital where the pilgrims most in need are treated. During the six days he remained there, he suffered two hemorrhages and several epileptic fits. But each day he was taken to the grotto and was bathed nine times. In addition he attended all ceremonies for the sick—even though his stretcher bearers told physicians and priests they were fearful he might die on the way.

Three days after his arrival, while bathing in the waters of Lourdes, his legs became suddenly agitated. He tried to stand, but his stretcher bearers restrained him, fearing this was another fit. They dressed him and took him to a place near the grotto, called Rosary Square, for the ceremony of the Blessing of the Sick.

Traynor later told his own story to Father Patrick O'Connor: "The procession came winding its way back as usual, to the church and at the end walked the Archbishop of Rheims, carrying the

Blessed Sacrament. He blessed the two ahead of me, came to me, made the Sign of the Cross with the monstrance and moved on to the next. He had just passed by, when I realized that a great change had taken place in me. My right arm, which had been dead since 1915, was violently agitated. I burst its bandages and blessed myself . . . for the first time in years.

"I had no sudden pain that I can recall and certainly had no vision. I simply realized that something momentous had happened. I attempted to rise from my stretcher, but the *brancardiers* (stretcher bearers) were watching me. I suppose I had a bad name for my obstinacy. They held me down, and a doctor or a nurse gave me a hypo. Apparently they thought I was hysterical and about to create a scene. Immediately after the final Benediction, they rushed me back to the Asile. I told them I could walk and proved it by taking seven steps. I was very tired and in pain. They put me back to bed and gave me another hypo after awhile.

"They had me in a small ward on the ground floor. As I was such a troublesome case, they stationed *brancardiers* in relays to watch me and keep me from doing anything foolish. Late that night, they placed a *brancardier* on guard outside the door of the ward. There were two other sick men in the room, including one who was blind."[1]

The effect of the hypodermic began to wear off in the night, but the man still had no knowledge that he had been cured. He lay awake most of the night, however, in the darkness.

"The chimes of the big Basilica rang the hours and half-hours as usual through the night, playing the air of the Lourdes Ave Maria. Early in the morning, I heard them ringing, and it seemed to me that I fell to sleep at the beginning of the Ave. It could have been a matter of only a few seconds, but at the last stroke I opened my eyes and jumped out of bed. First, I knelt on the floor to finish the rosary I had been saying. Then I dashed for the door, pushed aside the two *brancardiers*, and ran out into the passage and the open air. Previously, I had been watching the *brancardiers* and planning to evade them. I may say that I had not walked since 1915, and my weight was down to 112 pounds.

"Dr. Marley was outside the door. When he saw the man over whom he had been watching during the pilgrimage, and whose death he had expected, push two *brancardiers* aside and run out

[1]Don Sharkey, After Bernadette, Milwaukee: The Bruce Publishing Co., 1945. p. 143.

of the ward, he fell back in amazement. Out in the open now, I ran toward the grotto, which is about two or three hundred yards from the Asile. This stretch of ground was graveled then, not paved, and I was barefoot. I ran the whole way to the grotto without getting the least mark or cut on my bare feet. The *brancardiers* were running after me, but they could not catch up with me. When they reached the grotto, there I was on my knees, still in my night clothes, praying to Our Lady and thanking her. All I knew was that I should thank her, and the grotto was the place to do it. The *brancardiers* stood back, afraid to touch me."[2]

So stunned was he by what had happened that this man did not grasp the facts of his healing fully until he was en route back to Liverpool, traveling on the train with the archbishop of that city. The archbishop asked him if he realized how sick he had been, and that he had been cured by the Blessed Virgin.

As the archbishop asked this question, the memory came back to Traynor of all that had been suddenly blotted out in the emotionalism of his experience at Lourdes. The memory of years of illness, of the suffering of his journey to Lourdes and how ill he had been at Lourdes itself. "I began to cry," he told Father O'Connor later. "And the archbishop began to cry, and we sat there, crying like two children."[3]

The case of John Traynor is one of the accepted miracles of Lourdes. It is one of many equally dramatic cases. But, as already noted, only a small percentage of those who come to the grotto of this world-famed shrine receive physical cures. Of the nearly two million who visit Lourdes annually, approximately one per cent are seeking cures for physical ailments. Of that one per cent, approximately two hundred to three hundred receive cures of some kind. Of those claimed cures, only a handful, sometimes as few as two or three, will be certified as true miraculous cures.

But what of the effect on the many—the great majority, in fact—who come out of the icy mountain waters without physical healing in any instance? There is no easy answer to this. There are many severe critics of Lourdes, including Dr. Leslie Weatherhead who, in his book, *Religion, Psychology and Healing*, describes a trip in a train full of uncured pilgrims returning to their homes, many to almost certain death, lying on their cots with wordless despair in their eyes. But many who emerge from the

[2]*Ibid.* p. 144.
[3]*Ibid.* p. 146.

waters insist that they find new peace, new acceptance of God's will for them.

One of the most famous cases of this kind is that of Fred Snite, the American who was stricken with polio in 1936 and forced to live thereafter in an iron lung. His determination to live fully and happily in spite of his paralysis, including marriage and raising a family, won him millions of friends. In 1939, still in the iron lung, he went to Lourdes. The good wishes and prayers of the world went with him.

For ten days he remained at the shrine. In his diary he wrote: "Life here at Lourdes is so wonderful, such a series of unending thrills that I find it difficult to record my reactions. Everyone is happy, happy because they are in a place apart from the world, a place seemingly halfway to heaven. Here there is no talk of war, of politics, of business; life here is a prayer . . ."

In another entry he wrote, "Early this afternoon I had another new experience—a bath in the famous Lourdes water. In that I had to leave the respirator during the bath, I was quite nervous and excited. Everything went smoothly, however, and I was soon glad that I had decided to do it. The water was very cold, but I did not mind it. There was some kind of happiness in connection with it which I am unable to analyze, therefore unable to record."

The day before he left Lourdes, he wrote, "And so tomorrow is Saturday—the ninth day of our stay and Sunday the last day. I have not in any way given up or lost hope. I am praying very, very fervently, and if nothing happens, as I have so often said before, God certainly knows what is best for Him and for me, and for the world in general."[4]

Snite's close friend and spiritual advisor, Father James J. Walsh of Miami Beach, was quoted as saying, "Fred had a good faith, of course, before he went to Lourdes. He had already reached a degree of resignation. But as he used to point out, he never before had the deep well of peace that was his the day he came out of the water. . . . In later years, he had the depth of resignation to tell me more than once that if God gave him the choice of getting well or staying in the lung, he would stay put."[5]

Although he continued to live a prisoner of the iron lung until his death a decade and a half later, he never changed his attitude.

[4] *Ibid.* pp. 153-154.
[5] Leonard C. Hawkins and Milton Lomask, *The Man in the Iron Lung.* New York: Doubleday and Co., 1956. p. 141.

* * *

The Shrine of Lourdes and its story is known all over the world. The story is of a fourteen-year-old French peasant girl named Bernadette Soubrious, a not-too-bright child who, preparing for her confirmation, saw a vision in the grotto of a great rock in Lourdes—a rock they called Massabielle. She, her sister and another girl were gathering wood. The other two girls had gone on and she had remained by the grotto when she saw her first vision of Our Lady of Lourdes, who was standing in a niche in the shadows of this rock—a beautiful lady in a white gown with a blue girdle and a rosary of pearls.

That was February 11, 1858. Rarely has the story of a place of miracles been so fully and carefully documented, step by step. Here was the little French girl, on her knees before her vision in the grotto. And here were her sister and her schoolmate, watching, incredulous and disbelieving, yet full of awe. Massabielle is high and dark and frightening. Before the great rock is a brook and beyond the brook runs a little river, the Gave, an icy mountain fed torrent. Bernadette did not know why she saw the lady, who the lady was, what the lady wanted. But to the simple Bernadette this was a most beautiful creature, a being of love.

None in the community knew what to make of the story. Church leaders were aloof from these goings on. Civil authorities were alarmed but unsure of what action to take. Each day the growing crowds gathered at the grotto to watch Bernadette kneeling before a vision they could not see. The lady had instructed Bernadette to "do her the grace" of coming to the grotto for fifteen days

without fail. At first Bernadette's parents sought to forbid her; then they surrendered to the girl's obvious need to go there. When authorities questioned Bernadette, asked her who the lady was, and if she claimed it was the Blessed Virgin, Bernadette's reply was only that she was the lady.

On February 25, during one of her visits to the grotto, Bernadette received from the lady of her vision an order: "Go to the spring and drink and wash yourself."

There was no spring at Massabielle. The crowd of worshippers who watched this child did not hear any words or commands or see any vision. They saw a girl in simple dress running back and forth like a crazed creature, turning first to the brook and then toward the River Gave, but neither of these was correct and the lady of the vision so indicated. "Go to the spring and drink and wash yourself,'' the lady repeated. ''Go eat of the plants you will find there.''

They saw her now go to a patch of earth and herbs, and pull some of these herbs from the earth and eat. They saw her put some of the moist earth into her mouth. Then she became sick and vomited. And watchers said Bernadette was mad; the visions were madness.

When Bernadette told them about the spring the lady had told her to drink from and wash in, they pointed out that there was no spring. Still there were those who believed. A one-eyed stone worker named Louis Bouriette went to the grotto and removed a bagful of earth from the spot where Bernadette had scraped with her hands. He placed this earth upon his eye that could barely see light from shadow. When he removed the earth, he was startled by dazzling light. Although the light faded, his vision was obviously improved, and the following day he went again to the grotto for earth and saw a crowd of women standing around the spot.

''We were praying here,'' they said, ''when the stream of water began to run from the place where she dug.''

Bouriette continued to come to the spring and his sight continued to improve.

From that moment, there was no halting the story. All over France people were talking about it. Civil authorities who tried to board up the grotto and prevent Bernadette's visits there backed down before the multitudes who came there. After nineteen visions, Bernadette announced simply that the lady would come no more. But she had given instructions that a chapel was to be built at the Massabielle, and that ''processions come there.''

One of the first miracle healings of Lourdes involved a two-year-old child who had been paralyzed from birth, had suffered from rickets and had had frequent convulsions. At the point of death, he was carried by his distraught mother to the grotto. She dipped the infant into the icy waters of the spring. Others praying in the grotto cried out that she was killing the child by placing him up to his neck in the chilling water. She told them the child was dying in any case; this was her only hope. In the hush that followed, there was a small cry from the infant who only an instant before had been unconscious and probably in the throes of death.

The woman took the child home. He slept quietly through the night. The following day he took nourishment. The day after— for the first time in his life—he was able to sit up. Within the week, he was outside and playing, entirely cured of the paralysis which doctors had diagnosed as complete paralysis of both legs due to meningitis or poliomyelitis.

The "processions" the lady had commanded began to come— the sick and crippled and dying—to the waters of Lourdes.

There were some reports that the waters contained special minerals of therapeutic quality. But tests disclosed that the waters contained no material therapeutic agents whatsoever. It was ordinary mountain-spring water, harmless to drink, without any special chemical qualities.

Civil and church authorities, anxious to avoid open battle with the devout worshippers who thronged here, appointed a commission of scientific, medical and church authorities to investigate and report. The commission examined a number of cases of alleged cures, and found that at least fifteen of them fell into the area of the miraculous. These were fully documented cases of organic disease healed at Lourdes after physicians had given up. The records were studied with great care, to minimize the possibility that there had been wrong diagnoses. The commission's report, after exhaustive investigation, declared that there were cures at Lourdes which defied any normal explanation and must be considered supernatural. Physicians, scientists and clergy concurred.

From all over the world, gifts poured in, pennies and dollars— in some case, vast sums. Buildings and hospitals and places of worship—a whole new community of faith—began to take form around the craggy shadows of Massabielle.

Of the early cases, before the establishment of the *Bureau des Constatations Medicales* in 1882, the most remarkable and one of the most fully documented miraculous cures was that of a Belgian, Pierre de Rudder. On February 16, 1867, helping woodcutters on the estate of the Viscount de Bus, De Rudder, forty-four years old, had a tree fall on him. Both bones of his lower left leg were fractured. A physician reduced the fracture and put on a splint.

After several weeks, De Rudder was in unendurable pain. The splint was removed. He was found to have a large ulcer on the back of his foot. The fracture itself had not healed and appeared to be badly infected. Physicians removed a fragment of bone. All consulting physicians on this case agreed that the fracture would not heal and that amputation was inevitable. Despite his condition, De Rudder refused to allow them to amputate. A year later, he forced himself to leave his bed and walk on crutches, dragging his leg. His condition grew worse. In 1874, seven years after the accident, a Dr. van Hoestenberghe of Stahille reported after examining this man: "De Rudder had a wound on the upper part of the leg; at the bottom of the open wound could be seen the two ends of bones about an inch apart. There was not the slightest appearance of cicatrization [growth of scar tissue preceding healing] . . . The lower part of the leg could be turned in any direction . . . The heel could be lifted so as practically to fold the leg in half. The foot could be twisted until the heel was in front. . . ."

On April 7, 1875, with the blessing but skepticism of the owner of the estate on which the accident occurred, De Rudder and his wife boarded a train for Lourdes. Part of the trip to the grotto was made by bus. The driver protested angrily that blood and infectious matter seeping through the bandages of De Rudder's leg had stained the floor.

At the grotto, he limped to the waters, and stepped in.

Almost instantly, he was aware that something had happened— something was happening.

He lifted himself out of the waters and he stood up and he walked without crutches or any other physical support. He stopped and deliberately knelt down and then lifted himself again. All of the terrible swelling was gone from the leg and foot. The bones which had been separated by almost an inch were joined. The bleeding had stopped and the infectious matter was gone.

The man who had not walked without crutches for years walked with a steady step past the rows of pilgrims and threw himself down befor the statue of Our Lady of Lourdes. "I am on my knees, O God," he is reported to have cried out.

A full medical examination showed that the wounds had healed, the bones knitted and the two legs outwardly appeared to be normal and the same size.

For twenty-three years thereafter De Rudder lived a normal life, without any signs of being crippled. He died of pneumonia at the age of seventy-five.

Dr. van Hoestenberghe—who examined this man seven years after the accident and was one of the physicians who had called the fracture incurable and recommended amputation—obtained permission to examine De Rudder's body after death. Although the examination showed minor indications of the effects of the accident, it revealed that between the broken bones new bone tissue had apparently grown. It was whiter than the rest.

A Man Without Faith

Dr. van Hoestenberghe stated that this new bone could not be explained on natural grounds. The Medical Bureau stated that it could be explained only as an instantaneous miracle. Dr. E. LeBec said in his book, *Medical Proof Of the Miraculous*,[6] that one of the principal signs of intervention is the rapidity or instantaneousness of the healing. "Time is an absolute necessity for the progress of physiological processes and where it is lacking," LeBec wrote, "when anatomical structures are evolved without it, the progress of events *cannot* be natural."

Dr. LeBec, in fact, as head of the Medical Bureau at Lourdes, established three main conditions for classification of a "miraculous healing" at the Shrine. In generalized terms, these conditions require that there be a proven organic condition, a broken limb, a tumor, tuberculosis confirmed by X-ray, a blood condition, or other positively organic and identified ailment. Second, that cicatrization or some form of cure must occur either instantaneously or within a span of time too short for normal healing process to occur. Third, permanency.

Thousands of skeptics come to Lourdes. They leave with varying impressions. Some remain unchanged. Some who come as doubters throw away their disbelief as others do their crutches. One of the most extraordinary was the noted surgeon and Nobel Prize winner, Dr. Alexis Carrel, who came to Lourdes with a kindly skepticism and vast curiosity.

It was in the early years of this century. One of the men he met and talked with was a psychiatrist, Dr. Smiley Blanton, later author of *Love or Perish* and close associate of Dr. Norman Vincent Peale. Dr. Blanton was startled at Dr. Carrel's open agnosticism about Lourdes. Had Dr. Carrel looked into the De Rudder cure? More than twenty-eight doctors had been involved in that one; all had certified the authenticity of the facts. "How can you dismiss the evidence of twenty-eight doctors?"

Dr. Carrel stammered phrases but had no plausible answer. "If it is true," he told Dr. Blanton finally, "it would be the very signature of God."

Dr. Carrel himself was interested in a special case he had kept track of, as a scientific observer, on the trainload of sick and dying during his journey to Lourdes. The patient was in the latter category: Marie Bailly, suffering from tubercular lesions of the lungs.

[6]Edouard LeBec, Medical Proof of the Miraculous. New York: P. J. Kenedy and Sons, 1923. p. viii.

Peritonitis had developed. She was a pale skeletal creature whose skin was the color of death itself.

"She may last a few days more, but she is doomed," Dr. Carrel told Dr. Blanton. "Her heart is giving out. Death is very near."

Yet a little later, standing in the grotto, he saw an extraordinary change take place in the girl whom he said could not live more than a few days.

After Dr. Carrel's death there was found among his papers a report of this journey to Lourdes. Published under the title *The Voyage to Lourdes*, it tells the adventure of a man named Lerrac— Carrel's name spelt backward—and a girl he called Marie Ferrand. It was actually an account of his own experience, witnessing the cure of Marie Bailly. He described, through his picture of Lerrac, how he examined her, and gave her morphine to ease her pain en route to Lourdes. He then described, as a doctor, what he saw happen in the grotto:

"Lerrac made no reply. To him it was obvious that there was a sudden improvement of her general condition. Something was taking place. He stiffened to resist a tremor of emotion. Standing against the low wall near the stretcher, he concentrated all his powers of observation on Marie . . . He did not lift his eyes from her face. A priest was preaching to the assembled throngs of pilgrims and patients. Hymns and prayers burst out sporadically; and in this atmosphere of fervor, under Lerrac's cool, objective gaze, the face of Marie Ferrand slowly continued to change. Her eyes, so dim before, were now wide with ecstacy as she turned them toward the Grotto. The change was undeniable."[7]

Marie Bailly was taken to the hospital at Lourdes. When he examined her that evening, he found all of her symptoms in the abdomen and pelvic regions had gone. Marie left the hospital a few days later, cured of a disease Dr. Carrel had said would destroy her.

As he had told Dr. Blanton, Dr. Carrel doubted miracles in general. But the case of Marie Bailly was one he could not doubt: he had examined her himself, he had kept records of her condition as a physician, he had seen her instantaneous cure in the grotto with his own eyes.

In his book *Man, the Unknown*, he wrote, "In all countries, at all times, people have believed in the existence of miracles, in

[7] Alexis Carrel, The Voyage to Lourdes. New York: Harper and Brothers, 1950. p. 32.

the more or less rapid healing of the sick at places of pilgrimages, at certain sanctuaries. But after the impetus of science during the 19th century, such belief completely disappeared. It was generally admitted, not only that miracles did not exist, but that they could not exist. As the laws of thermodynamics made perpetual motion impossible, physiological laws oppose miracles. . . . However, in view of the facts observed during the last fifty years, this attitude cannot be sustained. The most important cases of miraculous healing have been recorded by the Medical Bureau at Lourdes . . . They prove the objective importance of the spiritual activities, which hygienists, physicians, educators, and sociologists have almost neglected to study. They open to man a new world."[8]

That miraculous cures occur at Lourdes is not in dispute any longer, even by the most unreconstructed skeptics.

The questions of how and with what cosmic implications are not so easily answered. For there are, indeed, many answers.

To Dr. Carrel the important point was prayer. Speaking of the miracles at this shrine, he said, "The only condition indispensable to the occurrence of the phenomenon is prayer. But there is no need for the patient himself to pray, or even to have any religious faith. It is sufficient that someone around him be in a state of prayer. . . ."[9] One recalls an incident nearly fifty years later, when a Communist looked down and saw a ten-year-old boy praying for him.

Others take a far less supernatural approach. Dr. Blanton, for example, who talked so fervently with Dr. Carrel, nevertheless clings to Freudian concepts in his explanations of these healings. One case Dr. Blanton analyzed concerned a man named Charles McDonald who had been for fifteen years a helpless bedridden tubercular patient, unable to move his hips or shoulders without severe pain. In September, 1936, when he went to Lourdes, there were open sinuses draining pus on his neck and shoulder. On September 6, he was bathed in the piscina and felt no benefit. On September 7 he was bathed again. This time on emerging he stated that he felt a "glow of health." Lying on the stretcher he began to move his arm and felt no pain. He loosened the brace on his shoulder and moved his shoulder and felt no pain. He moved

[8] Alexis Carrel, Man, the Unknown. New York: Harper and Brothers, 1939. pp. 149-150.
[9] Ibid. p. 149.

his hips and felt no pain. The following morning, he arose from his bed and walked, for the first time in fifteen months.

On September 10, he left for his home in Dublin, Ireland. Virtually all of his trouble had cleared up. The physician accompanying him on the pilgrimage, as well as his personal physician in Dublin, testified that he had gone to Lourdes with active tuberculosis; when he returned they were able to assert that the open sinuses had virtually disappeared. One year later, they were able to state, on a basis of X-ray examination, that he was completely cured.

Dr. Blanton did not call it a miracle in the accepted sense. Discussing this case before a joint meeting of the American Psychoanalytic and American Psychiatric Association in Chicago, Dr. Blanton pointed out that many who go there sick and come away well are individuals *in extremis* or individuals suffering from chronic ailments for which physicians have abandoned hope of cure.

"The important thing, we think," Dr. Blanton said, "is that they have reached the limit of their emotional and physical capacities to adjust to the demands of their illness . . . They cannot any longer accept life and yet they cannot accept death . . . Their ego has reached a state of depletion . . . In our opinion, it is only when they have reached this state of complete surrender that they can be cured by such a transference—in this case to the Virgin Mother Mary who, they feel, intercedes for them with the Creator Himself. It is now possible for the patient to give up his fear of love, to be willing to accept it without a sense of guilt and without reservation . . .

"The value of the Virgin Mother as a transference object is infinite. No crosscurrents of human authority can touch her. She does not threaten, as a human mother does, even those who love her. On the part of the sick person the guilt payment has already been made by the act of being so seriously ill. There is nothing in her love that can rearouse the sense of guilt. Moreover, there is no ambivalence in the surrender to the Virgin Mother, nor any insecurity."

It is in this surrender of self, Dr. Blanton believes, that the individual gives up the wish to die, gives up the right to be sick, gives up even the right to get well slowly, thereby explaining instantaneous healings. "It is my feeling then," he said, "that in this case and in similar cases at Lourdes there is a quickening of the healing process (due to the emotions aroused by the transference to the all-powerful, all-loving Virgin Mother) to an extent which has not yet been realized or accepted by the medical profession.''

None of this did he consider supernatural in the usual sense. It was rather an unfolding of some law of function not yet fully described or understood: ''There is something above and beyond the test tube which must come back into the relationship between the patient and the physician.''

But none of this analysis explains the miracles involved in the healing of a dying infant who could not have known why the icy water spilled over its convulsed body.

To Alexis Carrel, the essence of Lourdes is prayer. To Smiley Blanton, the essence lies in surrender to the Virgin Mary, symbol of the protecting mother. To Fred Snite, it was resignation to God's will and awareness that however great is our need there are others whose need is greater. To other religious leaders, it is the atmosphere of deep and abiding love.

Perhaps the greatest miracle lies in the possibility that all of these views are equally correct.

5

A House of Prayer

In one of the chapels of the soaring Oratory of St. Joseph, high on Mt. Royal in the heart of Montreal, a crimson light gleams on a vessel preserving a human heart—the heart of the man to whom hundreds came to find healing at his word or touch.

The Oratory was built through contributions sent in from all over the world. A flow of pilgrims came here to climb the high steps to the Oratory seeking help. Hundreds of letters arrive daily, asking for prayers or giving thanks for prayers answered. On the walls are crutches and canes and other paraphernalia of some who were cured.

One extraordinary fact about miraculous shrines and cures within the Roman Catholic church is that while magnificent chapels and basilicas often arise at sacred places—erected through the gifts of the grateful—the individuals who brought these healing shrines into being are usually persons of extreme simplicity, often uneducated, even illiterate, of the most unpretentious and unlikely beginnings.

The term "oratory" means house of prayer—and the lives of many of these Roman Catholic healers fit this term also.

Above all this was true of the little barber and porter known as Brother André.

Brother André was born in the village of St. Gregoire d'Iberville, east of Montreal. His name was Alfred Bessette. He was orphaned at the age of eight and went to live with an aunt and uncle at St. Césaire. Deeply religious, he performed acts of penance as a child, sleeping on the floor regularly at night, once wearing a barbed leather cincture around his wrist. "I promised to make this sacrifice," he told his aunt, who ordered him to halt such actions.

55

The family was poor. When he was twelve he left school and went out into the world on his own trying different types of work, remaining constant only to his religious faith. He was a cobbler's helper and learned to make lasts and sew leather. Then he tried blacksmithing, in spite of fragile health, and learned to shoe horses and work iron. He wandered the countryside, trying his hand at odd jobs. Once he worked for a farmer who purchased a crucifix at an auction. Seeing the adoration with which the boy looked at the crucifix, the farmer gave it to him as a present. That night the farmer found him in the barn, praying to the crucifix which was fastened to the unpainted boards. His extensive travels took him also to the United States when he worked as a mill hand in Hartford and West Warwick, Connecticut.

During all of this he kept in touch with his priest, the pastor of St. Césaire, who was the first to tell him of the wonders of St. Joseph, and to inspire him with love for this saint. On his return from the United States, this priest urged him to enter the church. The youth replied that he could neither read nor write. "God's work needs neither of these talents necessarily," the priest informed him.

In 1870 he entered the Congregation of Holy Cross and became Brother André. Because of his lack of education, important work in the church was out of the question. He was to become a lay brother upon whom fell the physical toil of the church.

At the conclusion of his novitiate in 1871, he was appointed porter of Notre Dame College in Montreal, a school for boys. His duties were many. He had to cut the hair of the squirming youngsters. He had to scrub the floors, wake the boys in the morning, answer doorbells, go for the mail, close up the school at night and handle other menial chores. He slept on a cot in the porter's cell—a closet six feet square.

But his devotion to prayer remained unabated and won him a reputation. Once he asked a brother to pray with him and they remained before the altar for several hours. The story spread around the school: If you value your knees, don't pray with Brother André.

Sometimes he would go alone to a grove high on Mt. Royal and here he would pray to St. Joseph. He would tell others at the school, "St. Joseph wants that piece of land on the mountain, and someday there will be a shrine there to honor him."

There was another part of his life that they did not know about in the school. When he went to pick up the mail, he often stopped at the homes of families in the community where there was sickness. He would give them a word of cheer, or suggest they pray to St. Joseph.

It happened that sometimes the sick became well after these visits and prayers—even when there had appeared little chance of recovery. The word spread that Brother André, who cut hair for the schoolboys, had powers like a saint—he could heal the sick.

The college bursar was ill with a leg injury and informed school officials that he would probably not be well enough to go to the chapel the following day. "Pray with me and you will be well enough," Brother André told him.

To the amazement of his confreres, the bursar was well in the morning.

A few weeks later, a well-dressed woman appeared at the school, supported on the arms of two men. "I want to see Brother André," she said.

A priest turned to the porter, at that moment scrubbing the floor in the front entrance. "Brother André, this lady wants to talk with you."

Brother André looked up from his scrubbing. The woman said, "I want you to heal me."

For only an instant, according to the accounts of this incident, Brother André was silent. Then he declared, "She is well. Let her walk."

The woman pushed back the arms of the men who were supporting her and walked forward—three steps. She was able to walk out of the school unaided, according to eye witnesses.

Cures attributed to Brother André increased. The number of visitors seeking his help grew to such a point that the school officials had to assign a building where these petitioners could wait for Brother André until he was through with his chores of the day. Sometimes he would take these visitors up to the grove on the mountain where he had erected a small statue of St. Joseph. On occasion during these prayers on the hillside, healings occurred.

Montreal's civic officials began to grow alarmed. There were complaints about this "healing Brother André." A delegation from the Montreal Board of Health was sent to order him to halt his healing. Brother André's answer was that he effected no cures whatsoever. All that he did was pray, or anoint with oil, or rub the afflicted part with a medal of St. Joseph. There was nothing medically harmful in this. It could hardly be called the practice of medicine. The delegation retreated.

The crowds continued to increase. By 1904 the throngs became so great that officials of the college at last saw that action had to be taken. The head of the college gave Brother André two hundred dollars; with this financing, plus the aid of the college carpenter, a chapel was built on the hillside.

The shrine had been started. By 1908, the crowds had grown so great that a pavilion was built to feed and care for some of the pilgrims, and additions were made to the chapel. Brother André was promoted from college porter to custodian of the church, the highest position he could receive as a lay brother. The oratory and the great building of the basilica came later.

The healings went on. One of the most extraordinary concerned a man who rushed into the oratory crying, "Brother André, come at once. My wife is dying."

Brother André hurried with the man to his home. The wife was so close to death that the doctor had pulled the sheet over her head and was writing out the death certificate. This story, as preserved in the records of Brother André's healing, states that he pulled down the sheet and touched the woman's cheek. She moved her head, opened her eyes, and said, *"J'ai faim"*—"I am hungry."

He gave her a piece of orange. The physician tore up the death certificate as he watched. Within a few days, this woman was restored to complete good health.

One of his associates wrote of his work: "During more than fifteen years, I came here nearly every afternoon to supervise the coming and going of the visitors to Brother André's office. I do not think a week passed in which I did not witness a miracle. Often a paralytic would be cured, or one blind, or again someone who had to be brought here on a stretcher. Brother André would say to me at times: 'We must not say they are always miracles; they are great favors which God grants to open the eyes of the world . . .'"[1]

In his own latter days, more than ninety years old, he suffered greatly from abdominal pain, but when asked why he did not alleviate his own suffering he answered, much as Bernadette had answered, "I can do nothing for myself."

After his death, the Oratory continued its growth. A Medical

[1] *A Visit to Saint Joseph's Oratory.* Montreal: Fides, 1955. p. 42.

Record Bureau was established to handle, index and investigate the claims of cures—numbering anywhere from one hundred to five hundred a month. The Medical Bureau comprises eight surgeons and physicians of unquestioned professional authority who investigate the facts behind the claimed cures and who serve without pay. A large percentage of cases investigated by this Board are described as either exaggerated, unsubstantiated or entirely hysterical or psychosomatic healings. But for others, the physicians have been unable to find any normal explanation.

The millions of visitors continue to come, some to watch, some to pray, some to seek cures. The heart of the little barber was preserved and placed in a chapel in the Oratory and many regard it as a relic of healing power.

The founders of healing shrines are mirrors of the mystical experiences of man.

To most of them religion was not a matter of debate, as it was to a scientist such as Alexis Carrel; to these profoundly uncomplicated people, faith was as integral a part of their lives as food or air.

Yet each story has its special drama.

The healing shrine of St. Anne de Beaupré, also in Eastern Canada, had its origin in a storm which turned the St. Lawrence River into a seething mass of tidal terror. Trapped in this storm one night in 1650, a handful of Breton sailors prayed to St. Anne, mother of the Virgin Mary, and patron saint of Brittany. They promised that if they made land safely they would build a chapel to St. Anne at whatever point they beached.

After a night of battling the waves of the river, they managed at dawn to beach safely on the northern bank. Coming ashore, they found themselves in a beautiful slightly rolling meadowland. Far in the north was the blue outline of mountains. They at once began the construction of a small wooden chapel in honor of St. Anne. In 1656, by order of Msgr. François de Laval, Bishop of Quebec, Beaupré was made a parish and construction was started the following year on a parish church.

The first miracle of St. Anne de Beaupré was said to have occurred while the foundation of this building was being laid. A man named Louis Guimond (also spelled Guimont in some reports), crippled from rheumatism, was nevertheless anxious to participate in construction of this shrine to the saint. Despite his ailment, he managed to carry three stones for the foundation of the chapel on the day the cornerstone was blessed. As he laid these three stones in place, he was instantly and completely cured of his disease, according to attested records of witnesses, affirmed by the studies of Roman Catholic authorities. Eugène LeFebvre, C.Sc.R., in his booklet on healings at this shrine entitled *Land of Miracles,* states, "The First Miracle was wrought also in 1658, when Louis Guimont, a crippled farmer of Beaupré, placed three small stones in the foundation of the Sailors' Chapel, through devotion, and was suddenly cured."[2]

This chapel was never finished, because of undermining by ice and tides. But in 1662, a new church of stone and wood was constructed on higher and dryer ground. The stories of healings, first in the unfinished and then in the new chapel, were known widely even in those days. The Venerable Mother Marie of the Incarnation, founder of the Ursuline Nuns of Quebec, in a letter written on September 20, 1665, said: "Seven leagues from Quebec . . . there is a church of St. Anne, in which Our Lord works *great wonders* in favor of this holy mother of the Most Holy Virgin. There the paralyzed may be seen to walk, the blind receive their sight and the sick, whatever be their malady, recover their health."[3]

The shrine had to be repaired and enlarged in 1694, and ninety-three years later was enlarged once more, to accommodate the increasing number of pilgrims. In 1759, British troops battled French and Indian forces throughout this area but the church was untouched. In 1876, construction of a new basilica of stone was begun. This building was later destroyed by fire and was rebuilt in 1923. When the flames destroyed the first basilica, two items remained untouched by the fire: the wooden statue of St. Anne, holding the infant Virgin Mary in her arms, and the relic of the arm of St. Anne.

By the mid-twentieth century, St. Anne's was the scene of a number of buildings: the basilica; the memorial shrine, on the site of the original Sailors' Chapel; the Holy Stairs; a monastery and a seminary; a hospital for invalid patients. Widespread criticism of commercialism at this shrine—of the shops selling religious articles and banners and other souvenirs—was met by the answer that none of these stores is in any way connected with the Shrine

[2]Eugène LeFebvre, Land of Miracles. St. Anne de Beaupré: St. Alphonsus Bookshop, 1951. p. 9.
[3]*Ibid.* p. 7.

itself. The official Guide Book states: "That the Shrine is not commercialized is obvious from the fact that it may be visited, at any time, by anybody . . . even with the official Guide conducting, without the visit costing them a single penny. . . . Any place in Saint Anne's charging admission or selling religious articles for admission has no connection whatever with the Shrine."[4]

Despite the remarkable series of adversities by way of flood, ice, fire and later-day charges of commercialism, the miracles apparently continue. In 1902, a two-hundred-page book was published containing reports of hundreds of cures at the Shrine. Later reports, particularly the collection of documented cures made by Father LeFebvre, reveal that healing continued and increased as the number of pilgrims increased annually. Although there is no medical board here, as at Lourdes, these records present evidence of cures of tuberculosis, cancer, epilepsy, heart lesion, infantile paralysis and other illnesses. One typical documented case concerns Graziella Dubois, who, in 1925, at the age of sixteen months, was stricken with infantile paralysis. Her physician, Dr. L. Poisson of Normandin, Quebec, treated her for a period of a year with only slight results. One leg was undeveloped, shorter than the other, and extremely weak.

"In March, 1935," the priest reports, "the child, then twelve years old, lost her father, and was placed in the Immaculate Orphanage, Chicoutimi. Her leg caused her constant suffering, and it was increasingly difficult for her to walk and to play. She had reached the point where she had to walk on tiptoe with it, and that with difficulty.

"The Mother Superior of the orphanage urged the child to make the novena to Saint Anne, and all the orphanage pupils made the solemn July Novena for Graziella's cure. On the Eve of the Feast, July 25, 1936, her leg was wrapped with several pages of the *Annals of Good Saint Anne*[5] and the child prayed herself to sleep."

Graziella herself wrote what happened following this evening of prayer:

"The next day, when I arose and set my foot to the floor, I did not at once realize what had happened to me. Then I suddenly noticed that both my feet were equally solid. I said to myself, 'I am cured.' Then I ran to Mother Superior to tell her. She replied, 'You know you are mistaken, Graziella, you can't be cured.'

[4]Guide Book for Pilgrims and Visitors. St. Anne de Beaupré, 1954. p. 82.
[5]A monthly publication containing records of cures at this shrine.

However, that day and the following days, I found that I could walk better. I accordingly returned and said, 'Mother, it is indeed true that I am cured. I know it.'"[6]

To prove it, while the Mother Superior and the nuns looked on, the little girl ran up and down the corridors of the orphanage.

On September 27, 1936, the Mother Superior of the orphanage, Sister Marie Francoise de Jesus, P.F.M., made a written statement.

"Little Graziella Dubois had formerly suffered from infantile paralysis, and had remained with one leg shorter than the other, being unable to stand on the infirm leg.

"Last July (1936), on the Eve of the Feast of Saint Anne, the *Annals of Saint Anne* were wrapped around her leg, and the next morning the child ran to announce to me that she had been cured. Since that time, she has been able to run and jump, even on her 'bad' leg, just as if she had never had any infirmity."

On December 24, 1948, Graziella's original physician, declared, "The child suffered from malignant infantile paralysis and the cure was instantaneous and lasting. It cannot be attributed solely to the resources of medical science and of nature."

On January 13, 1949, Graziella Dubois herself wrote, "I was only twelve years old at the time of my cure. I am now twenty-five. My legs are of equal length, and I do not limp. Since the age of sixteen, I have done housework for private families, and can do my work without fatigue. It often happens that after my day's work, I walk several miles, without tiring."

After speaking of her childhood suffering, she said, "All that is now a thing of the past. A mere detail remains, a slight thinness of the calf of the leg, which serves as a reminder of my cure.

"All thanks to Saint Anne who did not do things by halves. The cure was final and has been maintained since then. . . ."[7]

Her letter is one of hundreds on file at St. Anne's. They come from Protestant and Roman Catholic and Jew, from Canada, the United States and other parts of the world.

In 1947, a few days after the birth of Philip Albers, in Cincinnati, Ohio, a swelling was observed on the infant's lower right leg, between the two bones.

X-ray examination and a biopsy resulted in a diagnosis of ma-

---

[6]Eugène LeFebvre, Land of Miracles. St. Anne de Beaupré: St. Alphonsus Bookshop, 1951. p. 38.

[7]*Ibid*. pp. 38-39.

lignant cancerous growth. The child was given X-ray treatment without success. The disease affected not only the tissues but also the two bones of the leg. The doctor, a non-Roman Catholic, informed the parents that he did not know whether the X-ray treatments could halt the progress of the disease and held out little hope. He advised them to pray.

At that time the child's maternal grandmother urged that they try St. Anne. She had heard only recently of a miraculous healing at the Shrine at Beaupré. The mother and a neighbor and the child made a Novena of Communions and went to the Shrine. On their return to Cincinnati, the X-ray treatments which had been unsuccessful before were resumed. The doctors still had little hope. Then—slowly and yet seemingly miraculously—healing began. The medical report of this case states: "I hereby certify that several days after Philip Albers' birth, there appeared a growth, between the tibia and fibula of his right leg, which required immediate attention.

"In August of 1947, X-rays were made at the Good Samaritan Hospital, Cincinnati, Ohio, and a biopsy was done for pathology. The reports were very discouraging, for the diagnosis was made of a fibro-sarcoma, involving not only the bones, but also the connective tissue. Extensive X-ray therapy was started at once, but little hope was held for a recovery from this malignant disease.

"I tried to assure the parents, but I also told them that their only hope was to pray, and that if the Lord was too busy to listen to them, they would be out of luck.

"In March of 1948, a re-examination was made, which revealed that both the tibia and fibula were showing normal development, and that the pathologic destructive changes were healed.

"While due credit must be given to the medical profession in recognizing this serious condition, and the ability to provide the necessary treatment, I feel the cure was miraculous, and that a Power greater than ours must have managed the work."—Lee McHenry, M.D.[8]

Of special significance at St. Anne de Beaupré, as at any other Roman Catholic shrines, are the relics. Beaupré has five relics of the body of the saint, the largest of which is a wrist bone with skin and flesh assertedly still adhering to the bone. There is a story, which some Roman Catholic authorities claim is fully sub-

[8]*Ibid*. p. 80.

stantiated, that early Christians carried the body of the mother of
Mary from Palestine to the city of Apta Julia in Gaul—now the
city of Apt, France—where it was hidden in an underground crypt.
According to the legend, this body was miraculously rediscovered
in a concealed crypt in the Apt Cathedral in the eighth century,
by a boy who was deaf, dumb and blind—the son of the Baron
of Casanova—during services reconsecrating the cathedral after
the victory of Charlemagne over the Saracens, and the re-
establishment of Christianity throughout Europe. According to a
brochure, *Good St. Anne*,[9] with the imprimatur of the church,
"the miraculous discovery at once made the cathedral of Apt the
center of attraction for Christian pilgrims from every part of Gaul.
In the wars which followed the reign of Charlemagne, down to
our own times, the clergy and people of Apt have watched with
never-failing love over the sacred treasure which is the glory of
their city . . . The chief cities of Gaul hastened to solicit from the
Church of Apta Julia portions of the hallowed deposit thus miraculously discovered."

The large wrist bone at Beaupré was obtained, with authori-
zation from the Vatican, from the Church of Saint-Paul-Outside-
the-Walls in Rome.

While en route to St. Anne de Beaupré, in May, 1892, this
wrist bone was placed on exhibit in the Church of Saint Jean
Baptiste in New York City. Word of its arrival excited great
interest, particularly in Roman Catholic circles. Thousands of devout Catholics crowded into this church, many of them afflicted
with serious sickness, eager to beseech the intercession of Good
St. Anne to obtain cures for them from God. As these services
began in the church, one young man, of a prominent family,
collapsed in convulsions as he approached the relic. It required
several men to hold him. A moment later, he was touched by the
relic, and his convulsions halted. This abrupt cessation of the
convulsions had a tremendous effect upon the hundreds watching.
Reports of the incident circulated swiftly through the crowds outside; all day and into the night they continued to edge through the
doors. Healings were reported; the crippled walked out whole, the
blind could see. Throughout the city, rumors of miracles multi-
plied.

Instead of hurrying on to Canada, the bearer of this sacred relic

[9]Good St. Anne. Clyde, Missouri: Benedictine Convent of Perpetual Adoration, n.d. pp. 12-13.

from Rome, the Right Rev. Msgr. J. C. Marquis, agreed to tarry
a few days in New York. The few days became three weeks. The
relic remained on display and often the crowds were so great that
they could not enter and hundreds waited outside on Lexington
Avenue, where the Church of Saint Jean Baptiste is located, for
their chance to enter and see this relic. It was estimated that
between two and three hundred thousand persons came to the
church during those three weeks.

It was impossible to keep records of what happened, of cures
and claimed cures. Crutches would be found, leaning against the
altar, pairs of glasses fastened to the church wall. A few names
and addresses were kept, but the overburdened priests had little
time for anything except to carry out their duties within the church.
One eyewitness to this amazing episode, the Right Rev. Bernard
O'Reilly, wrote in a report on this event: "This last week must
ever remain memorable in the religious annals of this city. Of the
numbers and names of those who were daily said to be cured there
was no means of keeping an accurate account, if any account at
all. Everything, all through these three weeks, had been absolutely
unexpected and unforeseen. No one was appointed to keep a list
of those reported miraculous happenings. No one could register
the names, residence, antecedents, and the specific nature of the
disease, together with the witness to the old chronic condition of
the sufferer, as well as to the sudden and ascertained recovery.
Besides, the priests attached to the church were overwhelmed and
exhausted and, at first at least, few, if any, had a notion that they
needed assistance . . .

"The sidewalk above and below the church was densely packed
by all who had strength enough to stand and wait. On the opposite
side of the street stood hundreds apparently expecting their turn
. . . What a sight it was to look down from the sanctuary railing
on the slowly advancing throng of men and women, whose features
were lit up with an expression of faith and hope and ardent sup-
plication . . ."[10]

So great were the effects of this episode that the Vatican agreed
to send another relic of Good Saint Anne to the Church of Saint
Jean Baptiste—a bone of the saint's forearm. This arrived in New
York City in July, 1892, and the new Shrine of St. Anne opened
in this church. Healing services and novenas have been held since

[10]Right Rev. Bernard O'Reilly, The Good Saint Anne. New York, N. Y.:
Blessed Sacrament Fathers, 1919. pp. 17-19.

then, quietly and without publicity of any kind. Hundreds have come to these services, for more than a half-century, many seeking, and frequently claiming, to be healed.

There are other shrines to Good Saint Anne. Most noted is St. Anne D'Auray in Brittany, visited by thousands of pilgrims annually. There is the Shrine of Apt. There are relics of the saint in Rome, at Chartres, Périgueux and Bordeaux and Noyon, as well as in Beaupré and New York.

In the United States, one Roman Catholic healing movement began its rise on a day in 1937 when police were called out in Chicago to quell what were reported to be riots on Jackson Boulevard, in front of Our Lady of Sorrows Church.

Racing out in squad cars, police found no rioters but worshippers—thousands of them—waiting for their turn to participate in a new Perpetual Novena to Our Lady of Sorrows.

This Perpetual Novena, held every Friday, so that one can begin any week and make the nine weeks of prayer and petition, was only a few weeks old at that time. But already there were reports of many petitions answered.

The novena eventually spread to more than two thousand parishes in thirty-two countries. It was held in churches, universities, and even on aircraft carriers and submarines.

In 1957, on the novena's twentieth anniversary, with the number of answered prayers and miraculous cures claimed through this novena reaching close to seven million, Our Lady of Sorrows church, home of this novena, was made a minor basilica, one of the highest honors which can be bestowed upon a church by the Vatican.

In Wisconsin, a hill rises abruptly three hundred feet into the sky near the town of Hartford. The upthrust mound is called Holy Hill and there is a magnificent Roman Catholic church here, the Church of Mary, Help of Christians, run by Discalced Carmelite monks.

Pilgrims come here—two million a year—and many make the Stations of the Cross up the hill and many cures are claimed for themselves or others.

A century ago they called it Hermit Hill. Some called it Miracle Hill. There has always been a church here, as long as people recall. And there is also the legend of the hermit.

That began one evening in the mid-nineteenth century, when a farmer, returning from the fields near this mound, happened to see at the top, silhouetted against the sunset sky, the figure of a man on his knees before a Cross. The farmer climbed the hill and talked to the man after the prayer was ended.

He learned that this man had slain the girl he loved because she had betrayed him, and then he had fled and hidden in a monastery.

One day he had stumbled upon a diary of two early American explorers, telling of how they had found a hill on top of which they dedicated an altar sacred forever to the Virgin. As part of his penance, the man swore to find this hill from the facts given about its location, and rededicate the spot.

Although partially paralyzed, he had made the journey from Eastern Canada to Wisconsin, finally reaching this hill looming against the sky.

On his knees, he climbed to the top. He spent the entire night alone on the summit, in prayer to Mary. In the morning, his paralysis was gone.

He built a shack, erected the Cross, and each morning and night came to pray.

From this story as he unfolded it to the farmer, the legend began. The hill had healing power, people said; they began to come with their prayers.

The Stations of the Cross were built up the side of the hill. Cures of local people, farmers and their families began to be reported. There was no documentation to speak of. Only a few letters and the stories repeated from one to the other. But throughout the area everyone knew about the Hermit and Holy Hill, and the prayers answered at the hilltop shrine.

Today they come over wide highways to seek their cures in the beautiful church overlooking the Wisconsin countryside.

Throughout the world there are Roman Catholic shrines whose histories are rich with religious lore.

On the fringes of Mexico City, in what once was the town of Guadalupe, is a basilica to which come pilgrims from all over Mexico and, in fact, from all over Latin America, to seek the blessing and sometimes cures or special favor of Our Lady of Guadalupe.

Here there is a miraculous painting of the Immaculate Conception, and stories centuries old, but well-authenticated. Authorities tell of how the Virgin talked with Juan Diego, a youthful Indian convert, and how the picture appeared, and how in mid-winter roses bloomed. Many pilgrims come here, and many miracles are claimed.

To believer and non-believer alike, the story has a beauty rich and full of wonder.

In 1531, the report goes, an Indian peasant boy named Juan Diego, a convert to Roman Catholicism, looked up on a hillside and saw an apparition of a beautiful lady, as he walked on a road outside of Mexico City, at a place called Tepeyac; later the area was called Guadalupe.

The Lady urged Juan Diego to go to the Bishop and tell him that she wanted a "temple" built at this spot. The Bishop was kindly, but Juan's story was wild and difficult to believe.

Several more times the Lady appeared to the Indian youth of Tepeyac. At last she gave him a sign: a bush of fresh and dewy roses bloomed on the hillside where there were no roses at all; the Lady instructed Juan to take these roses directly to the Bishop.

Juan Diego carried them in his cloak, made of a coarse muslin kind of material. When he reached the Bishop's residence, he opened the cloak and the roses fell out. And, on the inside of the cloak in which they were carried, Juan and the others present beheld a beautiful painting of the Madonna.

This was the picture known today as Our Lady of Guadalupe. Strange, primitive, rich in its colors, fitting no school or known master's technique, it was painted with a smoothness and luminosity that for centuries has defied explanations by artists and technicians.

The Bishop took the painting on the cloak of the peasant and went into his oratory to pray and seek spiritual guidance and to give thanks to God. Later the "temple" the Lady had asked for arose in the form of the basilica of Guadalupe.

Thus runs the story. And there are historical records to bear witness to the facts of Juan Diego and the Lady.

In a land of imagination and age-old legends, some of the ancient thoughts and ways infiltrate the minds and legends of the people today. But apart from the reported healings and the devotion of those who come here to pray, there is another remarkable aspect of this story.

For centuries the picture has remained, unspoiled and undimmed, its golds and blues and reds bright and gleaming.

Guadalupe's climate is not good. Other pictures in that district have faded and cracked and rotted. But the painting of Our Lady of Guadalupe remains as fresh as the winter-blooming roses Juan Diego reportedly took to the Bishop as proof that the Lady had appeared to him.

There are also Roman Catholic saints believed to have power to aid in special illness. One of these is St. Peregrine, the cancer saint, who lived in the thirteenth century and who was reported to have been cured instantly of a cancer on his leg.

A shrine to St. Peregrine has been established by the Servite Fathers in Chicago. It has a following of thousands, many of whom claim healings received after making the novena to this saint.

These shrines and saints were dedicated to healing through the power of God. The dedication to prayer and faith appears in many cases to invoke the healing force.

An extraordinary example of this is the life of Pope Pius XII, born Eugenio Pacelli.[11] Few men have been as devoted or have given of themselves so completely to the service of their faith and their God.

By 1954, the Pope's health began to fade. He suffered a severe attack of hiccups, great pain and discomfort, and the inability to take food. By November, he could take no solid food; he weighed just over a hundred pounds, his face was that of a living skeleton. Leading medical specialists of the world were summoned to his bedside. Opinions regarding what should be done varied. Some of the doctors wanted to operate; others said the Pope's condition would not allow any operation.

By December 1, he was barely alive. Everyone knew now that he was dying. Outside the Vatican, crowds waited. In churches and temples around the world, men of many faiths prayed for the life of the Pontiff.

He was still conscious and his mind was still quite clear. That night, as he lay alone in his room, the Pontiff heard a voice. It said: "There will be a vision." The Pope believed it was a sign that his death was imminent.

The following morning, at dawn, as he lay with open eyes, he saw the figure of Jesus. The figure stood silent beside his bed.

As he saw this vision, the Pope is reported to have cried out with joy, believing that Christ had come for him, *"O bone Jesu!*

---

[11]Alden Hatch and Seamus Walshe, *Crown of Glory.* New York: Hawthorn Books, 1957. pp. 227-235.

Voca me; iube me vinere ad Te!'' (O good Jesus, summon me, order me to come to you!'')

But the vision remained a moment only, and turned and was gone.

The story of this vision ultimately was published and became a topic of debate. Many expressed the opinion that it must have been an hallucination. Many were unsure. Some believed.[12]

It is not for this writer to challenge the authenticity of this vision. But as a reporter of facts, I find certain other aspects of the story provocative:

All through the night following his hearing the words "there will be a vision"—although the public did not know he had heard them, of course—the world waited for Pius to die.

All through the following day, after he had had his vision—although the public had no knowledge of that vision—the world continued to wait for him to die.

And from that day on, he began to get well. From the brink of death, within a period of only forty-eight hours, the Pontiff, who had been given no hope of recovery, was taking nourishment.

Within three weeks he was strong enough to begin preparation of a peace message to the world, and was able to give it to the world himself, by radio broadcast, only a few weeks later.

Before spring, he appeared fully recovered and began to assume his full and arduous duties as Pope.

By 1956, he was conducting a crowded schedule of work and was giving audiences to groups totaling a million persons a year. And, upon examination, his doctors found this great religious leader, whom they themselves had given up, in the very best of health.

It might well be that in this instance—for one moment in the Roman dawn—the Great Physician had taken the case out of their hands.

[12]Roman Catholicism teaches that miracles and authentic visions continue to happen in our world, but Catholics do not have to accept the validity of any individual modern miracle.

6

Woman of God

On July 15, 1850, in the town of Saint Angelo of Lodi, in Italy, it is asserted that a flight of white doves, never seen before or since in that community, appeared above one of the houses. The owner tried to drive them away, fearful that they would destroy his grain, but failing this, he gave up and brought one of the doves into his house. Shortly afterwards, his wife gave birth to an infant girl.

She was called Frances Xavier Cabrini.

From earliest girlhood, she was devoted only to the service of God and Christ. At eleven, she made a vow to Jesus to remain a virgin: when she was nineteen she made this vow perpetual. Although at first denied a chance to give herself to the church because she was considered in too poor health, she proved her ability by managing an orphanage and preparing other young ladies for adult life in the secular world—and a few for life in the church.

In 1877, she was allowed to take her holy vows, and was immediately appointed a mother superior by the Bishop of Lodi. But the Bishop became pessimistic about the House of Providence, as her orphanage was called. He told Mother Cabrini: "You wish to become a missionary. Well, the time is ripe. I do not know of an institute for missionary sisters. You found one."

"I will search for a house," she replied.

Shortly thereafter, Mother Cabrini founded a new order whose work and missions were to spread across the world: the Missionary Sisters of the Sacred Heart. These sisters were to work with the children, to found orphanages and schools everywhere they went. Mother Cabrini went to various cities in Europe, and to Rome itself, and then she went to America to set up an orphanage, primarily for Italian orphans, at that time in the greatest need.

With the energy of an inspired being, Mother Cabrini traveled

71

throughout North America, Central America and South America, England and Spain, and Europe and back to North America, everywhere setting up new "missions," schools, orphanages, colleges, hospitals, dispensaries. She obtained ranches and farms in Denver, Los Angeles, outside Chicago and New Orleans, where food and livestock were grown and used to supply the needs of her orphanages.

When she died in 1917, her name had become known everywhere in Christendom. Many prayed to her for intercession in healing. A member of her own order, Sister Delphina Grazioli, was dying of cancer. It had been so diagnosed by two physicians, a Dr. Sturgis and a Dr. Leeds, of Columbus Hospital in Seattle. The first operation took place on October 14, 1921. "Pains, vomiting and a continual wasting away of the body," continued, however. Three more operations proved equally unsuccessful. In December, 1925, doctors considered her death only a matter of days or hours. She was given the last sacraments.

As Sister Delphina lay in her bed, she seemed to see Mother Cabrini appear, telling her there was some important work she had to do.

Suddenly—perhaps it was delirium or hysteria, but regardless of what explanation is given—Sister Delphina, close to death, was well. She sat up in bed, she reached out and ate a few grapes on the table beside the bed.

All day the sisters and the orphans had been praying to Mother Cabrini to intercede. Now, as they stood around her bed, the sister who had taken the last rites declared, "I am cured. Mother Foundress has obtained the miracle."

In three days she walked to the chapel for Holy Communion. Her cure was complete. Thirty-five years later she was still hard at work in Columbus Hospital in Seattle.

Following her canonization in 1938, Mother Cabrini's remains were placed on public view in a shrine attached to the Mother Cabrini High School on Fort Washington Avenue in New York City.

Other shrines in her honor have been established in other cities. Letters that come to the various shrines tell of extraordinary answers to prayers. Some give thanks for healings of serious nature—skin cancers, mastoids, severe burns that left no scars after prayers to Mother Cabrini, tuberculosis and arthritis. Other express thanks for favors ranging all the way from selling a piece of property, or getting a new job, to the return of a son safely from combat.

They are simple letters, too simple to be fabricated: "Thank God for your prayers. My son obtained the position he wanted . . ." "I want to thank St. Frances Cabrini for the disappearance of a growth on my face . . ." "Please accept my deepest thanks for two particular favors received through the intercession of St. Frances Cabrini; one, the bringing about of peace in a family where there was great tension; and the second, the restoration of health to me and ability to continue my daily work . . ."

For the non-Roman Catholic, much that happens in this area of Roman Catholic faith is difficult in terms of acceptance. The whole concept of relics, of visions, of white doves hovering over a house in Italy—such things present problems and often insuperable obstacles to the non-Roman Catholic mind. But these questions pertain not so much to the healing as to the interpretation, the meaning, and method.

But the fact of the healings at shrines and through prayer to saints cannot be brushed away merely because we may not understand, or pray in the selfsame words.

The miraculous does not lend itself to easy interpretation. There are areas of mystery that force us to grope for truth.

The interpretations of events and the dynamics by which they occur may differ on the surface as widely as the many minds of man and the many ways by which he reaches out to God.

7

He Commanded Them to Heal

The architecture of the church interior was singularly inornate; there were no shadowed arches or niches with sacred images or candles flickering. The lights were bright. High above the altar in gilt letters were the words: "God is Love."

A woman member of the congregation was standing and talking. "It is with such gratitude to God that I speak tonight. As Mary Baker Eddy, our founder, wrote, 'Divine Love always has met and always will meet every human need.' I was a chronic invalid; I lived in pain. Doctors could not heal me. I thought I was being punished by God. Then I turned to Christian Science. A practitioner told me that God did not want to punish me. God was love. My chronic illness was error. Through learning to understand Him and learning love for Him, I was able to shed this error from me, to demonstrate health. The error that had plagued my life was gone completely . . . I am deeply grateful . . ."

She finished her testimony and sat down. A hush came throughout the church. After a moment a tall, well-dressed man arose. He began to tell of another cure, that of his niece who had been injured in an automobile accident, and was cured by Science and prayer . . .

The Wednesday evening Christian Science testimonial meeting was a sharp contrast to healing services and rituals of other faiths—in the detail, the attitude, the philosophy.

There was about this service almost the atmosphere of a New England prayer meeting. The "reader" in the pulpit wore no religious robes, only a plain business suit. There was a hymn sung, and a silent prayer, and a reading from the Bible and briefly from the Science textbook.

But there was no kneeling and no incense and no repetition of creeds or litanies. To some it might have seemed a cold and meaningless service. To others, its simplicity was part of its deepest meaning.

As Mother Cabrini's life—from its earliest days in a small Italian town—was devoted to religion, so Mary Baker Eddy's—beginning in an austere New England village—likewise was a dedication to God. Before Mary was born, her mother and a neighbor woman prayed frequently together and read the Bible. After Mary was born, her mother read to her from the Bible. One story, relating how Daniel prayed three times a day, so impressed Mary that she began to pray regularly seven times a day, marking a check on the wall of the woodshed for each prayer.

Her personal life—often unjustly vilified—was one of considerable joy and even greater suffering. Married at twenty-two, in 1843, she was widowed the following year when her husband, George Washington Glover, died at their home in Charleston, South Carolina. In September of that year her son George was born. Her physical condition had always been frail; the birth of her son left her an invalid. In 1853, she was married a second time, to Daniel Patterson, who would not even permit her to have her son George in the same house with them. When Patterson was made a prisoner during the Civil War, she succeeded by strenuous effort in winning his release. After the war he ran off with the wife of another man and Mary obtained a divorce from him on the grounds of infidelity.

Later, in her religious studies she became briefly interested in the work of Dr. Phineas P. Quimby, who had developed a number of theories regarding hypnotic and mental healing. These theories had considerable influence on what might be called the new *avant garde* of religious thinking in the early post-bellum era. Mary Baker's health was improved by his treatment. Within a short time, however, she came to believe that his concepts were tied to the physical rather than the spiritual mind. To her, material mind had no power of its own; what existed was not man's mind, but the Mind of God, all-powerful and all-good.

On a winter night in 1866, in Lynn, Massachusetts, she slipped on the ice and was gravely injured. She was carried unconscious into a nearby home. Many believed she had suffered fatal injuries. For some days she lay in a critical condition. One day, alone in her room, she opened the Bible and read the story in Matthew of Christ's healing of the palsied man.

This passage crystallized in the injured woman the concept that the words and teachings of Christ offered mankind a science of living. This was the passage which pointed the way to the world-wide religion we know today as Christian Science:

"And, behold, they brought to him a man sick of the palsy, lying on a bed: and Jesus seeing their faith said unto the sick of the palsy; Son, be of good cheer; thy sins be forgiven thee.

"And, behold, certain of the scribes said within themselves, this man blasphemeth.

"And Jesus, knowing their thoughts said, Wherefore think ye evil in your hearts?

"For whether is easier, to say, Thy sins be forgiven thee; or to say, Arise, and walk?

"But that ye may know that the Son of Man hath power on earth to forgive sins, (then saith he to the sick of the palsy), Arise, take up thy bed, and go into thine house.

"And he arose, and departed to his house."[1]

When she completed reading this passage several times, although she was still believed to be in critical condition, Mary Baker arose from her bed, dressed herself and walked from the room. She was well, she was sound; she was able to carry forth her mission.

For several years after this instantaneous cure, she spent her time in study and preparation—"to ponder my mission," she wrote, "to search the Scriptures, to find the Science of Mind that should take the things of God and show them to the creature, and reveal the great curative Principle, Deity."[2]

From this study she emerged with principles and ideas which she later developed fully in her book, *Science and Health, with Key to the Scriptures,* the textbook of Christian Science. Of this period of study and preparation, she wrote: "I beheld with ineffable awe our great Master's purpose in not questioning those he healed as to their disease or its symptoms, and his marvelous skill in demanding neither obedience to hygienic laws, nor prescribing drugs to support the divine power which heals. Adoringly I discerned the Principle of his holy heroism and Christian example on the Cross, when he refused to drink the vinegar and gall," a preparation of poppy, or aconite, to allay the tortures of crucifixion.

---

[1] Matthew IX: 2-7.
[2] Mary Baker Eddy, Retrospection and Introspection. Boston: published by the Trustees under the Will of Mary Baker G. Eddy, 1891. pp. 24-25.

"Our great Way-shower, steadfast to the end in his obedience to God's laws, demonstrated for all time and peoples the supremacy of good over evil, and the superiority of Spirit over matter.

"The miracles recorded in the Bible, which had before seemed to me supernatural, grew divinely natural and apprehensible; though uninspired interpreters ignorantly pronounce Christ's healing miraculous, instead of seeing therein the operation of the divine law."[3]

In 1875, after a number of years of teaching, and healing, she published the first edition of the textbook. In 1877, she married Asa Gilbert Eddy, who had come to her as a student. In 1879, the Christian Science Association—which she had founded a few years before with her students and followers—voted to organize a mind-healing church, to be called the Church of Christ, Scientist. The charter was obtained in June, 1879; the founding members, twenty-six in number, extended a call to Mary Baker Eddy to become their pastor.

The growth of this church is one of the great phenomena of modern religion. From twenty-six members, it has grown to millions. From a first edition of one thousand copies, the number of copies of *Science and Health, with Key to the Scriptures* soared into the multi-millions, with translations in almost all languages on earth.

In its cradle days, Christian Science was looked upon as a sect of fanatics. Nevertheless, its adherents increased—along with continuing reports of Christian Science cures. Mary Baker Eddy herself performed healings but did not think of herself as miraculously gifted. In Christian Science, spiritual healing is built on scientific principles; any person who understands these principles can be an agent of healing. Thus began the corps of Christian Science practitioners, who work with and pray with those who come in need of aid. In the monthly edition of the *Christian Science Journal*, this list by 1957 numbered more than ten thousand practitioners and teachers, both men and women. Practitioners are supposed to devote their lives to this work. Like a doctor, they charge a fee; it usually is less than five dollars a treatment. Unlike doctors, they cannot—under church rules—bring any legal action to collect if the client does not pay.

From some in the medical profession came sporadic volleys of ridicule and denunciation. The ideas were a joke, they said. Her

[3]*Ibid.* pp. 25-26.

teachings, they asserted, were the gibberish of a neurotic female infatuated with words she did not understand. Much of her dogma came originally from the metaphysician Quimby, the more violent critics charged. In addition to medical science, a large part of organized religion believed that the healing ministry of Christ was of the past; miracles that happened centuries back were safe and respectable but any idea of such things in our own day was absurd. The command of Jesus to his followers to go forth to heal the sick was not considered by many persons to apply to modern times.

But as the new religion gained adherents and healings, a slightly altered course was followed by the army of detractors.

Perhaps you could cure some functional diseases by this method, some admitted. But organic diseases could not be so healed by such means. One leading exponent of this view was a distinguished Boston physician, Dr. Richard C. Cabot, who himself became part of a medical-religious movement in the Episcopal Church. In 1906, Dr. Cabot published an article reporting on his investigation of one hundred Christian Science cures. In this report he stated: "In my own personal researches into Christian Science 'cures,' I have never found one in which there was any good evidence that cancer, consumption, or any other organic disease, had been arrested or banished. The diagnosis was usually made either by the patient himself or was an interpretation at second or third hand of what a doctor was supposed to have said."[4]

One reaction of this statement was the publication of B. O. Flower's book in which he described in detail cases of organic ailments cured through Christian Science. These records cited dates, names, doctors, diagnoses and results. One of the most carefully-documented cases ever reported of a cancer healing is cited in this book, quoting a published report of a Dr. F. Burton. Dr. Burton had himself been healed of tuberculosis through Christian Science and, in his report, cited several healings he had investigated personally.

"The case of cancer referred to is Mrs. Belt, Bellevue Terrace Hotel, Los Angeles. The healing was done in November, 1906. Her brother, through whom it was done, is Mr. W. S. Alexander, 121 West First Street, Los Angeles. The case had been diagnosed by several physicians and at the time referred to was in charge of Dr. Barton Dozier, 412 Grant Building, Los Angeles. There were

[4]Quoted by B. O. Flower in Christian Science As A Religious Belief and a Therapeutic Agent. Boston: Twentieth Century Company, 1909. p. 69.

all the classical symptoms and signs of inoperable carcinoma of
the stomach. She was believed by two nurses in charge of her at
the Clara Barton Hospital, this city, to have died and such notation,
together with the hour of death, was made by the head nurse. Her
brother refused to accept this verdict and continued with Christian
Science treatment, with the result that she was restored to perfect
health, left the hospital in a carriage in a few days, and is today
a normally healthy woman.''

On March 26, 1908, Mrs. Ollie Malone, of the Clara Barton
Hospital nursing staff, made the following signed statement as
reported by Flower:

"I do hereby certify that I was a special nurse at the Clara
Barton Hospital in the city of Los Angeles at the time Mrs. Mary
A. Belt was brought there as a patient on or about the first of
November, 1906. She was almost continually vomiting and suffering; was unable to eat or sleep or retain anything on her stomach
for several days. Her stomach was very much bloated, and she
had been there suffering in that way for four or five days; phlegm,
similar in appearance as [sic] soap-suds, at times almost filling
her mouth and nostrils . . . this slightly mingled with blood from
the nose. Her ankles had both turned black, indication that conges-
tion had set in, and we were not expecting her to live through the
night.

"About this time she was treated through Christian Science.
Her brother, Mr. W. S. Alexander, remained at the hospital with
her practically all the time, day and night, for five days. (I understand there were two other Christian Scientists treating her.)
She appeared to rest easier and not suffering so much pain soon
after she was receiving Christian Science treatment, and I think
it was the second or third night after she was taking Christian
Science treatment, she appeared to have expired.

"I was unable to locate any pulsation. This was about twelve
o'clock at night. I immediately looked up the head nurse, and she
came to the room with me. She called Mrs. Belt, and then tried
to locate her pulse. In the meantime her mouth had come open
and the jaw turned slightly to one side, every symptom and indication that death had taken place, and the head nurse, in my
presence, recorded her death.

"It was then that Mr. Alexander, her brother, stooped in front
of her, and placing his hands to each side of her head, called her
by name, 'Mary,' the second time, and she opened her eyes, and
breathed a natural breath, and that morning she turned over on

her stomach and had a sleep for the first time while she was at the hospital. Within a few days she left the hospital, and I regard it as miraculous and the most wonderful case of healing through prayer.

"I am not a Christian Scientist, and have told others of this wonderful case of healing, which I could never have believed had I not witnessed the same with my own eyes."[5]

This and other healings, numbering in the thousands, involving every type of disease and injury known, made even the most dubious modify their original opposition. Nearly twenty years later, Dr. Cabot, then of the Harvard Medical School, was quoted, in the Harvard *Alumni Bulletin* of December 31, 1925:

"I see no reason why we should admit only one of the different ways through which healing comes to our bodies. I want to take them all, and in that I disagree with Christian Science, the good effects of which I see on all sides. I have not the slightest doubt that it does good, that it cures disease, organic as well as functional, only I do not want anybody to say, 'And nothing else cures.' I do not want to see anybody trust all his salvation to any single channel of communication with God."

On file in the main offices of The Christian Science Publishing Society in Boston are tens of thousands of testimonials. Unlike Lourdes, there is no board of physicians to determine when a healing appears to be "miraculous" within prescribed conditions. But published Christian Science cases do require an extraordinary degree of verification and documentation. Regarding these conditions, Will B. Davis, manager of the Committees on Publication, gave me the following facts:

"1. All published accounts of healing have been volunteered by the individuals signing them. It is not the policy of our church or our religious periodicals to solicit testimonies of healing.

"2. The healings published include virtually every known disease—cancer, tuberculosis, poliomyelitis, arthritis, heart trouble, diabetes, and all the rest. In a great many instances healings of this type have occurred after the patient has been given up by medical authority and turned to Christian Science as a last resort. Many of our church members have become Christian Scientists through 'first healings' of this type.

"3. In a majority of instances—particularly those mentioned

---

[5] *Ibid.* p. 94.

in paragraph 2 above—the healings are of long standing, ranging from ten to forty years ago. There has been ample opportunity to verify the permanence of the healing through medical examinations for insurance or entry in the armed services, or through the living of a normal and active life for many years.

"4. Every account of healing published in a Christian Science periodical is signed, giving the home city of the testifier. These people, of course, are known to fellow church members and other subscribers to our periodicals. In many cases their testimonies refer to hospital records, X-rays, medical diagnoses, etc., which anyone in their community can check on if he chooses.

"5. The number of accounts of healing submitted to the editors of our religious periodicals far exceeds the number that can be published.

"When an account is received, the editors require it to be signed by the testifier and to be verified by three members of The Mother Church[6] who know of the healing or can vouch for the integrity of the testifier. The account reaches its turn to be edited about six to nine months after it is received, and at this stage it is processed to be set in type. When the time comes for publication, galley proofs are sent to the testifier, and the verifiers. All are required to submit a signed statement that so far as they know the facts related are authentic and no condition has arisen which would render undesirable the appearance of the testimony in our periodicals. Only after this request is fulfilled is the testimony considered for printing. No testimony is published where any unfavorable information is turned up by investigation.[7] Date of publication of the account is ordinarily from one year to eighteen months after the testimony is first received. A complete file for every testimony is kept for three years after its publication.

"6. Selection of the testimonies for publication involves a very careful screening, the purpose of which is to insure that the healings reported are thoroughly established and authenticated beyond any doubt."

Christian Science has had its army of followers and its army of critics down the decades since its founding. At many levels and in many places, in my investigation of this faith, stories were told

---

[6]The First Church of Christ Scientist, Boston, Mass.

[7]To protect readers against misleading testimonies of healings which are not valid or permanent.

deprecating the work of Christian Science. Some of the criticisms were personal attacks on the character and life of Mrs. Eddy; some dealt with the pay received by practitioners; some concerned the limited training required to be a practitioner, although—in actual fact—no practitioner is registered until he or she has proved ability to heal by several healings and has given evidence of a complete understanding of Christian Science and a willingness to devote his life to healing.

To the individual healed through spiritual treatment, after having received a virtual condemnation to death, intellectual arguments and attempts to explain away the healings in materialistic terms make little sense.

One of those condemned to die was a woman named Mrs. Lois B. Estey of Geneva, N. Y. In 1930, Mrs. Estey was suffering from a large internal growth which had been called incurable. Her physician finally informed her that medical science could do no more to help her. Gently, in answer to her direct question, he declared, "You have a year or possibly a year and one-half."

Mrs. Estey told the doctor that she might as well try Christian Science. His answer was that he hoped it would do her some good. She went out and purchased a copy of *Science and Health*. Her condition continued to grow worse. She was in great pain, totally blind and almost completely paralyzed, according to her documented story.

She called in a practitioner and he gave her some help. One night, as she lay half in coma, she heard her husband say, "If Christian Science heals my wife, I'll become one too."

The practitioner answered, "If Christian Science is not the truth, you do not want it, even if it heals her. If it is the truth, you want it, even if she is not healed."

The words of the practitioner struck home to Mrs. Estey even in that half-conscious condition. She found herself wanting to understand this thing, the power called God, wanting to understand the meaning of Him. "And suddenly," she was to recount later, "the fear of dying left me in my realization that what I really wanted was to know God better."

She was at low ebb that night. As the practitioner was leaving he made Mrs. Estey promise to repeat one phrase from *Science and Health* whenever pain or fear struck: "There is no power apart from God."

Through the night, Mrs. Estey fought to cling only to this thought.

"Suddenly a pain would sweep through me and I would think, 'Well, isn't pain a power apart from God?' and then I would think, 'No—I don't understand it, but there is no power apart from God.'

"Then I would try to move and the thought would come, 'Surely paralysis is a power.' But then I would declare again, 'There is no power apart from God.'

"Then I would want to see and I couldn't see. And I would think, 'Well, certainly blindness is a power that isn't of God.' But I kept repeating—slowly and with effort—'There is no power apart from God.' And finally it dawned on me with understanding that either there wasn't any God or He must be all-power. He was the only power and presence there was or He wouldn't be God.

"That fact just dawned on me in radiance and beauty. I knew from that moment with an unshakable knowledge that I had found the truth concerning God."

Less than an hour later, on this same night, Mrs. Estey received what can only be described as instantaneous cure. "Shortly thereafter," she was to testify, twenty-five years after that night, "there was a sudden severe pain and a little later the entire growth passed from me. At the same instant the blindness and paralysis left. And within a few days I was out walking with my little girl."

Two years later, she saw the doctor who had given her no more than a year and one-half to live, and he examined her and stated: "There is not a trace of the old trouble."

"Since that time," Mrs. Estey reported in her testimony, "I have reared two daughters in Christian Science and have been privileged to become a worker in the vineyards of Christian Science healing . . . I add to the thousands of grateful testimonies my own deep and sincere thanks to God . . ."

8

Rebirth: The Episcopal
Revival of Healing

The roots of the revival of healing in the Episcopal Church date back to the early years of our century—to a meeting of two ministers and a physician in the mid-Victorian living room of a church rectory in Boston, Mass.

There were several items on the agenda of these men: They had to talk about God and healing; about Christian Science and disease; about tuberculosis and fresh air; about prayer.

The year was 1906. The place: the rectory of Emmanuel Church. Present were the Reverend Elwood Worcester, the Reverend Samuel McComb, both Episcopalians, and Dr. Isidor Coriat of the Tufts Medical School.

One important reason for this discussion was to discover what lay behind the great success of Christian Science. The men did not, of course, believe this Christian Science idea that sickness was a mere mistake of the mind, a non-existent nothingness. Yet people were crowding into Christian Science meetings and telling of extraordinary cures. They were turning also to other healing movements.

They were turning because many of the recognized Christian churches had neglected the healing ministry, the Rev. Dr. Worcester said. He was determined, he told his two friends that day, to help restore the healing ministry within the Episcopal Church. But he would do this in full co-operation with the medical world.

This meeting led to a series of meetings with other ministers and physicians of Boston, including Dr. Cabot whose investigations into Christian Science cures were published that year. The meetings were followed by an extraordinary group of "healing conferences" attended by neurologists, psychiatrists, psychologists and general practitioners who were interested in the possibility of working with Rev. Dr. Worcester and the Rev. Mr. McComb in setting up a new kind of clinic, where physician and minister could preach and practice as a team.

Elwood Worcester was a man of prodigious intellect and learning. A doctor of philosophy *magna cum laude,* he had studied at universities in America and in Europe under some of the leading theologians and psychiatrists of that day; he was a scholar of history and languages and religions. He was a man also of gentleness and compassion, driven by an insatiable need to help others.

His career as a minister had its beginnings in St. Stephen's Church in Philadelphia—a church later to become a center of healing. But it was not until he was called to Emmanuel Church in Boston that the Rev. Dr. Worcester launched into the field of spiritual healing and the relationship of God, man and medicine.

The clinic which he established in co-operation with the other ministers, physicians and psychologists working with him, was the forerunner of the kind of clinic later established at New York's Marble Collegiate Church by the Rev. Dr. Norman Vincent Peale and Dr. Smiley Blanton, in which ministry, medicine and psychiatry practice "team therapy" side by side. But in the first decade of the 1900s, the idea of organized medicine and organized religion merging was new. The goal of that early group was to cure the physical ailment and eliminate if possible the mental, emotional and spiritual causes behind that illness.

The first group of people to whom this odd assortment of spiritual pioneers turned their attention were consumptive men, women and children living in Boston's slums.

Leading in the plan was a former student and good friend of Sir William Osler—Dr. Joseph Pratt, later the founder of the Pratt Diagnostic Clinic in Boston, and one of the consulting physicians on the board of the new "Emmanuel Movement." Dr. Pratt's slum-dwelling consumptive patients were organized into classes holding weekly meetings at which Dr. Pratt examined the patients and prescribed—and Dr. Worcester and the Rev. Mr. McComb talked of the role of faith and God and of the force of the human mind when attuned to the will of God. They talked also of the force of love, and of the corroding effects of hate and defeatism.

Much of the medicine preached was based on a simple idea just beginning to be recognized: consumptives need rest and fresh air instead of the foul-smelling poisons of their badly-ventilated tenement flats.

The results of this radical employment of fresh air, rest and the word of God combined were extraordinary by any standards. In some cases hemorrhaging halted overnight; hacking coughs abruptly ceased. Others were more gradual. Enough persons were getting well to attract attention not only in the newspapers but also at the Boston Health Department. Investigators were dispatched by the Health Department to discuss this technique with Dr. Pratt and the Rev. Dr. Worcester. The investigators were all scientifically trained men. The classes were achieving these good results, they said, obviously by employment of the new idea of group therapy plus rest and good air, which probably helped in some measure.

The religious aspect, the preaching and prayer, they shrugged away, announcing that they would set up classes of their own, with some of these same patients and others out of the slums, employing the same techniques, with other physicians, and without any ministers.

Something was lacking. The new groups, operated by the health officials, did not get the same results. The sunken slum faces did not bloom; hemorrhaging did not halt. The city's experiment was a failure.

Meanwhile, Dr. Worcester, Dr. Pratt and Mr. McComb, and the others, were turning to new fields and curing other diseases through this collaboration of medicine and religious faith. Healing sessions were held regularly for individuals suffering from illness of the mind and of the nerves and physical illness of a functional character.[1] Present always at these sessions were either Dr. Worcester or Mr. McComb, speaking individually to each patient, and sometimes to the patients in groups. Dr. Worcester himself did not hesitate to use autosuggestion and even hypnotism in his phase of treatment. Most important in his therapy, however, was the infinite care and patience he employed in trying to make the individual realize what he called "the oneness with God." When this realization was achieved, Dr. Worcester insisted that great benefits were received.

Thousands came to this clinic. Many hundreds were healed. The Emmanuel Movement itself spread to other churches, and other clinics were established in New York and Chicago. For more than a quarter of a century, this movement reached out to the

---

[1]Few physicians accepted the belief at that time that organic disease could be cured by faith in God.

Episcopal faith, and to other Protestant faiths as well, into scores of churches. It represented a middle ground, between the shrine of the Roman Catholics and the sin-denying dogma of Christian Science. It appealed to the man who saw no reason to give up either his doctor or his prayer.

In 1928, the head of this movement resigned his ministry at Emmanuel Church to devote himself to training younger members of the ministry in the church-clinic techniques. In 1930, he established two clinics in New York City—one at Grace Church, on lower Broadway, and a second at Holy Trinity Church, in Brooklyn. The Brooklyn Federation of Churches and the Brooklyn Medical Association worked together in the Emmanuel Movement, co-operating in the establishment of "healing sessions" of doctors and clergy.

There is no doubt that a large part of the success of the Emmanuel Movement was due to the dynamic intellect and drive of the Rev. Dr. Worcester. At his death, in 1940, there was no individual to take his place and a year later the Emmanuel Movement was lost in the all-engulfing turmoil of war.

But the rekindled awareness of spiritual therapy did not die.

The healing work of the movement was carried on through individual ministers and churches within the Episcopalian fold, and through other groups and fellowships, largely interdenominational, devoted primarily to the healing ministry.

One of the most important of these was The Society of the Nazarene, founded by the Rev. Henry B. Wilson of Boonton, New Jersey. It comprised clergy and laity concerned with spiritual healing as preached and demonstrated by Christ. This movement was abandoned in 1932, but the work was carried on by a new order, the Fellowship of St. Luke, later The Order of St. Luke, founded in 1947 by the late Rev. John Gaynor Banks of San Diego, California.

According to the manual of this society, "The Order of St. Luke the Physician comprises clergy and laity within the Church Universal who feel impelled to make the Ministry of Healing a regular part of their vocation. Members of the order devote themselves to the study and teachings of the true relation between the Spiritual Life and Bodily and Mental Health. They know that by humble realization of their own spiritual nature and by God's Presence and Power they can enter into contact with deep sources of life and obtain new health and strength for the body as well as for the mind and spirit."

For twenty-five years previous to the founding of this Order, the Rev. Mr. Banks, an Episcopalian, had been conducting healing services in his church. For ten years he published a magazine called Sharing, devoted to the healing ministry and listing churches of all faiths in which healing services regularly were held. After the death of Mr. Banks, the work was continued by his wife.

By 1957, the interdenominational Order of St. Luke had hundreds of members from business, the clergy, professors, education, medicine, engineering and other professions. Its membership included Episcopal bishops of Boston and Pittsburgh and Los Angeles, and pastors of churches as widely separated as Rio de Janeiro, Brazil; Natal, South Africa; Dublin, Ireland; and Moratuwa, Ceylon.

This Order represented responsible and respected leaders of world religion and laity. The fact that such a group would join together for the purpose of promoting spiritual healing throughout the world is an indication of the extent of this revival of faith.

So apparent was the directional force of this revival by 1951, that the Liturgical Commission of the Episcopal Church in the United States made a number of startling recommendations for revision of the official Prayer Book section devoted to "Visitation of the Sick." Among other things they found wrong was the word "visitation" itself; it had the medieval connotation that in sickness God "visits" us for our sins, again, it seemed too meager and private a word, whereas the service was intended for both public and private use.

The Commission urged the return to some practices of the very early church, before Christ's healing injunctions had been abandoned in large measure by his followers, particularly rituals "which employed a sevenfold order of ministrations upon successive days, thus achieving a continuous and cumulative effect, instead of the medieval attempt to do everything for the purification and preparation of the soul in one single Office of inordinate length . . ."[2]

They suggested also the revival of public services employing ancient rituals of the Laying on of Hands, and Holy Unction or Anointment for healing, at regularly held public services.

---

[2]Prayer Book Studies, III, The Order For the Ministration to The Sick. p. 13.

"In these days of psychosomatic medicine," the report stated, "it ought to be clear that spiritual ministration in sickness is of great importance, and that the point of view of the New Testament and the undivided Church is perfectly sound scientifically as well as theologically. At any rate, throughout the Anglican Communion there is a large and growing movement to obey our Lord's command, and to restore the healing ministry, not as a substitute for the work of the medical profession, but in co-operation with it, especially in dealing with the spiritual causes of sickness.

"The results of this revised ministry are most encouraging, sometimes as amazing as the accounts in the New Testament. Of course there are some failures, but these are to be expected. Medicine does not always cure either, but we do not give it up for that reason. However, we do need a more adequate service in the Prayer Book, both as a liturgical tool for the clergy, and as a means of cultivating that confident faith in our Lord's continuing power to heal, and that real repentence for hindering sins, which are necessary prerequisites for healing."[3]

These new approaches have, in large measure, been put into actual practice in many Episcopal churches in the United States. They have been carried on by a number of pastors who are exploring new methods, drawing upon the Emmanuel Movement and yet beyond it to the idea that any disease or difficulty may be cured and overcome, functional or organic, trivial or serious, even at the point of death.

Probably no man in America exemplifies more fully this new therapy of faith within Episcopalianism than the towering preacher who became head of the Order of St. Luke in 1956—and some of whose cases we have already discussed—the Rev. Alfred W. Price of St. Stephen's in Philadelphia.

This booming-voiced man of God believes and preaches that God wants us to be well; the Lord is on the side of health: "It is my firm conviction that God is always longing to pour out His power and love into the world, and by our co-operation we can help to release and direct that divine power through our prayers of intercession." He believes also that every genuine prayer is answered according to the measure of our faith. "Each of us brings a chalice of faith to the altar," he declared in one of his sermons, "and each is filled according to its size."

[3]*Ibid.* pp. 14-15.

The six-foot-four pastor is an ex-Marine who holds a Purple Heart from World War I and was for many years National Chaplain of the Military Order of the Purple Heart. He came to St. Stephen's in 1942, from a ministry in New York. Although interested for many years in the subject of spiritual faith and its relationship to medical science and pastoral counseling, he had never thought of himself as a healer.

But St. Stephen's was in a business district in Philadelphia. The people who drifted into the church out of the crowds on Chestnut Street were often in great trouble or sickness. The church, just around the corner from this endless river of human beings, reached out to those who sought a place to put down their bundles of pain.

While the Rev. Dr. Price pondered his course of action, two things happened to him which made up his mind. The first was the receipt of a pamphlet telling of how the ritual of Laying on of Hands could be used in public healing services with great results. The second was his remembrance of a quotation from the Book of St. James: "Is there any sick among you? Let him call for the elders of the church, and let them pray over him, anointing him with oil in the name of the Lord: And the prayer of faith shall save the sick. . . ."[4]

Alone in the large, drafty silence of the church, he sat in the pew and thought about these words. As an ordained minister of God and Christ, he was one of those duty-bound to carry on the healing ministry.

One Sunday morning he announced to his congregation that the following Thursday at noon he would hold services for any persons seeking special help or healing. A total of twenty persons attended the first Thursday. But it was not long before word of these services spread, and the numbers increased to a point where two services had to be held, at noon and in the late afternoon, and the numbers attending reached into the hundreds.

The sick came, and the stories of how they were made well became known. Doctors and surgeons and psychiatrists learned that here was a pastor who worked with physicians and believed in utilizing medicine and psychiatry, in making use of every means available in healing, natural and supernatural.

Nor was this any new Milquetoast administering pink-pill preachments. His searching of the motives and minds and resentments and envies of the people who came to him was neither

---

[4]James V: 14-15.

gentle nor superficial. One woman who came to him cried out angrily, "Why, I got more sympathy from my psychiatrist than I get from you." To this he thundered, "I'm not here to give you sympathy but to help you find healing by making your peace with God. Let's get down on our knees and pray for a little Christian humility."

His first question to those who come seeking help is: "Do you really want to be healed?" And his second, "What have you done to help yourself?" He will not accept those who refuse to go to physicians or psychiatrists, those who are too frightened to face the truth, those looking for short-cuts.

His method of healing involves three main steps. The first stage is the preliminary interviews with the individual seeking help. Often, he finds they are what he calls, "spiritual illiterates" who have to be led slowly to understand the road signs of the spirit. The important purpose of this stage is to find out what is wrong— not on the surface, but below; the underlying spiritual dislocations behind the physical. Then comes the second step, in which he puts the individual upon what he calls "the operating table of pastoral counseling."

Every person who crosses his door is a pastoral opportunity, in his view. Frequently they can not understand the purpose of his often embarrassingly difficult questions. "What does my private feeling about my wife have to do with my heart condition?" demanded one man.

Dr. Price tells them of the interrelationships between bodily, emotional and mental illness.

The third phase comes with the laying on of hands in the service before the altar. Sometimes there is immediate healing; sometimes healing occurs only after months or years of counseling and prayer. About 40 per cent of all who come receive affirmative answers to prayers. Dr. Price does not emphasize communion or strictly Episcopalian rituals because of fear that these might keep away people in need of help.

The Prayer Healing Fellowship of this church comprises almost one hundred persons, all of whom have been healed at the altar and each of whom agrees to give an hour a day to prayer. Twenty-four hours of every day members of this group are praying for the hundreds who come to St. Stephen's Church seeking help for themselves, or for a relative or friend.

No attempt is made to keep official "case histories" and documentation of healings, but hundreds of letters tell their stories.

and hundreds of individuals personally have returned to render thanks.

Among the early cases was an elderly lady who came to Dr. Price, explaining that she was the widow of a Lutheran minister and they had always planned to come over but never got around to it. Now she had some sort of abdominal tumor. X-ray examination had been made, and her niece, a doctor at Woman's Hospital in Philadelphia, and other doctors at the hospital agreed that she had to have an immediate operation or she would die. "You see, I don't want an operation and so I thought I'd just drop over here and let God cure me."

They talked for two hours. Here, the healer realized, was a woman of unquestioning faith. When she came to the healing service, according to her report to Dr. Price, she experienced a wave of great force sweeping over her and through her as she knelt, and as she felt the pastor's hands upon her and heard his prayer to God to use him and his hands as a channel for healing, and as she heard his words. "Go in peace, believing you have received God's healing."

When she returned home, the hemorrhaging she had been suffering ceased abruptly. Within forty-eight hours she felt "renewed and almost reborn." Her niece, however, insisted upon her going to the hospital for further checkup and X-ray examination, stating that this could be nothing more than hysteria or suggestion which would wear off in a few days.

She returned to Dr. Price and told him this, explaining that she did not mind going to the hospital but it seemed to her it would look as if she doubted her healing, if she insisted on proof.

Dr. Price answered: "We use X-rays because God has given them to us to use. You should give thanks to Him that you have this means of proof, not for yourself but for your niece."

The X-rays revealed no tumor.

That was in 1949. Seven years later, she was still coming regularly to healing services, to pray for others because, as she told Dr. Price, "I'm a firm believer in preventive medicine, for body and soul."

The number of healings at St. Stephen's and the letters that poured in about them, became legion. These were neither official documents of proof nor advertising testimonials; they were simply letters of thanks.

There were cases of every type; a clubfoot boy, a psychoneurotic young girl, a man with a gall bladder disorder, an alcoholic, a little girl in Children's Hospital with meningitis. These people were not concerned with scientific proof of spiritual healing; all they knew was that they or someone to whom they were close had been sick, or even given up by physicians as incurable, and now they were well. "I attended the healing service," wrote the little girl's aunt, "and heard her name included in the prayers. I am happy to inform you that she is entirely well again . . . With all the good people praying for Barbara, I am sure somehow the prayers were heard."

Of course it is no proof. The girl might have recovered without the prayers; she might have died in spite of them. But the fact was that she did get well after many had despaired, and after the prayers of this healing fellowship of men and women. "There are people who want to put this healing on a scientific basis," the Rev. Dr. Price told me. "They want to test it and examine it and perform it scientifically. I do not believe it can be done."

The ministry of healing, as expounded by Dr. Price, is based on an awareness of the individual and his relationship to God. It is, in his view, the experience of "making contact" with the Almighty. It is a reaching out to this power which is always there. We do not have to beseech the electric power company to give us light, Dr. Price declares; we do not have to cry out against the darkness, we have only to press the switch. "We need the faith, the unreasoning trust and confidence of a little child. Do not bemoan your little faith but thank God for the little you do have, and use it, and the increase will come."

Other ministers of the Episcopal faith have followed similar patterns.

There are divergent methods and approaches. Some perform healing rituals in private pastoral conferences; some hold public healing services intermittently; others on a regularly weekly or bi-weekly schedule. Some, like Dr. Price, dissociate their service from Episcopalian ritual in order not to discourage those in need of this ministry, regardless of creed. "The sacraments are important—but they must wait until those who come seeking help are able to understand them," Price declares.

Others insist strongly that healing comes most effectively through the sacraments. The Rev. John Ellis Large, of New York's Church of the Heavenly Rest, relies in his healing almost exclusively on the sacraments. "We live in a sacramental universe," he states. "The sacraments are the channel through which pure spirit comes into us. Pure spirit is completely unknown by us humans until it is mediated through some physical force. There must be a mediating force of our world."

The Rev. Dr. Large says that in his opinion the force of the spirit comes in the services at his church through the sacrament prayers and the laying on of hands at the altar. "I believe that this power of pure spirit comes through the prayers of the congregation, and flows from them to me, and through me back to them."

Another Episcopal healer who puts strong emphasis on the sacraments, particularly upon the power of Holy Communion, is Mrs. Agnes Sanford, founder of the first clinic for the instruction of ministers in techniques of spiritual healing.

Mrs. Sanford came into spiritual healing after she was cured some years ago of a serious mental depression. She believes that most people who sincerely desire to heal can learn how to use the powers God gave them for healing; it can be learned by study and spiritual discipline, she told me. "But there are some persons who have talents which help. Vivid imaginations which give them the ability to visualize fully, for one. And the power of concentration. Above all, the power to understand what the Bible is saying to us."

Mrs. Sanford referred to one passage of the Bible as indicating that, while the art of healing through faith and prayer may be learned, it is also specifically one of the gifts of the Holy Spirit. She referred me to a passage in Corinthians:

"Now there are diversities of gifts, but the same Spirit.

"And there are differences of administrations, but the same Lord.

"And there are diversities of operations, but it is the same God which worketh them all.

"But the manifestation of the Spirit is given to every man to profit withal.

"For to one is given by the Spirit the word of wisdom; to another the word of knowledge by the same Spirit;

"To another faith by the same Spirit; to another the gifts of healing by the same Spirit . . ."[5]

This healing gift, Mrs. Sanford believes, whether developed through discipline or received intuitionally, can be used in three ways: first, in words and rituals which employ the healer as a channel; second, when the power of pure spirit works through the mind of the healer, in intercessory prayer; and third, still largely an unknown area to us, "the power of pure spirit working through pure spirit."

I asked her to explain this third method.

She replied: "In such instances, we do not know that we are healing, there is no conscious effort, no direct channel or contact between the individual who needs and the person serving as the channel of Divine power. In effect, neither is aware. Both healer and healed achieve a state of prayer in which the channels of healing are open and the cure is worked seemingly automatically, without conscious prayer, without contact, without knowledge, without awareness."

Divergent views of many Episcopal healers contributed to the concept of "total healing," involving many disciplines that work to help man—psychiatry, medicine, pastoral guidance, physical therapy and clinical psychology. All of these can be used, and they have no argument with faith or prayer.

In a statement published in the magazine *Sharing*, Bishop Austin Pardue of the Diocese of Pittsburgh, declared: ". . . We must also realize that His supernatural feats of healing were not ends in themselves. For example, the cure of leprosy meant little if it did not lead to the making of a whole man whose inner spirit would find the joy of sacrifice in serving people for Christ's sake. If He healed a blind man and did not give him a new inward vision, it would have been better had the man remained sightless. Our Lord's aim was to make people whole. To this end, in many instances, He began with the healing of physical handicaps.

"One of the sad developments of modern healing movements is that some tend to make physical welfare an end all by itself. Our Lord is not interested in being a physician to the human body without administering to the total man: Body, soul, spirit, nation, and world. Wherever little healing groups are stressing only physical cures and answers to private prayer, without equal interest in

[5] I Corinthians XII: 4-9.

curing the persecution of minority groups or the welfare of those who are unjustly exploited, you may be well assured that Our Lord is not interested. Under such circumstances, these groups become a mere cult, remote from the real teachings of Christ."[6]

It is the outgoing prayer, for the help of others, say these theologians, which produces the great effect. The Rev. Dr. Large and his group at the Church of the Heavenly Rest always say a prayer for some particular hospital at each healing service, a prayer for the nurses and doctors and patients in that hospital, and the hospital is always informed of this fact in advance, and the exact hour of the prayers, and nurses and doctors at that particular hour remember the people praying.

"Thus there is a tremendous flow of power," Dr. Large said, "between these two groups working in different ways to bring help to people in need."

Such experiences could not fail to have their effect upon the people in the hospital and in the church. And similar experiences were occurring in other churches and other hospitals.

Without fanfare or publicity, the winds of the Protestant healing revival began to sweep across the land.

[6]Bishop Austin Pardue, Imagination, Vision and Faith, *Sharing*, Volume XXIV, No. V, April, 1956. p. 3.

9

Grassroots Miracles

By 1950, the Department of Pastoral Services of the National Council of Churches in America began to receive reports and rumors with startling and somewhat disturbing implications.

There were reports of miracles. Not miracles in great shrines like Lourdes, or through Christian Science or other major movements devoted to healing—but miracles in obscure, unheard-of Main Street churches.

The stories straggled in unsought—a postscript to a letter, a word in a conversation. The ministers and the churches involved were not seeking to become shrines, or to gain world fame.

So persistent and dramatic were some of these reports that the Rev. Dr. Otis Rice, then director of the Council's Department of Pastoral Services, decided upon a survey to determine how many if any of the reports were based on fact.

The questionnaire, sent to a cross-section of American ministers, was carefully drawn up to explore what these men had been doing in the field of spiritual therapy, what they thought about it, and whether they wished to explore it further. It asked for details of cases of healings in which they themselves had participated.

Many Protestant theologians were dubious about the wisdom of such a survey, or its possible results. Some believed it was invading the privacy of the rector's office, where he counseled with parishioners in need. Others feared that the survey would show that most of the rumors were exaggerations. Some hoped it would do exactly that. The "faith healing" rumors would then be put to a stop; at least in the well-mannered, down-to-earth, "realistic" outlook of some clergymen.

The findings of the survey did not bear out the hopes of those anxious to halt spiritual therapy in the Protestant church. Answers received indicated that one minister in four had had some experience with spiritual healing. A smaller percentage—approximately 18 per cent of those replying—had had more than one such experience. About 5 per cent stated that they had had many experiences in this regard. Far from being unusual, many in the last two groups stated that healings achieved through prayer were a normal and accepted part of their ministry.

There were, at the time of this survey, approximately eighty million Americans of Protestant affiliation. The survey indicated spiritual therapy touched the lives of hundreds of thousands of these people, in some degree.

Yet many members of the Council, and most Americans, had little awareness of this fact, even when they themselves were directly involved in individual cases.

A report on the survey was drawn up by Dr. Charles A. Braden, Professor of History and Literature of Religions at Northwestern University. It is an unusual document.[1] It lists the facts and figures, it analyzes and cross-analyzes, it probes the interpretations of the ministers as revealed in their replies, the methods employed, the results achieved.

It shows that of the 460 ministers replying to the survey, 160 had actual cases of healings to report.[2] Regarding methods employed, alone or in combination, the report states:

"Tabulations of the healing methods for all cases . . . is as follows: prayer, 117; laying on of hands, 37; anointing, 26; rituals, 18; affirmation, 49; assurance of forgiveness, 57; and other methods, 24; in most cases not specified, though three did specify reading scripture, one listening, and one counselling."

The report shows that the ages of those cured ranged from one year to seventy-nine. It indicates that Methodists had the highest number of practitioners of healing, with the Episcopalians second, followed by the Lutherans, the Baptists, the Disciples, the United Brethren, the Congregational, the Evangelical and Reformed, and Nazarene churches, in that order.

The questionnaire was carefully designed to elucidate sound statistical findings; the Braden analysis was equally objective. Questionnaires were sent to 982 ministers, in a cross-section of

[1] A statistical summary of the report's findings is included in an appendix.
[2] It must be recognized that the small numbers do not affect the validity of the report. As in a Gallup Poll, the cross-section is chosen to reflect the patterns of ministries throughout the country.

large cities and small, rural districts and urban, large churches and small in upper, middle and lower economic levels.

Of the 982 sent out, 460—an unusually high 46.8 per cent—replied. It was discovered that 70 of the questionnaires were misdirected and did not reach the ministers for whom they were intended. All replies were signed, with names and addresses of the minister and the church.

"Of the 460 who replied," the report states, "142 gave an unqualified 'yes' answer to the question, 'Have you ever as a minister attempted to perform a spiritual healing?' Eighteen qualified their affirmative answer somewhat. This means that 160, all told, have had such experience at least once. This is 34.7 per cent, or a little more than one-third of all those who responded to the questionnaire, and 16.3 per cent, or almost one in every six, of the 982 to whom questionnaires were sent . . .

"Of the 460, only 248 gave an unqualified 'no' answer to the question. This is just under 54 per cent. Forty-eight, or 10.4 per cent of our respondents, qualified their negative answers. . . ."

Many ministers, the Braden report continues, were confused by exactly what was meant by spiritual healing. Some thought it involved only the spectacular instantaneous healing. Dr. Braden made a spot check of a number of ministers who did not reply and found that many had experiences to report but had not been certain that theirs was the kind of healing information desired. "If there had been half the percentage of healings among those who did not answer as among our actual respondents," Dr. Braden states, "the total number would have reached about 250, or 25.4 per cent. That is, it seems wholly probable that as many as one-fourth of all ministers of the larger denominations do resort to spiritual healing on occasion. This is, I think, rather a surprising figure. I confess that I am myself surprised."

I examined these questionnaires at the offices of the National Council, checked them against the Braden findings, and examined the reports of certain cities in a special spot study of replies. In Toledo, Ohio, for example, I found that a total of eighty questionnaires went out. Of the eighty, there were twenty-seven replies, somewhat below the general average. Of the twenty-seven, nine ministers in Toledo gave an unqualified "yes" to the question of whether they had attempted spiritual healing. One gave a qualified "yes." There were sixteen unqualified "nos," and one qualified "no." Those replying "no" included churches of several major

denominations, although other churches of the same faiths in Toledo stated that they employed spiritual healing.

Answers were usually terse and lacking colorful details. Here
is a sample of replies given by a Baptist minister to questions for
information on at least one case of spiritual healing:

(a) *Age and sex of person:* 48, female.

(b) *Nature of illness, describing the symptoms:* Cancer—
been in hospital and treated with radium. The doctor had not given
any hope for her recovery.

(c) *How long had she been ill?* Four months.

(d) *Had a qualified physician diagnosed the case?* Yes.

(e) *Had the patient had adequate scientific medical attention?*
Yes.

(f) *Was the person deeply religious before the healing?* No.

(g) *Was the patient hopeless of cure by any other means?* Yes.

(h) *Was the initiation yours or the patient's?* Both.

(i) *What method did you use?*

    (1) *Prayer*—I went twice a week for prayer with the patient.

    (2) *Laying on of hands*—no.

    (3) *Anointing with oil*—no.

    (4) *Use of some ritual*—no.

    (5) *Making of affirmations*—I did assist her in straightening
        out her thinking.

    (6) *Assurance of forgiveness*—She did find forgiveness for
        things in her past life.

    (7) *Other*—She read devotional books, the Bible, and stud-
        ied the Bible a great deal.

(j) *What was the result?* She gradually came back to health,
is now back to work, and is working in the church.

(k) *Was it temporary or permanent?* It has been four years since
that experience.

(l) *What was the reaction of the patient?* Was more religious.
She got into activities through teaching.

(m) *How did it react on yourself?* It was a stimulant and I believe
that God worked very definitely to cure this person.

(n) *Has the patient developed any other illness since then?* No.

To later questions, this Baptist minister stated that he did not
conduct a regular healing service, did not desire to do so and
believed the pastor had to be extremely careful in dealing with all
such cases. ''He cannot go too far but he must always suggest

that God can do much more than many times we are willing to permit Him to do.''

He suggested that ministers should be trained in counseling and if possible given some training in hospitals. "They should be trained not to go too far," he said, "and to know when to refer a patient to a medical hospital or a psychiatrist."

To the question of his opinion regarding the place of religion in health, he replied: "Religion and health go together. They cannot be separated."

Other replies, from other pastors in the churches of our country, echoed this idea. "Religion is basic to health," a Dallas pastor wrote. Another in the same city stated: "I believe that it is God's will that we be healthy . . . in all ways."

From one side of the country to the other came this chorus of belief:

"A well soul seems to express itself in a well body, and vice versa," wrote a minister in Madison, Wisconsin.

And one in Denver: "I believe it is God's Will to heal bodies, minds and souls."

A pastor in St. Paul, Minnesota: "It (spiritual healing) is a source of profound help little used and much neglected—in most cases never discovered."

And one in New York: "My hope is that eventually there will be established in the Church a guild or order of healers composed of clergy, psychiatrists, and physicians working closely together, it being taken for granted that all are deeply religious and desire to bring all available resources to bear on the problems of illness."

Of the healings themselves, Dr. Braden states:

"On tabulating the variety of diseases reported healed, I found I had listed sixty-four which were different enough to note separately. On closer examination many of these fell into broad general classes. It was interesting to note that the largest number of physical healings were of cancer, of one kind or another; of the lungs, three; of the spine, two; of the mouth, one; duodenal, one; of the bone, one; and just cancer, otherwise not specified, ten; or a total of eighteen all told.

"Did the patients really have cancer? In almost every case the informant declared that the diagnosis had been made by a competent doctor and that there had been medical attendance for a longer or shorter period. One case of cancer of the lungs had persisted two years, had been properly diagnosed and treated by

a physician. After the healing, which consisted of laying on of
hands, some ritual, and prayer at a healing service, X-ray tests
disclosed that the condition had cleared, and in a period of six
months prior to the time of reporting the case, there had been no
recurrence.

"Still another cancer case—that of the bones, her skull, ribs,
hip and leg bones being already involved, diagnosed and treated
as cancer by a physician, and the patient hopeless of cure—was
reported by a Mission Covenant minister in a midwestern city as
having been completely arrested and permanently cured. A Methodist minister in a midwestern city reported a case diagnosed as
lung cancer by not one, but a group of physicians in consultation,
who gave the patient, a woman of thirty-seven years of age, one
week to live. On his own initiative, the minister prayed with and
for her, she confessed, and forgave a person she hated. Next day
he reported the lungs were clear of cancer and after two years the
woman was still well.

"What shall one make of such reports? These are not anony-
mously given. Nor are they the more or less spontaneous testimonies given in a public meeting, where one's enthusiasm,
perhaps stimulated by other testimonies, might lead him to
exaggerate his statements, but they are written statements,
made deliberately, in reply to specific questions, and
signed."

From the evidence of these questions and Professor Braden's
analysis, the Baptist minister of Toledo, in calling health and
religion "inseparable," spoke not only for himself but apparently
for a large segment of the Protestant clergy.

The Department of Pastoral Services, through its Commission
on Religion and Health, announced in 1957 plans to pursue its
investigation of healing even more intensely through seminars and
"spiritual workshops."

The Reverend Mark Shedron, executive director of this department, said:

"We encourage any properly qualified person who honestly
wants to try spiritual healing to record the results and explore
the actual possibilities of serving human needs. We will work
to translate unknowns into definitely known and tested procedures. We are interested in systematizing experiments in healing
and open procedures to public inspection for verification and
improvement.

"We are working to discover new resources for health and

spiritual growth to share with all who suffer or hunger for a more abundant wholeness.''

It was a program in which many ministers in cities and towns across the United States—and, indeed, around the world—had started to take part.

10

A Man Named Day

In 1907, a newly-ordained Methodist minister in Ohio found himself suffering from tuberculosis. Hemorrhaging badly, he was shipped off to Colorado Springs. Doctors informed him that he would either have to live there for the rest of his life or die within six months after he left Colorado.

Still in his twenties, he did not want to die. Yet at the same time his life had been consecrated to God and Christ. One night alone in his room, a short time after his arrival in Colorado Springs, he prayed to God that he might have only twenty years allotted to him to preach from the pulpit. This was all he asked. The following morning, he arose, packed, went back to the doctor and informed him, "I am leaving for the next train to go back East."

The doctor tried to argue. Then he saw that the young patient had made up his mind. "As you will," he said. "But you are going home to die."

The young preacher, Albert E. Day, returned to his church, his wife and children. Hemorrhaging halted the moment he made his decision to return. Although future examinations revealed that the original diagnosis of tuberculosis was correct, he never experienced one further symptom of this disease.

In the early 1940s, Dr. Day became part of what was called the New Life Movement within the Methodist Church—a vigorous effort, launched immediately after World War II, to bring increased vitality into Methodism. In the midst of this strenuous work, he suffered a severe heart attack. X-rays revealed that his heart was seriously enlarged. Physicians warned him he must cease all work or he would kill himself. Dr. Day decided that he had work to do for the church that could not be halted at that stage. He left the question of whether he lived or died in the hands of God, and continued with his work.

Dr. Day was never again seriously bothered with this heart condition. He went everywhere in the country with this work—lugging suitcases up and down stairs, traveling and making speeches explaining the new Methodist programs.

In 1947, after a slight attack (which proved to be digestive and not cardiac) Dr. Day had a complete examination by one of the nation's top heart experts, Dr. Edwin Jarrett. Dr. Jarrett's exhaustive tests revealed not only that there was no block, but also that the heart had regained its normal size, a fact the doctors called unusual.

The healings he had received were more than personal favors, Dr. Day decided. He felt he had no right to keep these gifts of God to himself. He came to an awareness that his healings were illustrations of possibilities available to all. These possibilities could be disclosed only through a program of action launched from his own pulpit at the Mt. Vernon Place Methodist Church in Baltimore, Maryland.

One Sunday morning, in 1950, Dr. Day announced that the following Tuesday special services would be held for any persons who wanted prayers for any problem.

In this simple way, with a few words from his pulpit, the New Life Healing Clinic—which was to become a center of healing to which hundreds were to come weekly—came into being.

The morning after his announcement, alone in his study, Dr. Day sat in silent prayer. He was embarking upon an adventure that he himself did not fully understand. He believed in prayer, in the power of God, in the force of faith. Through his own life and experiences, he had come to understand prayer in its spiritual depths, not merely as empty entreaties but as a deep striving of the consciousness toward God. The effective prayer was the prayer of quiet, of meditation, of "letting the ego vanish into the embrace of God," as he put it.

"Prayer," he told me in one of our interviews, "becomes not mere words repeated but a personal and moving experience, which begins with surface emotions openly poured out, and deepens slowly as the infinite merges with the finite beings, into awareness and strength."

In his book *An Autobiography of Prayer*, he wrote, "True prayer is not a demand but a dedication."[1]

---

[1] Albert E. Day, An Autobiography of Prayer. New York: Harper & Brothers, 1952. p. 142.

To this man of prayer, alone in meditation at his home, at eight-thirty in the morning, came the moment when he knew that he needed help, that he was not yet ready to conduct any full-fledged healing clinic by himself, despite his announcement from the pulpit. His knowledge of the techniques of healing was limited to his own experiences. He was asking God to send him help.

At nine o'clock that morning a woman who identified herself as Mrs. Olga Worrall called at the church. She explained that she wanted to help Dr. Day work in the new clinic she had heard he was starting. Her husband, Ambrose Worrall, was an official in a large aircraft firm in Baltimore. He was a layman with a gift of healing. She, too, had a similar gift and she had worked and studied in this field.

Dr. Day's assistant informed her that the minister was not in his office and was not expected in until the next morning. As she was leaving, Dr. Day walked in. His startled assistant inquired, "Dr. Day—what are you doing here? You aren't supposed to be in."

"I don't really know why I came, why I'm here," Dr. Day answered. "Something told me I had to come over to the church."

Mrs. Worrall then told the minister that earlier she had had the impression that she must call Dr. Day. "I had to offer my services. Not for money—only to help. I had the impression so strongly that it was like a physical blow striking me."

Dr. Day regarded the dark-haired woman curiously. "What time was that?"

"It was early today—about eight-thirty this morning."

The clinic which they opened—in a small chapel at the side of the church—was the scene of many unusual cases and cures. Here, on Wednesdays, gathered old and young, the sick and crippled, the emotionally and mentally disturbed. The chapel itself quickly grew too small for these petitioners, and an added room was opened on one side to accommodate others.

The services were simple. There was a hymn, a talk by Dr. Day on the sacraments, on church ritual and their meaning. Dr. Day would explain: "To discourage any false thinking and to keep healing within the framework of Christian faith, we insist on educational talks each time, the theology of healing and its application in our lives. In this kind of work, divorce of the head and the heart can be disastrous."

I first interviewed Dr. Day in his office at the church. I found him a man of understanding and compassion; there is warmth behind his soft-spoken reserve. A visitor cannot but be aware that this is a man of prayer and meditation, which have brought him close to Divine forces. It was nothing hypnotic or overwhelming; it seemed to me rather like an emanating glow of absolute assurance.

He talked of his early experiences, and his own searching, and the first cases in the opening days of the clinic, conducted with the assistance of Mrs. Worrall.

One of the first was a woman suffering from a "falling down" sickness that none of the doctors or world-famed clinics of Baltimore had been able to diagnose, beyond the fact that she had lost her equilibrium and could not stand up. When she came into the church, she was supported by two men. "She looked like living death," Dr. Day recalled. "Her face was thin and white and emaciated. The two men half carried her forward to the altar for the silent prayer and the laying on of hands."

This woman continued to attend the services. Two weeks later, he saw her come forward to the altar, alone and unaided. "Within one month, she was well. She seemed to have changed inwardly; outwardly she radiated health and happiness. At the end of that month, she was downtown bargain-hunting in the department stores."

Her doctors were amazed and delighted. One told her, "I don't know what it is you're doing—but whatever it is, go right on doing it."

The variety of cases ran the gamut of trouble and need, from the merely imagined and psychosomatic to advanced organic illness. Many cases have been helped; some resulted in cure, some in failure. Dr. Day does not believe that every failure is necessarily the will of God.

"Christ," he said, "does not preach in the New Testament that it is God's will that anyone be sick or indeed that anyone die. Instead, we see Him heal the sick and raise the dead. The message Christ brings is one of health, happiness and life. He is saying that God wants us to live happily and fruitfully and to die only when our time comes, not prematurely, and not, certainly, in pain. Nowhere in His teaching is there any such idea recorded."

Through years of preaching and healing, Dr. Day has studied and analyzed the dynamics of prayer and spiritual healing. The real answer to prayer, he says, comes in our understanding of a God who assures us life and beauty and love beyond the grave; the message of the Resurrection.

"Right prayer brings one to this ultimate and impregnable security," he declares. "Not the frantic, egocentric prayer that on the battlefield expects God to deflect the bullet coming one's way to someone else who isn't praying and never prays! Not the fanatic prayer that would turn the tornado moving toward one's home to the home of another! Not the competitive prayer that would save one's business in an economic crash while one's rivals go to the wall! Not the purely earthy prayer that would get from God a guarantee against all the losses, bereavements, and sorrows incident to our human lot. The saints never sought such guarantees and never received them. Jesus did not enjoy such immunities. The crown of thorns He wore, the lashes mercilessly laid on His quivering back, the thirst which wrung a cry of agony from His heroic lips, the cross where He hung amid the railings of the mob and where He died in untellable agony, all speak a language we ought never to misunderstand. There are no complete immunities provided even for the best. A prayer that 'tries to organize the universe around ourselves' and in behalf of our all too human wants, is not a Christian prayer. It will not only not secure immunity, or bring the world to heel, or marshal circumstances to coddle us; it will lose for us the only real security.'"[2]

The real metaphysics of divine healing involves this awareness of the meaning of God and of love. This is true, in Dr. Day's opinion, in all religious healing.

"At Lourdes, the individual is given things to do. First they must make a good confession, purging all the guilt out of their consciousness. Second they must step into some icy cold mountain water. They are given the sense of having done their part in faith, of having completed their demonstration of faith, so that they do, in full sincerity leave their problem, their illness, their pain to God. It is when they do this fully, most often when they so forget themselves that they pray for the healing of others, that they find healing themselves in many cases. If you open your life to God, you open your life to infinite love that is waiting for you."

Many letters have come into the church telling of healings and answered prayers. Some have been verified by medical reports and physicians. Although Dr. Day is exceptionally careful in any stories and claims made, he is not attempting to keep dossiers. All persons seeking healing, however, received, as part of their

[2]*Ibid.* p. 176.

healing, pastoral counseling with Dr. Day.

Some cases are special. One involved a young minister, of another city and another faith, who had suffered a breakdown so serious that he not only could not preach but refused even to leave the room of his rectory. For several weeks Dr. Day and this young minister prayed and counseled together. Among the causes of this breakdown, the sessions revealed, was the fact that he had been brought up to be a perfectionist; every error he made, even a slight slip in a phrase in the course of a sermon, seemed to him catastrophe. This fact was brought out by a simplified "psychoanalytical" technique Dr. Day employs in some instances of counseling. But recovery lay in a spiritual change, enabling this man's mind and emotions to clear where he could comprehend the difference between his own finite limitations and imperfections and the infinite perfection and limitless forgiveness of God. This was accomplished not by instantaneous cure, but slowly, through days of prayer and counseling of these two men. Within six months, this young minister was back in his pulpit, recovering from a mental breakdown which might otherwise have required several years of hospitalization.

Some cures occur away from the church, some right at the altar. One woman with a growth on her eye came to the clinic to pray the day before she was to have the growth operated on. When she appeared at the doctor's office the following day, she reported, the physician found to his astonishment that the growth had become so loose he was able to lift it off with a pair of tweezers.

Many types of illness have been cured at the clinic. In a case of a youth with a brain tumor, intercessory prayers at the clinic were followed by the surgeon calling off his projected operation only a few hours before it was to have taken place. Within a week the man was home, well and healthy again. Nor was there any reported return of his illness.

"We do not pretend in any sense to be healers," Dr. Day stated in a brochure for the clinic. "It is God who heals. We do not have all the answers. In spiritual therapy, as in the other therapies, there are still many unsolved problems. Sometimes we fail where conditions seem most favorable to success, and sometimes there is success where many of what we believe to be the essentials are lacking.

"But in the light of our experience and our study and our growing conviction, we could do no other than to begin a research in this field, bringing to it some of the same intensity and devotion, intelligence and honesty, self-criticism and humility, that must characterize successful research in any field. We do not attempt to conceal or explain away any failures that may occur. We try to recognize coincidence as coincidence. Our unanswered questions become the stimulus to more earnest research and to a more critical appraisal of our methods.

"We have never permitted any antithesis to be raised between what we are doing and what capable physicians, surgeons, psychiatrists, and psychotherapists are doing. We believe with Dr. Richard Cabot of Harvard that it is God who heals, whatever therapies are employed . . .

"No money is requested or received in connection with this work. We believe that, especially in this adventure, fees are a threat to our own sincerity and devotion, and confusing to the people who come. We began, not knowing whether there would be any response in this conservative community and in a city famous for its schools of materia medica and surgery and psychotherapy. But the people have filled the chapel each week and most of the time there has been an overflow into the adjoining room.

"Whatever has been accomplished has not been because of our merits or skills, but because God has worked in mercy, through the efforts of us, the humblest of His servants, to be the mediators of His grace and the interpreters of His holy will."

One of Dr. Day's hopes for the future is the establishment in America, under Protestant auspices and "in harmony with our religious faith and practice," of a healing center open to all.

The proposed center would make use of many of the operational techniques successfully employed at Lourdes. His outline of this project includes the following suggestions:

"A center, in a quiet place, surrounded by the beauties of nature and structure, isolated from the fevers of our competitive life and yet accessible to those in need.

"A small but beloved community composed of dedicated persons who truly love people of all sorts and conditions, have a living experience of God and an indefatigable faith in God's power and willingness to heal, and will give all or part-time service to those who come for healing.

"A carefully planned regimen that will stimulate the imagination, which is the matrix of faith; make the patients feel that they are loved and inspire them to love; by symbol and sacrament and teaching and witness make real the presence and love and power of God; give the patients something to do that is related to healing, something that requires courage and effort and lifts them out of the passivity of self-pity.

"A God-centered therapy that will direct the patient's attention to God and create a sense of personal partnership with God, not only in the quest for healing, but in all of life, and deliver him from dependence upon a healer.

"A required residence of perhaps two weeks, in order that there may be the time essential to change the patient's ways of thinking, lead him into redemptive contact with God, and promote his wholehearted dedication to God.

"In the beginning, at least, a careful screening of applicants, not for the purpose of selecting easy cases, but to bring to the Center people who have some basic understandings of the Christian Faith and some disposition toward humanitarian service, and to prepare them for treatment, by instruction, as to what to expect on arrival and what they may do at home to begin the therapy of the spirit before they make the journey.

"A recognition that God is not merely 'energy' operating under fixed laws, but 'personal,' having such freedom within law as we finite persons know daily, and such transcendence over law as the Absolute, who is the source of all being, must have; and that our relationship with Him in moral and spiritual as well as in physical renewal is not a matter of an impossibly perfect obedience to law, but of compliance with those conditions of faith and love which in person to person relationships are determinative. The function of the Healing Center should be to help people understand and effect within themselves these essential conditions so that the way is open between them and God, and thereafter the Healing Center itself becomes dispensable as far as they are concerned, and they will know how to find God for healing wherever they are and whatever the illness."

As to the establishment of scientific procedure at such a center, Dr. Day says:

"Obviously such a philosophy and practice render impossible the establishment of the strict 'controls' so dear to the scientist. The presence of an investigator 'breathing down one's neck' or the effort to trace and measure all the forces operative in a healing situation, would destroy that unself-consciousness, that concentration upon God, so essential to true spiritual healing.

"Besides, it seems folly to try to trace all the divine ways of working within and upon the human spirit . . . This, however, does not preclude before-and-after testing to make sure that the disease and its cure were real, something which should always be welcome!''

In the spring of 1957, the retirement of Dr. Day was announced. At the same time it was stated that this healing work begun in this church would go on, and new clinics were established, under the guidance of Mrs. Worrall, in several other Methodist churches in the area.

The Methodist church itself has approached the revived ministry of healing with faith, hope—and moderating caution. Its leading spokesman on this subject, Dr. Leslie Weatherhead, the noted British clergyman and healer, emphasizes the results of counseling with psychiatrists and physicians and ministers working as a team. In general, Dr. Weatherhead disapproves the larger, public healing with its attendant hysteria potential.

But Dr. Weatherhead does not speak for the whole Methodist clergy; each minister is allowed to determine his own policies on this subject. One Methodist spokesman informed me that the church is eager to see the healing ministry carried forward in whatever way the ministers themselves find most effective.

As Dr. Day points out, it is difficult to get scientific proof of religious cure. The elements which make the cure possible religiously often preclude the scientific method of examination. The healing could be coincidence—it ''could be'' many things.

In the town of Woodbridge, N.J., in 1951, a commuter train called ''The Broker'' leaped the rails and careened over an embankment, crowded coaches piling on top of each other in one of the worst train wrecks of our history. Eighty-five persons were killed, hundreds injured. All night, rescuers worked to bring out the bodies of the victims, alive, dead, conscious and unconscious, while relatives of the victims stood by, many waiting through long hours for word—or to make identification.

Among the victims was a man named Robert Stout. He was carried from the wreckage to an ambulance and taken to Perth Amboy General Hospital in a coma. His wife, Mildred, was notified. His minister, the Reverend Roger J. Squire of the First Methodist Church of Red Bank, N.J., had already called Mrs. Stout and told her he was praying for her husband, knowing the man was on the train that had crashed. The Stouts were members of his church and sang in the choir.

A tentative diagnosis of skull fracture had been made, although Bob Stout's condition was so serious that it was impossible to make a full examination. For hours Mrs. Stout and her sister-in-law, Bob's sister, kept vigil in the silent hospital room. Three days after the accident, he was still comatose and physicians decided that, in spite of the danger, exploratory brain surgery appeared essential to save his life.

Several times, the Rev. Mr. Squire called at this room to pray and to give the wife and sister encouragement. On Saturday he told Mrs. Stout, "Tomorrow I will ask my congregation to pray for Bob. And I've called other ministers and they will do the same."

Mrs. Stout was grateful for the pastor's words. She had the feeling, she said afterward, that all the prayers of the world would be said that Sunday for her husband. But on that Sunday morning there were other things scheduled also; X-rays and surgery. Her husband's head had been shaved for the operation when the wife and sister entered the room Sunday morning. Mr. Stout lay motionless as he had for days, his face like carved marble.

At the church, the Rev. Mr. Squire, in the midst of his service, suddenly came down from the pulpit and called upon the congregation to pray for Bob and Mildred Stout. In a matter of moments, Bob was to undergo surgery. It was 11:15—the time of the operation was almost at hand.

"Let us surround these two with our prayers and our love, let us concentrate on Jesus and His healing power for Bob Stout," he told them.

His prayer was a spontaneous prayer from the heart, asking Christ's healing for this man, asking Christ to touch him and make him well.

All that they had to offer there in church was prayer and love and faith. Yet at the exact moment when they prayed, in the quiet room in the hospital, an extraordinary happening occurred: Bob Stout opened his eyes and sat up in the bed. Then he sank back again. The nurse, the wife, the sister, were astounded. The nurse insisted there could be no medical explanation that made sense; she rushed out to relate this incredible event to the doctors and surgeons waiting to perform the operation.

When they wheeled the man to the X-ray room, the surgeon made a close examination and, seeming to see an indication of consciousness, he pinched Mr. Stout. The man who had been unconscious uttered an exclamation of pain. The operation was called off. The surgeon informed the wife and sister that it would not be necessary because the tide had turned and the man was now on the road to getting well.

He continued to get well and recovered within a few weeks. Six years later he still was well except for occasional lapses of memory.

At the time he first opened his eyes in the hospital, his wife remarked, "Isn't it a strange thing, that it should happen right at this hour. They're all in church now. Do you suppose all the people are praying?"

They were.

11

Faith and Fears

Some church leaders of the upper echelons of Protestantism found themselves in a quandary over the healing revival. They were for abundant faith but fearful of faith healers; they were worried that millions might be misled; they were afraid of over-emphasis on physical healing rather than spiritual insight. They believed in Christ's miracles but wondered how many modern "miracles" were merely coincidence. They were concerned that the faithful might be led down a path of medical neglect to needless illness and death.

Some of the leading church magazines, in the mid-1950s, were sounding words of warning. "Grave perils have attended the faith healing movement wherever it has appeared," declared an article in an official publication of the Reformed Church in America. "One danger has been the morbid interest in bodily ailments rather than a real concern for spiritual misery . . . Happy are the healed, but how despondent are the many who have waited and hoped in vain. . . ."[1]

But after warning of these and other dangers, this article explicitly disclaims, a paragraph later, that it is denying "God's ability to heal through faith." And it quotes the words in the book of James, enjoining the elders of the church to anoint the sick and to pray, that they may be raised up.

It was a difficult but understandable dilemma for many church authorities. No one wished to put up barriers to faith, yet wisdom and prudence indicated that progress should be achieved with caution. Most major denominations were insisting that healing methods should be based on the Holy Bible and the Sacraments

[1] John Frey, Faith Healing Fads and Faults, *The Church Herald*, Vol. XIII, No. 34, September 7, 1956. p. 9.

of the Church, not on willpower, suggestion or vaudeville shows and mass hysteria. The were insisting on medical and psychiatric support; they were insisting that no claims be made that could not be authenticated; they were warning their followers to be on guard against "false prophets."

Yet against all of this doubt there were healers and healing in almost every faith.

The Lutheran church is an example. Here one finds a mixture of emotions; the Lutherans believe in healing but, in general, favor private counseling and prayer. Lutherans ranked third, after Methodists and Episcopalians, in the number of cures reported in the National Council survey.

But official Lutheran publications have repeatedly warned their ministers to beware of the sensational and "misdirected" aspects of faith healing. "The Lutheran Church has been wise and scriptural," states an editorial on this subject in *The American Lutheran,* "in declining recognition to any ministry which is not a ministry of the Word and Sacraments. If those who are stewards of this ministry have special gifts from God, He will also enable them to give evident and unmistakable proofs of such capacities. The burden of proof must always remain upon such as claim gifts of healing. . . ."[2]

Similarly in other faiths—Congregationalist, Baptist, Presbyterian and others, large and small—we find a duality of approach and opinion, where individual ministers and individual churches and clinics are on the one hand reporting remarkable case histories, while church authorities themselves take a far more cautious stand.

In the Presbyterian faith there is both a sounding of alarms and the appointment of Commissioners on Christianity and Health to explore the relationship of health and religion. This committee was established on a permanent basis at the ninety-sixth General Assembly of the Presbyterian Church in the United States (Southern) because "a continuing concern for healing is a part of our commission as Christians." The group affirmed its belief in the "power of God to heal the whole man in body, mind and spirit." It further affirmed its belief in a "co-operative ministry of those professions concerned with healing"—medicine, religion and psychiatry. Although constantly warning against "spectacular" faith healing, the Assembly went so far on another occasion as to state in one report adopted, "Prayer may be just as much one of the conditions through which God sends His healing as is penicillin or the surgical removal of a diseased organ.''

Only a short time after the permanent committee on Christianity and Health was approved, a leading Presbyterian theologian, Wade H. Boggs, Jr., professor of English Bible and Christian Doctrine at the Assembly's Training School in Richmond, Virginia, writing in his book, *Faith Healing and the Christian Faith,* made what amounted to a serious attack on the entire field. Starting out with a plea for the Church to use extreme caution in examining, with the most exacting critical scrutiny, ''the theology and practices of the faith healers,'' Professor Boggs later poses what he sees as the heart of the issue:

''But even if we were to suppose, contrary to the teaching of all the Scripture we have been considering, that ability to perform amazing cures is proof of a divine mission, we should be immediately thrown into a state of hopeless confusion over which of the healing movements to embrace. Even if we wished to do so, it would be quite impossible to accept as true all the healing movements which can point to certain successful cures, because their beliefs and practices differ so radically, and contradict one another at so many vital points. . . .

''Sometimes these cures are attributed directly to the healing power of God. Again, the faith of the sick man, or of his friends, is said to play a part. Prayer is considered essential by many. Value is often attributed to such means as sacramental oil, or the laying on of hands, or to annointed handkerchiefs. Or, the successes of Christian Science healers are said to result from their fierce denials of the reality of matter in general, and of sickness or pain in particular. Others attribute healing power to the guidance of spirits, others to the Virgin Mary; others to relics of dead saints. . . .

''The theories behind these healing movements vary widely and in fact are often radically opposed to one another. . . . Yet all of them alike can point to certain successful cures, and all of them alike have a high percentage of failures. . . .

''Nor are we able to make a sensible choice between the various faith healing movements on the basis of doctrine. To be sure, some of us might prefer the religious healers over the non-religious, although there is no evidence that the one is superior to the other in terms of successful cures. Some of us might prefer the more orthodox healers who stand nearest to the Protestant religious tradition which we ourselves have embraced. But . . .

these Protestant healers are orthodox only in those areas of doctrine which have nothing to do with healing."[3]

The alarms and cautions are not to be taken lightly; they are neither whimsical nor mere pettifogging dogmatism, but the real concern of religious men grappling with a serious emerging situation. The fact is that ministers themselves, often in the very denominations which most urgently entreat caution, are performing spiritual healing, sometimes in open services, more often in private pastoral counseling and ritual.

We know this from the replies to the National Council, which showed for example that 39 per cent of Presbyterian ministers polled stated that they had performed healings, some on a regular basis, some as the need was presented.

Regarding the methods employed, there is most certainly a wide range from which to pick and choose—all the way from kissing an ancient relic of a saint to kneeling in wordless prayer before a candleless altar, or praying alone in one's room. The question may also be posed: Are differences in method and theology as important as the similarity of basic Christian attitudes and results? For certainly, if one accepts the belief, which all these denominations do, that God can intervene in our personal lives as He chooses, it is surely equally possible that He will heal Presbyterians and Christian Scientists and Roman Catholics, by whatever candlelit or non-candlelit road each may elect to follow. Christ employed many methods of spiritual healing—by word, by touch, by spittle and mud.

Following its surveys into this subject, the National Council sent out an unpublished "spot-check" survey to four Episcopal churches and to the Reverend Dr. Otis Rice, just prior to Dr. Rice's move from the Council to become Religious Director of St. Luke's Hospital.

Five questions were asked, several of them dealing with procedural matters: how frequently services were held, on what days and hours and similar details. Two of the questions went to the heart of practical belief.

The first was: *What is your philosophy and theology of spiritual healing?* Here are the replies, as made by four churches and one chaplain:

Christ Church Cathedral, New Orleans, La.: "The theology of

[3]Wade H. Boggs, Jr., Faith Healing and the Christian Faith. Richmond, Virginia: John Knox Press. pp. 33-35.

healing is based upon the sacramental nature of all creation. In proportion to the *wholeness* which comes to the soul by the operation of the Holy Ghost, the body and mind express that wholeness.''

Calvary Church, New York City: ''I believe that God does heal through Jesus Christ—that it is a result of our faith in Him that God would have us whole.''

Dr. Rice: ''Granted that God's will for us is 'wholeness'—salvation of personality—it thus follows that body, spirit and mind are an indivisible entity of integration, and that Holy Unction through the Laying on of Hands is one of the several channels for the enriching and deepening of that 'wholeness.' ''

St. Paul's Cathedral, Buffalo: ''In expressed need on the part of the individual seeking healing, and faith in God's willingness or readiness to heal according to His will.''

Church of the Good Shepherd, Houston: ''I believe that our Lord meant what He said when He told His Church to preach, to teach, and to heal. Because the Church is our Lord's body on earth, His life and His power are mediated through the church.''

Indicative equally of differing but not necessarily contradictory points of view, were replies to the second question: *What do you believe to be the actual dynamic in the healing process?* The same group of churches answered:

Christ Church Cathedral: ''The Holy Ghost, the Lord and Giver of Life.''

Calvary Church: ''The actual dynamic in the healing process is a test of our faith, complete trust in God so that one lets go our own anxieties and is completely willing to let God do for him as He wills.''

Dr. Otis Rice: ''Since we are spiritual beings whose souls are housed in a temple of flesh, it follows that *sacramental* means of grace are the most efficacious. As in the Incarnation itself, pure spirit is mediated through *sacramental* channels, *outward* in character but *inward* in result.''

St. Paul's Cathedral: ''Faith, of course; however, certainly in conjunction with faith in the physician as well as the Divine.''

Church of the Good Shepherd: ''(a) Faith in God through Christ upon the part of the one who is doing the ministering. (b) A willingness to be healed by the ones who are being ministered to. (c) Faith on their part when they know they are being prayed for.''

Despite seeming divergencies there are similarities, especially concerning faith on the part of the person seeking help, and putting the problem into God's hands. There is the similarity also, expressed in different ways in almost all creeds (with the outstanding exception of Christian Science), that one should utilize the physician and medicine and surgery and all materia medica as part of the healing tools given to us by God.

"It is my conviction that every medical man is an agent of God whether or not he acknowledges this fact," the Reverend John Sutherland Bonnell of the Fifth Avenue Presbyterian Church said in a sermon on spiritual healing. "He is a channel through whom God works for the well-being of His human children. But he becomes far more effective when he is a conscious agent cooperating with God. As one of the great leaders of medicine in former days once remarked, 'I dressed the wound but God healed it.' How foolish, therefore, for anyone to point to those who work in the field of spiritual healing and say, 'God is working only here.' God is working in both these vital areas, for He fulfills Himself in many ways.

"I see the hand of the Creator in every advance of surgery and medicine and in those newer medications that are arresting and curing diseases long considered beyond the skill of the physician. Proper and necessary medicine is a creature of God just as truly as is the food on our tables and just as legitimate for our use."

Healing and the power to heal is also a claim of the Church of the Latter Day Saints, the Mormons. The men who reach the age and acceptance to be part of the Mormon priesthood have the power, they believe, by Biblical command, to heal through the laying on of hands and prayer.

Mormons do not publicize these healings. But one woman of this faith wrote to me that she doubted if there was a single Latter-Day Saint who could not testify to such a healing in his family.

"This is accepted humbly," she declared, "as a constant gift from a loving Father to his children. It is with us always. It is not necessary for one to go to any particular place, or shrine, for the Lord's power is not so limited.

"These healings take place in the home, hospital, at the scene of accident, or wherever it is needed, and administered by humble, ordinary men who are unique only in that they possess the priesthood, which is the authority from God to administer and act in His name."

* * *

There are also many healing groups outside the churches—individual mind-healing groups and local healers having nothing to do with major organized religions. Some of these call themselves churches but are not part of any affiliated group.

Other groups are investigating healing as a part of a scientific probe of the workings of the mind and its powers beyond our present understanding. One of these, the Parapsychology Foundation, with headquarters in New York City, was founded in 1951 for the support of investigations of parapsychology and the evidence of paranormal healing. The president of this Foundation, Mrs. Eileen J. Garrett, is herself a charismatic healer.

Spiritual healing also has played its role in some of the great ethical movements such as Moral Rearmament, where the reemphasis of moral values has in some recorded instances produced a spiritual reaction and physical healing.

One of the most distinguished unaffiliated "individual healers" was the late Rebecca Beard, a former physician who gave up medicine to tour the country with her husband Wallace Beard, preaching and teaching the "spiritual laws of healing" learned in her long years of medical practice.

In 1947, she and her husband helped establish Merrybrook,[4] an estate near Wells, Vermont, as a center of spiritual group therapy. Although the Beards have died, Merrybrook has been continued under the direction of the Rev. Dr. R.W. Simpson and his wife, Helen. The Merrybrook program is interdenominational and interracial and is centered around group discussion, personal counseling, meditation, prayer and the ministry of the laying on of hands and Holy Communion.

In the midst of the quiet beauty of the Vermont hills and trees and skies, this site has produced many reported healings.

However wide the differences of doctrine in the higher echelons of the larger denominations, in individual churches themselves, it is a story not so much of dogma as of day-by-day results. Those who work by prayer in their daily lives, live by the daily products of prayer.

In my search for these facts, one of these front-line men of faith I wrote to was my friend, the Reverend Mr. William M. Hunter, author of *God and You*, and at that time pastor of the First Pres-

---

[4]This estate was donated to "Foundation Farthest Out," then directed by Dr. Glenn Clark. It was operated on his metaphysical ideas.

byterian Church of Robinson, Illinois.[5] Here was a man not particularly concerned with the subject of spiritual healing, as far as
I knew; he ran no healing clinic or service in his church.

It was some weeks before I had a reply. When an answer finally
arrived, it contained not only a typewritten letter but also a copy
of the weekly church bulletin, with one paragraph marked for my
special attention: "The pastor and his family wish to thank all
who extended their good wishes and prayers during the illness of
Mary Ann Hunter this past week. There is abundant evidence that
many were praying for her . . . her recovery, as of the writing of
this Bulletin (Thursday afternoon) is nothing short of miraculous—
considering all possible complications. . . ."

The letter explained: "The enclosed bulletin for this morning's
church service contains an announcement which will partially explain my delay in answering your letter . . . On the day you wrote
that letter, my 13-year-old daughter was operated on for a 'rup-
tured, perforated, abscessed and walled-about' appendix. The doctors and nurses frankly did not expect her to live the day out—
but she did! As you can see, we have actually been *experiencing*
the healing power of faith this immediately past week! . . .

"I was aware of the profound dangers inherent in her situation.
The doctor and nurse tried to 'prepare' me for the 'worst' without
actually telling me how dangerous was her condition. However,
having been through several truly critical illnesses in my own life,
and having tried to help people through such in theirs, I found
that it wasn't necessary to 'keep on praying' in an actual, literal
sense of the word. It wasn't fatalism in any form, actually, but
simply a placing of the entire matter in God's hands, as it were.
Generally speaking, whenever a person has faith, he tends not
only to pray in the more formal, or spoken, sense of the word,
but to live on the assumption that one's needs are also one's
prayers."

Perhaps in these words of this pastor and his personal attitude
is the answer to some of the questions about which many of the
theologians concern themselves. If one can accept the idea that a
need, to the truly faithful, is itself a prayer, then how can it matter

[5]Rev. William M. Hunter, *God and You*. New York, Chicago: Fleming H.
Revell, 1957.

to our Lord in what precise way we lay our problem at His feet—whether in words, spoken or unspoken; or at an altar; or at a shrine; or telling our beads; or even seeking spiritual aid and prayer from some healing center over the long-distance telephone?

12

Switchboard

Of all techniques employed in religious healing, the one universally accepted as most effective is prayer. All religions accept prayer as the basis of the individual's personal relationship with the universal being or spirit which men call God. Yet prayer itself has many techniques, and many approaches. On one side the Roman Catholic asks a saint to intercede for him in Heaven; on the other, the Christian Scientist prays for full awareness that the evil is unreal and has no force to hurt him and must dissipate in the light of truth, as darkness dissipates in the sun. There is personal prayer for one's own needs, and prayer for others, and impersonal prayer for the world.

And there are some who give their lives to prayer for others—for strangers, for people they have never even seen.

In a place called Lee's Summit, Missouri, there is a room where a light burns throughout the night—every night of the year—and a man or woman sits at a switchboard waiting for calls. All the rest of this community sleeps. This switchboard attendant is a worker for a group known to the world as Silent Unity.

The telephone operator here is waiting to take the calls of those who are seeking guidance, help, direction, encouragement—and prayer.

Calls late at night come infrequently. But they do come in from many kinds of people, for many reasons. A woman calls about her child who has a cold: will Silent Unity pray for him so he can be well for school in the morning? A man whose wife has been injured in a fall calls to ask for prayers.

In a few days, a letter comes from the man, thanking Silent Unity. Almost from that first moment when he called, he writes, his wife began to get better. Now she is almost completely re-covered.

All day and all night, there are groups of workers praying, here at Unity Village in Lee's Summit. But this telephone room on the second floor of the Silent Unity Building is a front-line listening post where trouble pours in from all sections of the continent.[1]

Sometimes people call at night to say they are going to take their own lives or to commit acts of violence against others. The phone worker's job is to calm the individual and reason with him and set his thinking on other solutions to his troubles. Always they assure him that he is receiving the prayers of Silent Unity.

One man called to inquire of the worker who answered at this curious switchboard of prayer: "What do you do when you want to kill?"

The worker told him that first of all she would have to know the man's reason for such a desperate course.

He began to tell her his story. His former wife had threatened him and was trying to ruin his second marriage. His second wife, whom he said he deeply loved, was pregnant. The man had obtained a shotgun and started after his first wife who was trying to make the trouble.

"Then—just as I got out of the door," he told her, "I remembered something from my early childhood. I had a grandmother who used to read to me from a magazine called the *Daily Word*. It was put out by Unity. So I'm calling you people for help. Everything inside me says to kill her and I know it's wrong and everything says I have to."

The worker talked with him calmly, not on moral grounds but in terms of whether it would solve the problem. Wasn't he merely substituting a more terrible problem in the agony he would bring upon his second wife, and the child she carried? Gradually he began to calm down, to see her reasons, to recognize the consequences not to himself but to his second wife and his unborn child, had he surrendered to his murderous hate.

The calls concern everything and anything that might hurt or frighten or destroy human beings. They range from prayers for the sick to prayers for business or romantic success. They come from alcoholics in need of spiritual conversations and from persons

[1]There are Unity Centers in many cities with phones open at all hours, but calls come to Unity headquarters at Lee's Summit from thousands of miles away.

with chronic illnesses who suddenly become alarmed in the lonely dark of night.

Youngsters sometimes call the night before a high school or college examination. Actors and actresses call in before an opening of a play—sometimes only minutes before they go on stage—to calm "the butterflies in my stomach." One mother used to call for prayers of protection every time her daughter went out on a date. Finally, according to a letter the mother wrote, the girl got married, and the calls stopped.

There is never a catastrophe, flood, fire, earthquake or bad accident that calls do not come in from that area, asking for prayers of protection. There are requests for prayers for pets, for dogs, birds, cats, even for wild things. There are people who call asking for prayers for individuals whose troubles they know only from reading about them in the daily press.

More than half of the countless calls coming to this switchboard are requests for prayers for others.

In addition, letter requests for prayer come to Unity Village daily by the thousands, from every part of the world. Hundreds of letters are received that give thanks for the prayers and for affirmative answers for problems solved and sicknesses cured.

Silent Unity, the most far-flung prayer group in the world, was launched in 1982, following the healing of a woman named Myrtle Fillmore in Kansas City.

Charles and Myrtle Fillmore, Silent Unity founders, were products of the post-Civil War years of Indian troubles, railroad building, upsurging industrialism, immigration, invention, expansion and growth.

Charles Fillmore was born on an Indian reservation near St. Cloud, Minnesota; his family lived on the reservation because his father was a trader with the Indians. As a youth Charles worked on a railroad in Texas and mined gold in Colorado and drove a mule team. Then he became a real estate man in Missouri. In Clinton, Missouri, he met a school teacher named Myrtle Page. The young frontiersman-turned-real-estate-agent and his school teacher sweetheart discovered that both were deeply religious and yet both were unsettled in their ideas of theology and metaphysics. Gropingly, they reached out to a force they thought of as the divine spirit.

Young Fillmore moved west again seeking his fortune, this time with his frail, titian-haired wife, Myrtle, sharing the adventure.

They lived through frustrating, sun-baked months of mining ventures in a West still wild, and finally gave this up and returned east, to Kansas City, Missouri. Fillmore went back into real estate.

Myrtle was ill. All her life she had been semi-invalid and her family had constantly reiterated that sooner or later she would come down with tuberculosis as had so many others in her family. Now, at last, their dire prophecies were fulfilled. In Kansas City, she was stricken first with malaria, and then tuberculosis. For a time they debated whether they should go west again, to the clear mountain air. Then, one night, Charles Fillmore had an unusually vivid dream. It was so real to him that he considered it almost like a vision. It impressed itself upon him, as he later reported, so strongly that he would never forget it. Of this unusual experience he was to write:

" . . . An unseen voice said, 'Follow me.' I was led up and down the hilly streets of Kansas City and my attention called to localities I was familiar with. The Presence stopped and said: 'You will remember having had a dream some years ago in which you were shown this city and told you had a work to do here. Now you are being reminded of that dream and also informed that the invisible power that has located you will continue to be with you and aid you in the appointed work.' When I awoke, I remembered that I had had such a dream and forgotten it."[2]

They remained in Kansas City, but the condition of Myrtle Fillmore grew worse. The doctors appeared helpless. Fillmore himself had tuberculosis of the bone and also was under tremendous strain because of the serious condition of his wife and their ever-growing debts.

As a counteractive to their own despair, the Fillmores turned to metaphysics. They looked into the numerous metaphysical movements of that day. There were many such movements, some spurious and worthless, some built around hypnotism or mesmerism, some valid and honest, some seeking to understand the workings of spiritual forces in their relationship to materialism and material science. They studied and were greatly influenced by the new religion of Christian Science.

One spring night, at the suggestion of a friend, they went to hear a lecture by a man named Eugene B. Weeks, who came from Chicago, representing the Illinois Metaphysical College, founded

[2]James Dillet Freeman, The Story of Unity. Lee's Summit, Mo.: Unity School of Christianity, 1956. pp. 39-40.

and operated by Emma Curtis Hopkins, one of the most famous lecturers and teachers of metaphysics in that day. Mr. Weeks was lecturing on spiritual and mental healing. It was a lecture which seemed to Myrtle Fillmore to expound important truths about the universe and the human soul. All her life she had believed that she had inherited within her the seeds of tuberculosis which now had reached fruition. But this man was stating that one could inherit only Godliness and health, if one could only realize this and affirm it and know its truth.

"I am a child of God," she said in her mind, "and I do not inherit sickness. I am a child of God."

Outside, she repeated this statement to her husband. All the way home, in her mind, this thought drove at her: "I am a child of God." She began to try to explain the experience to her husband, and she began to realize that she was no longer defeated, no longer the beaten creature of a few hours before.

Within hours, her physical condition began to improve. Within days, this woman who had been dying was on the road to recovery.

Mrs. Fillmore, apparently through her prayers, and her grasp of the spiritual force available to all who turned to it, had become healed. Others heard of this and came seeking aid. A crippled man from across the street put aside his crutches one day and walked across the room when Mrs. Fillmore told him to. He never carried them again and years afterward, when Charles Fillmore met this man striding along the street, the man said, "I'm the cripple for whose healing your wife prayed years ago."

There was a maid who suffered from asthma and was cured. There was a blind boy who, according to the boy's father, would never see. Mrs. Fillmore had the boy brought to her. After a few visits the boy who they thought would never see again had his vision completely restored and normal.

Such things could not happen without the stories being repeated widely. Charles Fillmore, however, was far from serene about all this. He was delighted that his wife was well; he was pleased that she was able to bring healing apparently to others. But he was cautious about discussing such things with associates in the real estate business.

Nevertheless, he himself was sick and suffering agony. He was aware that there was tremendous need for resources on which the chronically ill could rely for help. He began to explore the subject and at last attempted to become healed, going into seclusion and—as he put it—sitting in quiet "to wait for God." Healing did not come quickly—but it came. Within a few years, his tuberculosis of the leg bone was healed to a point where he no longer wore a brace.

In 1889, Mr. Fillmore started a magazine called *Modern Thought*, to bring to the world the ideas he and his wife had been exploring. Later this magazine was changed to *Christian Science Thought*. The term "Christian Science" at that time was used almost as a generic term for religious healing. Mrs. Eddy, however, was opposed to its use except within authorized areas and, on her representations, the name was again changed, this time to *Thought*.

The Fillmores had also started a prayer group in their home. Every night the group met at ten o'clock, for no less than fifteen minutes, to pray for those who were sick or in trouble or in need of money or guidance. They prayed in silence; no word was spoken during that fifteen-minute period. One night, as the prayer period ended, Charles Fillmore cried out to the others, "I have it—Unity. That is the name of our magazine. That is the name of our group."

The magazine and the prayer group were the two basic outward operations of Unity. The prayer group was known first as The Society of Silent Help. Anyone was welcome to send his troubles into the group for their prayers and to join with them, at the same hour in the evening, in prayer, silently turning to God and affirming His presence and continual help. "Whatsoever ye shall ask in prayer, believing," Jesus said, "ye shall receive."[3] This was the approach of the prayer group. This was united prayer, united understanding, the united force of good will, of dedication to infinite truth and love. Any individual who attuned himself to these prayers could partake of their strength.

Letters began to come in from the sick and weary and lost—all seeking to touch this new force the Fillmores and their group and their magazine spoke of. The prayer hour was changed to nine o'clock so that more persons at great distances could participate. In the magazine *Unity* special prayers were written for those who wished to make affirmations during the fifteen-minute prayer period. Across the country, separated by hundreds of miles, thousands of men and women were praying together, the force of their prayer silently reaching out to God.

Such was the beginning of Unity.

As this organization developed, there was no thought of profit.

[3]Matthew XXI:22.

Money would come from the same source health came, to carry on this work. Workers originally served for nothing; as funds came in, they began to be paid wages. The one magazine grew to a number of magazines and books, telling the story of Unity and providing helps in the form of prayer. The front-room prayer group expanded into a full-fledged office and eventually into Unity Village with its array of buildings, provided by funds which poured in from the adherents of this vast reservoir of prayer.

A small charge was made for the magazines and books, insufficient to cover costs. Everything that was done at Unity was done for Unity—for the expansion of the movement, never for the personal profit of the Fillmores or of any individuals connected with this organization. When they needed funds to support the home, the Unity School for training Unity teachers, the printing plant, or whatever—they prayed. Serious business conferences at Unity would frequently start with someone saying, "Well, it's a serious problem. Let's pray about it."

No great industrial plant, no home or organization or business, ever stayed more faithfully to this basic idea of praying and doing. Whether it was a question of funds for a new project, or the life of a woman who had been told she had twelve hours to live— Unity prayed.

A day at Unity is an extraordinary experience. It is unlike any other place on earth. Here is a small and beautiful community, with a number of handsome buildings and hundreds of workers, a sudden and exciting world set down in the Missouri grassland, its tower rising like a strange pagoda against the prairie skies. There are student cottages, the Unity Inn, the Silent Unity Building, largely given over to prayer groups, the Administration Building, the printing presses, the bindery, the correspondence school— power plants in a workshop of faith.

Each day begins at eight and before it begins—precisely at that hour—each worker pauses for a moment of silent prayer at his desk or the place of work, to prepare himself to give the best service he can to those writing or calling or coming in personally. A major activity is the handling of the thousands of letters and cards received daily. Before the letters are opened, they are blessed by Unity workers. This is a spoken blessing—the Fillmores taught that the spoken blessing has great power.

As letters are routed through various departments—the Order Department, the Subscription Department, the Letter Writing Department and the rest—an additional blessing is given to the mail. After the letters have been handled in whatever way indicated— the subscription filled, the prayer requests cared for—replies are written and the outgoing mail receives a final blessing in the Mailing Department. The blessing usually is given in a few words of affirmation: "The Christ consciousness of peace, power, and plenty is expressed in this outgoing mail."

Center of the entire Unity movement is the Silent Unity ministry, the group of workers praying at the Unity center, in a continuous flow of faith in behalf of those who call, write or telephone. One of the important tenets of Unity is that prayer reaches across time and space; it does not matter if the individual is near or at great distance, the power of prayer is transcendent. One Unity brochure states:

"Unity believes that God's will is that His children have every needed blessing; that religion can and should be practical; and that when men learn to pray aright there is nothing that their prayers cannot accomplish. For more than sixty years Silent Unity has been co-operating in prayer with persons in every part of the world.

"Friends turn to Silent Unity for help in solving every conceivable problem. Not only do they request prayers for healing, but also for prosperity, employment, protection, better grades in school, freedom from undesirable habits, the adjustment of misunderstandings, and the solution of domestic and various other problems.

"There is nothing secret or mysterious about the way in which the Silent Unity ministry is carried on. Those who pray simply enter into the spirit of oneness with the Father and with the persons with whom they pray . . .

"Silent Unity claims no special power that is not within everyone. It is not Silent Unity but the Spirit of God that accomplishes healing. Unity believes that through faithfulness in prayer and obedience to the teachings of Jesus anyone can be illumined, healed and prospered."

The printing department and bindery turn out half a dozen magazines for adults and children, as well as pamphlets and books. Many of the magazines are printed in other languages and shipped overseas; some are printed by Unity groups in other nations— Italy, Brazil, Finland, Germany, France and others. These are sold at nominal prices; in addition, millions of copies are given away to more than five thousand institutions, homes for elderly people, YMCA and YWCA groups, Red Cross organizations,

Army and Navy hospitals, penitentiaries, leper colonies, orphanages, children's hospital wards and schools for underprivileged children. Free Unity literature is also sent to the Navajo Indian Reservation; *Unity* is often the only magazine found in a Navajo home.

The free literature is sent out through a Unity department known as "Silent 70." The name is based on a quotation from Luke: "The Lord appointed other seventy also, and sent them two by two before his face and into every city and place wither he himself would come . . . and he said unto them, The harvest truly is great but the laborers are few . . ."[4]

Unity also operates a training school and correspondence school for those who wish to prepare as Unity leaders and those who wish to follow systematic study of Unity teachings. In addition there is a "field department" which operates some two hundred eight Unity centers in American cities, providing devotional service, Sunday school and classes in Unity concepts. (But Unity is not itself a religion and does not ask anyone to leave his or her religion; Unity is a prayer group on a worldwide scale and all faiths are welcome to join its brotherhood of prayer.)

At its core, Unity is a state of awareness, of thankfulness, an expression of gratitude to divine spirit. "Metaphysicians have discovered," Charles Fillmore wrote, "that words that express thanks, gratitude, and praise release energies of mind and Soul; and their use is usually followed by effects so pronounced that they are quickly identified with the words that provoke them.

"Let your words of praise and thanksgiving be to Spirit, and the increase will be even greater than when they are addressed to man."[5]

It is awareness that God is present within each of us, that we can reach out to Him in our minds. Awareness, expressed in silent prayer, affirmation, stated with true faith, is Unity's key to health and well-being.

Unity's metaphysical interpretation of evil is close to that of Christian Science. "Unity believes that evil is the result of man's disobedience to divine law," one pamphlet on the movement's

---

[4]Luke X:1-2.
[5]Charles Fillmore, Jesus Christ Heals. Lee's Summit, Mo.: Unity School of Christianity, Inc., 1952. p. 137.

precepts states. "It does not exist as an entity in and of itself."[6]

According to a statement of Charles Fillmore quoted in one pamphlet, in the symbolic fall of Adam and Eve man came to know good and evil; had they obeyed the injunction of God and held to the good, only good could have manifested itself.

"We are prone to think of the 'fall of man' as something that happened long ago, in the infancy of the race, told, as indeed it is, in allegorical form. Instead we should realize that the scene depicted in the Garden of Eden is being reenacted in our own lives every day. Whenever we accept a restricting condition as having reality of finality, it proves that we have eaten of the 'forbidden fruit' and our eyes are open to evil. We are hearing its voice instead of the Lord's. Otherwise we should not worry, for God tells us to trust; we should not condemn for He bids us to love; we should not envy for does He not declare, 'Thou shall not covet'? . . .

"Unity affirms however that as man turns to the Lord, serving Him in thought, word and deed, evil in the form of distressing circumstances for the individual, in the form of social and economic difficulties for nations, and in the form of world problems for the race will depart as Satan did when overcome by Jesus in the wilderness."[7]

Every issue of *Weekly Unity* and the monthly magazine *Unity* carries letters of gratitude from persons who state that they received blessings and help through the Unity prayers. Unity itself makes no attempt to "check" on these cases or to follow up the case at a later date. Yet from the letters themselves they are able to see a broad picture of healings that last, of prosperity that is sound and that remains, of happiness that appears to be built on solid foundations.

Many who telephone for help call again and again, sometimes about the same problem. Workers are not allowed to give their names over the phones but many callers write in to say how much help they received from talking with the worker who was on some specific hour. Many persons, either by mail or over the telephone, keep Unity informed on what happens. In reply to my own request for fuller information on some of their operations, Unity officials

[6]Elizabeth Sand Turner, *What Unity Teaches*. Lee's Summit, Mo.: Unity School of Christianity, Inc., n.d. p. 15.

[7]*Ibid*. pp. 16-17.

sent, along with the additional information requested, the following special report:

"The day we received your letter we received a call from a woman who said that she had previously called for prayer for a sister-in-law who was threatened with a dreadful and disfiguring operation for cancer, and the cancer had miraculously disappeared. Now she was calling for prayers for her husband and two sons who were lost in a boat at sea. Later she called again to tell us that within an hour after her first call, the coast guard had called her to tell her they had a tentative identification, a short time later that the identification was positive, and then her husband himself called. The motor on the boat had failed but the coast guard had found them. . . .

"Many of the calls are long-distance and costly. Yesterday one of the phone room workers said she was touched with how much the prayers of Silent Unity must mean to people. A call came from California. She heard the operator say, 'It will be $3.45 for three minutes.' Then she heard the coins being dropped into the box, one by one, and the operator finally said, 'Go ahead.' The caller said she had just put her mother on the plane for a distant city and had hastened to the phone to call us right away as she wanted to know that Silent Unity was enfolding her mother with their prayers for protection. . . .

"Often those who call are distraught and sobbing. Then, of course, it is the Silent Unity worker's first need to get the caller to be calm and coherent . . . Sometimes the calls are calls of thanksgiving.

"Yesterday one woman called just to tell us how grateful she was for her awareness of God's ever-present Spirit, and to ask us to pray for her continued awareness of God the good. She had fallen down and injured her hand the night before and it had been cured almost instantaneously, this caller said, adding that she had been studying Unity for twenty-five years and every time she called Unity for help, 'things worked out.' "

One of their pamphlets states: "It is difficult to find a few words that explain exactly what Unity School is. It is a big publishing house. It is a place of prayer, a shrine to which hundreds of thousands of people all over the earth turn in their thoughts when they are in need of spiritual help. It is a recreation center. It is a school and a retreat to which hundreds of people come every year to study and meditate and pray. It is a farm with orchards, vineyards, and crops in cultivation. It is all these; and yet it is more than all these, for it is a place of God...."

There is a cool strength in these words, in a day when many voices are raised and many claims are made.

13

A Brash Young Man of God

There are two stories of Oral Roberts.

There is the story as the world knows it on the surface. And there is the story as this writer heard it and drew it from Oral Roberts himself, sitting across from him and talking it out—as I threw at him all the criticisms I had heard, all the denunciations, and listened to his answers.

They were good answers. They were not in any way evasive. They presented the picture of a man who has become—in a very real sense to many thousands of people, a channel of healing.

I set down my findings about Brother Roberts, and his own statements to me, in some detail because the words and his ideas and preachings today affect the lives of millions and the public has a right to unbiased facts.

One of the most controversial figures to emerge in the 1950s was this booming-voiced ex-stutterer who combined the forensic fervor of a Billy Sunday or Billy Graham with the homey drawl of a Will Rogers. By 1957—not yet forty years old—he had become America's best known evangelistic healer. His accomplishments in terms of "output" and personal achievements were stupendous. His radio program was carried on an international network of more than four hundred stations. His television program was seen on one hundred eighty stations throughout the United States and Canada, as far as Hawaii and the Philippines. His monthly magazine, *Abundant Life*, published at his Healing Waters[1] headquarters in Tulsa, Oklahoma, was reaching more than a million persons a month, not counting other magazines, books, tracts, pamphlets, an autobiography and a cartoon magazine de-

---

[1] *Healing Waters* was the original name of the magazine.

picting stories of the Bible and healing in this media, aimed especially at reaching the youngsters.

Most important was the television show, with its climactic "healing line" in which the sick, crippled, blind, deaf and dying walked, limped or were assisted up the ramp to Oral Roberts, who was waiting to place his hands upon them and pray for their healing. These healings occurred at services held in the Oral Roberts tent, before "live" audiences of as many as eighteen thousand, with television cameras grinding film for later showing over the airwaves.

"Filmed right in the big tent," declared one of Roberts' releases, "and showing the unrehearsed scenes of the revival campaigns, the Roberts program gives millions of viewers a 'front-row view' of the sermon, the call for sinners, and the prayer for the sick. Every week thousands of people write to tell how they accepted Christ as their Saviour right in their own homes while watching the Oral Roberts television program, and others write to tell how they have been healed of sickness in answer to faith and prayer as they viewed the program. . . ."

The dynamic personality and tactics of Roberts, his skillful use of the traditional techniques of the sawdust trail approach, won him hundreds of thousands of followers, many of whom regard him as truly anointed of God. It won him also a corps of critics, some of whom were leaders of other religions, and most of whom assailed his techniques and his claims.

Many of these critics demanded that Brother Roberts allow physicians to examine his patients before and after the alleged healings; that medical records and hospital records and similar responsible documentation be made available for examination by the public along with the claims of cures.

At the outset, any objective critic was forced to admit that Mr. Roberts—like other great evangelist "soul-savers"—was reaching millions of persons who might otherwise never have given a thought to God or faith or the teachings of Christ. In the area of soul-saving he was in a time-hallowed America evangelistic tradition.[2] In one of his books, Roberts describes a meeting with a fellow evangelist who dropped in to the big tent one evening. The visiting evangelist had brought along his small son who gazed

---

[2]Evangelist Billy Graham limited himself from the start to "conversions" of sinners, claiming no special gift of healing.

with great intentness at the five poles required to hold up the huge canvas of this vast tent.

"Daddy," the boy said, "I always thought you were the greatest preacher in the world but Brother Roberts is greater. You're only a two-pole preacher but he's a five-pole preacher."

Two-pole or five-pole, when the evangelist moves into the arena of spiritual healing, there can be no question that grave perils arise. Evangelism is by its very nature a high-pitched approach, a fervent crusade to rescue the unsaved, often rising to a height of near-frenzy. Under such conditions the danger of "hysterical cures" is constantly present. The crippled walk, the blind see, the arthritic's limbs straighten. Hysteria may produce extraordinary surface changes; it has the glitter of fool's gold. But when the hysteria goes, the seeming cure may go also, the temporarily displaced symptoms of the primary ailment may reinstate themselves and the victim may be plunged into renewed and infinitely more pernicious despair.

Some years ago a grim sample of this occurred in a small midwestern town where a woman evangelist was staging a revival. Present on the platform was a twelve-year-old crippled girl. Everyone in town knew her and her story. She had been a hopeless cripple since infancy. Now she was here before them, seeking healing.

The woman revivalist accepted the challenge. From across the platform she spoke to the child: "You can walk, darling. Drop your crutches and come to me."

The girl stood irresolute for an instant, leaning on her crutches. The revivalist called to her again, her words almost militant: "Drop your crutches, dear. Drop them and walk. You can walk, dear. Come to me."

In the hush that followed, everyone heard the crutches clatter to the floor. The girl took one halting step forward, and then a second. She gave a little gasp and walked forward, step by step, to the beautiful revivalist who waited with outstretched arms.

The gathering of townspeople broke into cheers. Here was a miracle in which the whole town took part; this was their own little crippled girl; they knew her, they knew she could not walk before and now she was healed. Many in the gathering openly sobbed.

But three days later, after the revivalist and her entourage had moved on to their next city, the little girl collapsed on the street and had to be carried, sobbing and in pain, to her home. The hysteria whipped up by the white-robed lady was over, and so was the "healing." A child's faith was crushed and the community, stunned by its own naïveté, will wait a long time before again talking about "miracles."

Such is the dynamite—at once mystical and mortal—with which the evangelist plays. Not all claimed healings by evangelists are hysterical or short-lived. If there are cures in the water of Lourdes, in a Christian Science practitioner's office, or by means of a telephone call to Unity there can be cures also in a tent or before a television camera; man does not tell Deity where and when He may work His miracles. Moreover, the sawdust trail does represent, to hundreds of thousands of persons, a true road to faith. For them it is the road, and has validity in its religious meanings.

And in this tented arena of faith, in the mid-twentieth century, Brother Roberts stood out as the outstanding "evangel" of healing in the big tent itself, and over radio and television networks—as the stellar minister of the Holy Word for the Pentacostal Holiness Church, the largest group of which is called the Pentacostal Assemblies of God.

Oral Roberts was the child of the sawdust. His father was a revivalist minister and frequently went off with his family on trips, holding meetings along the way. Sometimes the collection plates were full and the Roberts family ate well; sometimes there was hardly enough to buy a meal. Oral Roberts' father always believed that of his five children, Oral was the one on whom God would set His finger. Others in the family found this difficult to understand; not only was Oral a thin, pale, overgrown tubercular, but even if he recovered from this illness, they asked, how could he be a minister when he stuttered?

When he was sixteen, bedridden with consumption, Roberts had an experience in which he felt the presence of God, while he and his father prayed. It swept through him so strongly that despite his sickness and hemorrhaging, he stood up. ". . . the power of God came upon me with such force that it lifted me right up in the bed, and I found myself standing up in the bed with my hands upraised, praising and magnifying God and saying, 'I am saved! I am saved! I am saved!' "[3]

[3]Oral Roberts, *Oral Roberts' Life Story as told by himself.* Tulsa, Oklahoma: Oral Roberts, 1952. p. 46.

One day, after he had been in bed five months, his brother Elmer announced that he was going to take Oral to a service held by a revivalist and healer known as Brother George Moncey. Elmer had borrowed an automobile to transport Oral to this service. Of this momentous experience in his life, Oral Roberts writes in his autobiography:

"While I lay on the mattress in the back seat of the borrowed car with Mama and Papa and Elmer up front, everything grew very quiet. Suddenly I heard a voice. I didn't know who it was. It was calling my name. 'Oral Roberts! Oral Roberts!' It scared me, for I had never heard a voice like it. Then in an instant I knew it was God. I had never heard His voice before. What I knew about God I had learned from Papa and Mama. They had told me many times that His hand was upon me and that He had special work for me to do. Then just as clearly as I had heard Elmer speak, I heard God speaking to me. 'Son, I am going to heal you,' He said, 'and you are going to take my healing power to your generation.' "[4]

According to his own story, Oral Roberts was healed that night, both of tuberculosis and of stuttering. When Brother Moncey ordered the "cursed disease" to come out of the boy, Mr. Roberts recalls that something seemed to strike his lungs, he felt a tingling sensation throughout his body, a beautiful light engulfed him and the next thing he knew he was racing up and down the platform with his hands upraised, shouting, "I am healed! I am healed; I am healed!"

"Most of the people in the audience knew my father and mother and knew about my having tuberculosis," Roberts recalls in his autobiography. "Most of them were very sympathetic and anxious that night to see me healed. The power of the Lord struck them about the same time it struck my lungs. When I began racing up and down the platform, that huge crowd leaped to its feet, some ran down the aisles, some waved their handkerchiefs, some fell on their knees and began to pray. Papa later told me that more than one thousand people were on their feet shouting and praising God at the same time. My healing almost broke up the meeting . . ."[5]

When the minister then quieted the gathering and asked Oral to stand up to the microphone and tell the people what God had

[4]*Ibid.* p. 49.
[5]*Ibid.* p. 50.

done for him, the boy began to talk and to his astonishment found that he no longer stuttered.

Later, Brother Roberts states, he had several more "talks with God," and from these came to realize that he had both the power to preach and the power to heal. This power to preach rose to such a peak on one occasion that he leaped from the platform halfway through the sermon while the crowd below surged forward to touch him.

"There was shouting and rejoicing all over the audience," Roberts wrote of this experience. "Some were crying and weeping. I never learned how that healing line formed, but there was a long line of people coming to my left toward me. I started laying my hands upon them one by one and praying in the name of Jesus Christ of Nazareth for God to heal them. I laid my hand upon an old German woman who had had a stiff hand for thirty-eight years. Suddenly she screamed at the top of her voice and shouted that she was healed. She raised up her hand and began to open and close it to show the people how God had taken the stiffness away and given her the perfect use of it. Those close by saw this miracle, and it greatly increased their faith. A lot of people were healed that day, for people kept coming in the healing line and I prayed until six o'clock."[6]

Such was the beginning of the saga of the great mid-century outburst of evangelical healing. From this came the eighteen-thousand-person tent, the "crusades" in America's great cities, the Healing Waters headquarters at Tulsa, where some four hundred persons work producing the magazines and pamphlets and books published and sold by the Oral Roberts Foundation, the broadcasts, the whole tremendous operation.

Not all healings or "failures" are put on the airwaves. The technique is to bring the limp and halt and blind into a prayer tent, set up beside the main tent. Here, Brother Roberts goes and prays over individuals. Some are healed, according to claims, right in the tent. Others are healed, according to the claims, in the "healing line" which is photographed and recorded during regular meetings in the main tent for rebroadcast over the airwaves.

Questions have been raised as to the techniques employed in selecting those who go into the healing line in the big tent, and particularly on nights when television pictures are taken. (Roberts

[6] *Ibid.* p. 94.

states that these persons are taken in their turn and are not "selected.") Are the healings that are claimed before the viewers actual healings? Do they happen as claimed? Are they permanent?

In the Roberts magazine, a number of reports on these cases are listed each month. To check the facts, I interviewed those listed among the healed. In interviewing these persons, I did not prejudge the issue in any way; I asked questions and recorded the answers.

One of the healed was Doyle Wills, of Greensville, Tennessee. This man said that in 1948 he was dying of tuberculosis. He had been bedridden for twenty-eight months and was hemorrhaging almost constantly. He was not strong enough to walk or even to stand up. Physicians had given up all hope of this man's recovery, and told his family so.

The man's brother and sister took him in a car three hundred miles to Durham, North Carolina, where Brother Roberts was holding one of his "tent crusades." When Mr. Wills was carried in on a stretcher, Brother Roberts ordered him to get up off his bed and walk. Filled with faith, Mr. Wills did as ordered, according to his own story as he told it to me, and received strength he had not imagined he possessed.

"In that single instant, I was cured," he said. "I knew it, right then. There was no doubt in my mind. God had heard the prayer of Brother Roberts and healed me. I went out to the car immediately afterwards and I sat up and ate and I was strong again. I was perfectly well. When I got back to Greensville, I had new X-rays taken and they showed that the TB was gone.

"Since then, I've been working in a factory and doing hard physical work too. Furthermore, I had to go through a complete physical examination to get the job. And they found nothing wrong. I've got a family, a wife and three children, and I'm teaching Sunday school and I hope you'll tell this story so that it'll help other people to know about this wonderful thing that happened to me."

Another man I talked with, T. J. Rathke of Cameron, Wisconsin, is a television salesman. Mr. Rathke had been suffering from heart trouble brought on by a rare skin ailment which produced coronary insufficiency and angina pectoris. He had had a number of heart attacks, had developed nodule-like welts on his legs, and his eyes were so bad that he had to wear thick glasses to see. Gradually he grew weaker. His doctors informed him that his disease was incurable and that he did not have long to live.

Despite this, he continued to try to work. One evening, after helping to install a television set, Mr. Rathke saw the Oral Roberts show. The idea came to him, he told me, that if he could just get to Brother Roberts he would be healed. He and his wife got in the car, leaving their son with relatives, and started out for Cincinnati, where Mr. Roberts was holding a crusade.

They drove one hundred and fifty miles a day. He was forced to halt because of a heart attack at Holland, Michigan, and was treated in the hospital there. One of the physicians in that hospital, hearing his case history, told him that "beyond alleviating the symptoms for brief periods, there's nothing medicine can do for you." Finally they reached the "crusade" in Cincinnati. The night he went through the healing line, they were making television pictures and something went wrong with the lights. There was delay and confusion and when Mr. Rathke finally reached Brother Roberts, the evangelist got the cards mixed up and began praying for a totally different case.

"When he touched me, I felt nothing at all. I was terribly disappointed. I walked down the ramp unchanged in any way."

Before Mr. Rathke and his wife started home, they stopped at the house of a minister they knew in Cincinnati and Mr. Rathke told him of his experience. The minister said that Mr. Rathke, in coming to Cincinnati, had been carrying out the will of God; now he should have faith that God would hear the prayer of Brother Roberts.

He also told Mr. Rathke that whenever pain struck, he was to repeat a message from the Bible; "They shall lay hands on the sick, and they shall recover."[7] All the way home, he did as the minister had suggested, and each time he repeated this passage, Mr. Rathke told me, "To my amazement, the pain went away instantly."

When he reached his home he had a good night's sleep, and the following morning he awakened feeling strong and well and without pain. He did not go to the physician that day but waited a few days. He still felt completely well. When finally he went to his doctor, the physician was astounded at the results of his own examination. "Your heart is strong and your blood pressure normal," the doctor stated.

Mr. Rathke went back to work. Neighbors in his home town of Cameron were surprised to see him apparently well again. A

[7]Mark XVI:18.

few weeks later he drove to Billings, Montana, through heat of 106° F. because he wanted once again to go through the healing line; he did not question his healing, but he had to know if Brother Roberts had the "charge" in his touch that others talked about but that he had not experienced.

"I found out that second time," Mr. Rathke told me. "This was like a charge of electricity. I'm an electrician and I know what that means. It starts at the top of your head and the bottom of your feet and it goes right through your whole body."

Mr. Rathke continued to work at his television business and almost ten years later there had been no recurrence of the disease which doctors had said would be fatal to him.

I talked to others, and examined other "testimonials" published in the Oral Roberts magazine. Many of these are cases of functional ailments that could well have psychosomatic roots. A number of cases of healing involved allergies that might well have had emotional roots. Some of the cases, however, like the two reported in detail above, are too remarkable to dismiss lightly.

Every healer has his supporters and detractors, particularly as accounts of his achievements spread, and Roberts, with his tremendous appeal to vast audiences, reaching out halfway around the globe, has received his full share of attacks.

The critics of Oral Roberts were many and noisy, from the start. Here was a man who was active in a field about which millions were skeptical, even when healing has been attempted under the most conservative orthodox auspices in the churches. The man claimed he was performing miracles over the airwaves.

"Enlightened leaders of both the clergy and the medical profession," wrote Jack Gould, radio and television critic of *The New York Times*, "recognize that theirs can be a fruitful partnership, that often one may achieve what the other cannot. But this has nothing to do with a gospel preacher making his own extemporaneous medical diagnosis and claiming magic results unsupported by the slightest shred of rational evidence. Brother Roberts, it may be noted, carefully avoids rigid comparative tests before and after his miracles."[8] This columnist further suggested in his article that Brother Roberts could exploit hysteria and ignorance if he so desired but it hardly seemed to him "in the public interest" for the television industry to go along with this kind of program.

[8] *The New York Times*, February 19, 1956.

The result of this column was a deluge of mail into *The New York Times* office. About fifteen hundred letters piled up. More than 90 per cent were in favor of Brother Roberts, and heartily denounced Critic Gould for his audacity in criticizing the healer. Defending Oral Roberts also were ministers of other faiths. There were some ministers, however, who supported Jack Gould.

One of the most stinging assaults was made by W. E. Mann, a leading Canadian Anglican, who wrote in *The Christian Century*: "The 'healing' section of his television shows is deceitful because, through careful editing, it omits the failures and near-failures. Thus it implies that practically all who go before Roberts receive a personal hearing and a healing. In actual fact, only the first fifteen or twenty people in a line numbering hundreds are given any personal questioning, and invariably there are quite a number of fairly obvious failures. The abrupt manner in which Roberts treats many of these failures is disillusioning."[9]

But in spite of his outrage, Mann refuses to dismiss Oral Roberts out of hand. "What may we conclude about this man?" he asks. "He must be given credit for spreading among the masses the new idea that Christianity involves healing of the body and the emotions as well as salvation of the soul.[10] Undoubtedly his homiletical theme of deliverance from ills meets a need that is all but universal today. On the other hand, the dangers connected with his mass healing services are great . . ."[11]

Another radio and television critic, J. C. Wynn, writing in *Presbyterian Life*, said, "One comes away from his half-hour TV spectacular vaguely disturbed and fascinated. The man is utilizing a genuine and recognized power. The connection between prayer and health is widely conceded, and a resurgence of interest in this phenomenon is spreading throughout the churches today. Some persons apparently are gifted in healing, and Oral Roberts quite possibly possesses this gift.

"But how he uses it! No gentle laying on of hands is to be seen in his techniques. Roberts slaps his patients on the brow or the face; and his far-from-reverent prayers shout at God with imper-

[9]W. E. Mann, Super Salesman of Faith Healing, *The Christian Century*, Vol. LXXIII, No. 36, September 5, 1956. pp. 1018-1019.

[10]How a learned churchman can consider this a new idea, in view of the healings of physical ills by Jesus, as recorded in the New Testament nearly two thousand years ago, is difficult to understand.

[11]*Ibid.* p. 1019.

atives: 'Lord, when I put this child down, he's got to walk!' Then
the child gets off the healer's lap and runs away on his once-
useless legs.''[12]

In our interview, I asked Brother Roberts about the power he
claims comes into his hand. ''Sometimes it is like liquid fire,''
he told me, ''I never felt liquid fire but I think that's what it would
feel like. Usually, it is more like a warmth.

''I was brought up in a home of deep religious faith in the
Pentacostal Holiness Church. In my home, from the earliest days
I remember, when somebody was sick we did two things—we
called the doctor and we prayed. I believe in doctors and we try
to co-operate with them wherever we can. Sometimes people come
to me when the doctors have said they can do no more.

''I don't heal. God heals. I am only a point of contact. When
the woman with the flow of blood touched the hem of Jesus, she
was healed. The hem of His garment had no power in itself. It
was a point of contact. I have no power in me as such, any more
than the piece of cloth had power in it, as such.

''You must understand that I am two persons. One is just when
I am myself, and the other is when the Spirit of God takes possession of me, and I feel the presence of God, usually after my
sermons. Then I can do things of which I am not normally capable.
I am still in control of my faculties, you understand. I can still
think and act. But there is a spirit in me then that is different,
using me.''

I asked him about the criticism that he prays as if he were
commanding God, ordering God to hear.

Oral Roberts leaned forward, his hand touching my arm. ''When
I was sick with tuberculosis and the doctors practically gave up
hope for me, people told me I was sick because God wanted me
to be sick and that if He wanted He would heal me. I didn't believe
that. I didn't want to believe in a God who wanted me to be sick.
That didn't seem right. And it was my mother who told me, 'Oral,
God didn't make you sick. He doesn't want you to be sick. The
devil made you sick. The devil doesn't want you to be well, but
God does.'

''I don't believe it is the will of God that man be sick. It cannot
be the will of God that man suffer. It cannot be the will of God

[12]J. C. Wynn, The Oral Roberts Show, Seen and Heard, *Presbyterian Life*,
Oct. 13, 1956. p. 41.

that man endure poverty and despair. These are things of the devil. And nowhere in the New Testament does Jesus say or indicate that His teaching requires us to believe in a God of punishment. He loves—and He forgives.

"I pray with what some call authority, because the spirit is upon me and because I hate sickness, I hate disease, I hate evil, and when I am close to someone who is sick I suffer and I want to help him, I feel that if I do not pray for them I will burst. I put my hands on people in the healing line with force because I want to drive that evil out of them. I've tried to do it gently and it doesn't work."

I asked him, "What about the causes behind the sicknesses, hatred and resentments and other emotions that lie at the root of many illnesses? Pastors like Dr. Price in Philadelphia insist these have to be eradicated before God's healing can take effect."

His answer was that he was completely in favor of this pastoral counseling, and believed that ministers should do this work, and explained that in all of his campaigns and crusades he worked with ministers in local communities. "Counseling is the pastor's work," he told me. "For myself, I simply don't have the time for it physically. There are too many thousands seeking help. Their own pastors can and should and do help with counseling. But when they come to me what they want is not counseling but healing."

About himself and his work, Oral Roberts reacted with some feeling to the criticisms which have been leveled at him. "I claim only to be a Christian, a believer in Christ. They criticized Jesus, too; they criticized Him for healing. I wish some of my critics would read the four gospels and the Books of the Acts of the Apostles and find out what really happened in the life of Jesus and what He did and the example He set and told us to follow. Do you know that eighty per cent of his ministry was spent in healing?

"I don't keep a full check on all the people who come through the healing line, although we do keep records on all whose cases we publish in the magazines; we check on them and try not to publish any case in the magazine until at least a year has passed.

"I believe that everyone who has come to me has been helped in some way, and I know that many have been healed. I've had them come back to me to thank me for healing. I try to get them to go back to their doctors for checkups, to make sure they are healed if they believe they are. Sometimes they do and sometimes not. We can't make them go.

"A little girl came with her parents, her face was swollen up with cancer. I put my hand on the child and prayed. Later, she came back much improved and the parents tried to explain that the doctors couldn't understand the miraculous thing that had happened to her, the chemical change. I didn't understand that chemical change either, I'm not a doctor. But I could look in their faces and see new hope and new faith. I don't claim this as a healing. But there have been healings. You yourself have checked on them. And I say that if there is just one healing, this is an indication that God is willing to heal everyone."

He was willing and anxious to answer questions and criticisms. Despite statements that he earns one hundred thousand dollars a year as salary and has several Cadillacs and lives like a multi-millionnaire, Roberts told me this:

He has a wife and four children and they have a ranch of two hundred forty mortgaged acres in Bixby, Oklahoma. "In Oklahoma," he told me, "two hundred forty acres is not considered very big, even when not mortgaged." He has no Cadillacs; only one car—an Oldsmobile. He has had many offers of personal gifts but refuses to take them. Any gifts must be made to the Oral Roberts Foundation.

He has no church pastorate and does not draw any salary and has no pension funds or retirement funds. He believes that ministers and priests and evangelists are entitled to their livelihood and that there is no merit in the fact that most clergymen are underpaid.

"Our crusade in a city lasts around ten days. The crusades take a great deal of planning. The budget for each ten-day campaign— we can only make a limited number of them a year—is twenty-five thousand dollars. We usually have about ninety thousand persons attending. One of these services is the 'love offering'— traditional in the Pentacostal church—for the preacher and his family. I'm not going to tell you how much I make from a love offering because that's nobody's business but my own. Is this not a personal matter? And do not the top ministers of big churches receive good salaries? But almost everything we make goes to the Oral Roberts Foundation which is used to help bring the word of God to millions of people, and to bring His healing to the afflicted. The Oral Roberts Foundation pays for the television and radio shows. We have no sponsors, have never had and never will. The

Foundation gets all the royalties and profits from my books, except for six books.

"On those six books, which sell for a dollar each, I make about eight cents a copy, and all together they sell about one hundred twenty-five thousand copies a year. That and the love offerings constitute my total earnings. And let me tell you this: I'd settle for an average of twenty-five hundred dollars a love offering, any day."

All of the Foundation's books are gone over by government officials; funds contributed to it can be used for no purpose except the advancement of religious faith. In the event of Oral Roberts' death, the funds of the Foundation will go to six religions to be used only for specific religious endeavors.

"I am trying to do the work of God," he told me. "My mornings are spent in work, my afternoons alone in my room in prayer, meditation and preparation. Except for a moderate income for my wife and my four children, my entire earnings go into the Foundation, to carry on this work. I believe in my ministry because there are things that I know about God that I am sure of, because God has spoken to me directly."

I asked Mr. Roberts, "Did you actually hear God's voice?"

His answer was: "Yes. God spoke to me and I heard it, it was His audible voice speaking. Once on the occasion when I was in the car, and He told me to carry His healing to my generation. And again, in Hong Kong, when I was praying with missionaries and He told me to seek His joy, His pleasure, and His faith, and He would reward me with a million souls in ten years. By souls, I believe He meant conversions in my ministry."

On another occasion, in a hotel in Seattle, Washington, while he was shaving, he told me, the Lord called to him, "Oral . . ." and Brother Roberts became afraid and turned around. "But He was gone and there was no other word on that occasion because of my fear."

"How did you know," I asked him, "that this was God speaking to you?"

He started to answer, stopped, hesitated, and said finally, "I cannot tell you. It is an area we dare not talk about. But I knew."

14

"Who Touched My Clothes?"

One of the most beautiful episodes in the New Testament concerns the woman who touched the garment of Jesus.

"And a certain woman, which had an issue of blood twelve years,

"And had suffered many things of many physicians, and had spent all that she had, and was nothing bettered, but rather grew worse,

"When she had heard of Jesus, came in the press behind, and touched his garment.

"For she said, if I may touch but his clothes, I shall be whole.

"And straightway the fountain of her blood was dried up; and she felt in her body that she was healed of that plague.

"And Jesus, immediately knowing in himself that virtue had gone out of him, turned about him in the press, and said, Who touched my clothes?"[1]

It is a vivid and strangely modern picture which Mark paints; the woman who has spent all her money on doctors who cannot make her well and who pushes through this crowd to touch the healer.

His followers are surprised. Why, with such a crowd, hundreds pressing in upon them from every side, should he talk of one person touching him? But Jesus knows and the woman knows, and she throws herself at his feet and tells him what she had done, she is healed and yet she is afraid. "And he said unto her, Daughter, thy faith had made thee whole; go in peace, and be whole of thy plague."[2]

Few stories in the Bible illustrate more dramatically an example

[1] Mark V:25-30.
[2] Mark V:34.

of healing by touch, by physical contact between healer and healed. Yet it is to be noted that Jesus says only that faith has made her whole—plainly her faith in Him, in the power obtainable merely from touching His garment.

There are a number of other instances in the Bible and in the ministry of Jesus in which touch plays an important role. "Now when the sun was setting," reports St. Luke, "all they that had any sick with divers diseases brought them unto him; and he laid his hands on every one of them, and healed them."[3]

The power of touch, from biblical days to our own, has been of great importance in spiritual healing. It had in the days of Christ the symbolic meaning of a blessing as well as a communication of healing force. It later included belief in touching the relic of a saint, of a bit of cloth from the garment of a martyr. Some of the healing bishops employed the laying on of hands in the Middle Ages, notably at Tours. The concept that healing resided in the touch of a Bishop or Pope was strong throughout that period.

In a medieval era of ignorance and superstition, however, it is not surprising that much in religious faith was subverted into sheer superstition. There were people who believed that power lay in the touch of a powerful individual—any individual of temporal or military authority, or in a witch or some person possessed who could do evil or cast spells.

One of the most widespread beliefs centered on the power residing in the Royal Touch, an idea dating back to the eleventh century in England; the belief that royalty, through its Divine origins, had a special power of healing in its divinely appointed hands.

Literally hundreds of thousands of persons in England, under successive monarchies from the days of Edward the Confessor to the eighteenth century, believed in this royal gift from God. Monarchs of Spain and France also were said to have this power. On a single day, Louis XIV of France was said to have touched nearly sixteen hundred persons. Other monarchs are reported to have touched—and healed—tens of thousands in a single year.

Documentation of these healings were usually made by those close to the throne, with the result that few failures are recorded but alleged successes are set down with painstaking detail.

With the advent of modern times, the dawn of science and new social ideas, belief in the divine right of kings was inevitably

[3]Luke IV:40.

destroyed. And with it, the efficacy of the Royal Touch, in curing scrofula, epilepsy and other serious ailments, was similarly ended.

Healing by touch, however, continued. The Sacrament of the Laying on of Hands continued. Faith healers who claimed power in their hands continued. There were individual ministers, such as Dr. Albert Price of Philadelphia, who seemed to develop in their hands a force of which they themselves had not been aware. Oral Roberts was one of those who healed by touch. Harry Edwards, who rose to fame in England with his work in spiritual healing after World War II, also used this method.

One of the most unusual examples of a man with this gift is Ambrose Worrall of Baltimore, a business executive who heals by this method because he considers it a gift he has to use for the service of men and God.

Ambrose Worrall was associated from the start, along with his wife, Olga, in the healing work of Baltimore's New Life Clinic. Mr. Worrall was born in Barrow-in-Furness, Lancashire, England. When he was a child of eight he saw a blind man on the street and later, in Sunday school, heard the teacher tell of Christ's healing of a blind man with spittle and mud. At once young Worrall demanded, "Why cannot I go out and put some mud and spittle on that blind man and heal him?"

The Sunday school teacher hurriedly replied that the power to heal spiritually ended centuries ago and people could not do that any more.

The boy simply did not believe it was true.

Some years later, his sister was injured in an accident. The neck was damaged so that her head was twisted and doctors said there was no way it could be corrected. She would be paralysed that way all her life.

One day, Ambrose Worrall, then seventeen, was reading the sporting page when—as he told me—"the paper grew so heavy that I could no longer hold it in my hand. I was forced to drop it and rise and go to my sister and I felt impelled to put my hands on the back of her neck. I don't know what made me do any of that; I just had to do it. And in only a matter of minutes after I touched her, she was completely healed; the neck injury was gone and stayed gone."

That was how he began to have a realization that he had healing power, a healing touch in his hand. Mr. Worrall is what spiritualists and others in psychic and extrasensory research describe as a "sensitive." In my interview with him he related a number of psychic experiences which had happened to him. One of the most unusual concerned a time when he was about eighteen years old and had gone to the YMCA for the first time, because he was anxious to play football. While Ambrose waited in the lobby, the YMCA secretary came out. A kindly looking man some years older than Ambrose, he told the youth to follow him into the office. There, without a word, he handed young Worrall a bracelet, and said, "Hold this a moment, please," then walked behind the desk, sat down and began writing a letter, paying no attention to the youth whatsoever.

Young Worrall sat down and, with nothing better to do, began to examine the links of the bracelet, the odd markings of which he tried to decipher. "Suddenly," he told me, "I felt something strike me, it was like a lash across my back. It was so real that I jumped up from the chair and spun around to see who was striking me. There was no one behind me at all."

The secretary said, "What's wrong?"

"Who hit me?" the young man asked.

The YMCA official said, "You were lashed by a whip, that's all."

Then, Mr. Worrall told me, the man replaced the bracelet in the desk and explained, "You see, I was writing this letter when I became aware that there was a sensitive outside. I was sure, when I went out there, that it was you. The bracelet was merely a test. It belonged to an Algerian slave who was whipped to death."

Mr. Worrall came to America where he met Olga, who was to become his wife. Also "gifted," Olga later worked in the New Life Clinic at the Mt. Vernon Place church, and also helped to launch similar clinics in other churches. Neither Mr. Worrall nor his wife will accept any money for healing, or even small presents. He told me that both believe that if they accept any gain for their work, they may endanger their gifts.

Most extraordinary about the Worralls, as this writer saw them, is the complete lack of the extraordinary in their manner or mode of living; there is an everydayness about them found in any average home in any suburban community. As an engineer in a large aircraft concern, Ambrose Worrall goes to work in the morning with his briefcase and papers and returns in the evening like all the other men along the block; and his wife goes shopping and belongs to the neighborhood garden club and works in the garden.

Yet there is a world beyond the everyday world in which the Worralls seem also to live but which one would not guess from surface appearance.

Early one evening the Worralls were out buying groceries when they stopped off to visit a girl whom Ambrose had been asked to help. She and several others had been injured in an auto accident; the girl had become paralyzed and in addition had developed heart trouble. She was so sick that many despaired of her recovery; some even thought it might be better if she did not recover, because she would be mangled, bedridden and in pain all her life. But others had called the Worralls and asked them to help.

Ambrose Worrall stood in the doorway of the child's sickroom in her home in North Baltimore. Without knowing what prompted him, he said, "Don't worry about her. She'll be playing baseball before the season's over."

It was a ridiculous statement and he knew it even as he said the words. He looked at the child's scars. He said, "I can't work here. You come home with us and I'll see what can be done."

It was a warm spring evening. The Worralls forgot their shopping. They carried the child down the stairs and they took her to their home to the room where they go to pray, and he laid hands on the child and her twisted limbs.

Then she went home. She seemed much improved. She came again for his help the following week and was able this time to walk down the stairs herself. The next time they went to see her, they were told that she was downtown shopping.

She didn't play baseball, actually, but she could have, before the season was over. A few years later, she was married. She has had two children.

Was there a healing force in Ambrose Worrall's hand, in his prayers, in his body and spirit? Was the child's seeming paralysis and heart trouble hysteria to start with?

Mr. Worrall does not claim to understand the answer completely. The doctors who examined her did not consider it hysteria; the X-rays revealed serious physical damage. Their prognosis was that she would be permanently bedridden if she lived. The doctors might merely have been completely wrong in their diagnosis. But they were competent physicians, and such an opinion would be stretching the arm of coincidence beyond sensible bounds. Mr. Worrall does not try to explain these things. He is not concerned with why she didn't die or remain a cripple, or who was right or wrong, but is overjoyed that she was healed.

He does know that in his healing effort he waits until he can "tune in," as he calls it, on the individual. This may take from five minutes to an hour of just sitting and waiting, until he feels that on the spiritual level he and the person seeking help are on the same wavelength. Then, he believes, his health and vitality, of which he is a channel, drives out ill-health, the negative force of the sickness.

In a lecture that he gave on "The Gift of Healing," he tried to tell others interested in this field how they could develop and build this "gift." There is a strange, other-worldly ring in these words: "If we recognize completely our spiritual heritage, our sonship, our at-one-ment with the Supreme Being, then we would indeed be blessed for we would be pure in heart and see God. Under this condition of purity we would be perfect channels through which the power of the Spirit could flow unsullied to reach those less enlightened than ourselves, to restore them to a condition of health, to bring them peace of mind, and provide such guidance that, if followed, would lead them into the paths of righteousness, and the attainment of the knowledge of spiritual truths."

Not everyone who seeks the Worrall's aid is helped, but many are. I went through scrapbooks they keep of letters of appreciation. They are scrapbooks full of gratitude and an overtone of love. There were letters typewritten and handwritten, on fine stationery and ruled pieces torn from copybooks, letters from persons of all kinds and degrees of wealth and position and education, all of them writing to thank the Worralls for healings and blessings received, after this quiet, stocky pleasant man and his rather gay, high-spirited, yet deeply devout wife prayed for healing.

Not all the cases require actual personal touch. One night, while the Worralls were entertaining friends in their home, another friend called; her baby had the croup. The doctor said there was nothing he could do. The spells were getting worse. She was afraid the baby might choke to death. Ambrose had helped this mother previously in another case. The woman said she was calling from a drug store near her house. "Go home," he told her. "Take the baby on your lap. Put one hand on its back and one on its chest and think of me."

The woman said she would do this. Mr. Worrall returned to the living room and entered into the general talk. He told me that ten minutes later, he felt what he described as "an extrusion from the solar plexus—about twelve inches in diameter and eight inches thick." He told me that he believes this extrusion is a kind of force within him.[4] It seemed to pull him around in his chair, he declared, to turn him in the direction of the street where this woman lived. "I felt that the force within me," he said, "pointed like a searchlight in the direction of that house. I felt a power flowing through me and out of me. It was like a breath drawn out of me, but a little more substantial than breath."

The following day the mother came to see Mr. Worrall and brought the baby. "I want you to know," she said, "that I have witnessed a miracle. I went home as you said and put the baby on my lap and put one hand on the chest and one on the back and thought of you. Almost instantly I felt warmth and vibrations pass down my arms into the baby. Then the baby gave a terrific cough and coughed up the phlegm."

After that, the woman told him the baby went peacefully to sleep. The crisis was over.

Mr. Worrall asked her how long it took her to go from the store where she had phoned to her home. Her answer was: "Oh, about ten minutes."

Olga Worrall has performed many healings herself—at the clinic and in a few outside cases.

One of the most interesting cases, however, involved a cyst that grew to be as big as a walnut on Olga's hand. The Worralls believe in the use of medicine to its fullest extent, and Olga went to the best physicians in Baltimore. They informed her that removal of the cyst by operation would be difficult. The pain from the cyst was severe. One night, after she had been lying in bed for some time sleepless with pain, she said to her husband, "Dear, would you heal my hand?"

Ambrose was half asleep but he said, "I've been waiting for you to ask me that." Still half asleep, he reached out and touched her hand. The pain seemed to diminish and in a little while she fell asleep.

In the morning, she was talking with a neighbor when the neighbor remarked casually, "I see you've had that cyst removed on your hand."

Only then, she told me, did she look down and discover that the cyst was gone.

"It's one thing when this happens to others but quite different

---

[4]Worrall states that he felt this same extrusion pulling him out of his chair the day he healed his sister's neck injury. This invisible substance he described as "a homogeneous substance, but like a filter."

when it happens to you," Olga Worrall said. "I was so startled I ran into the house and burst into tears. And the funny thing is that Ambrose cried too, when I told him about it that night, after he got home from his engineering duties at the plant."

One notable fact about individuals who appear to have the healing touch is that most of them differ little or not at all from the average person except in regard to their power.

The writer has investigated several instances of individuals who are not seeking money or fame, who are not in the clergy, yet who appear to have the gift of the healing touch, so that friends come seeking help.

One of the most interesting of such individuals was the late William J. MacMillan, an American who went to England and was told by a spiritualist at a dinner party one evening that he had the power to heal.

Mr. MacMillan was neither a spiritualist nor a healer and moreover had no desire to become either. But later on—at what to him was a highly embarrassing evening, according to his autobiography,[5] the group asked him please to heal his hostess who was suffering badly from a sinus infection.

With his hostess insisting, there was no way to refuse. While they stood and watched, and while the spiritualist issued directions, he applied his fingers to the face of his hostess and then made a series of motions at the direction of his spiritualistic mentor. Throughout the proceeding, Mr. MacMillan regarded the whole thing as foolishness. The only thing that disturbed his equilibrium more than the episode itself was the aftermath. Following his ministration, his hostess was obviously relieved of pain. The infection was apparently gone.

Mr. MacMillan was still reluctant about the whole business. However, a short time later, while visiting a clergyman in the country, he was informed that the housekeeper had a large and painful bunion on her foot.

Impelled by urgings he could not explain, Mr. MacMillan went out to the kitchen and informed the rather severe-looking woman, who was apparently in great pain, that he could remove the bunion.

Surprised, she went with him to the servant's hall, removed her

[5]William J. MacMillan, The Reluctant Healer. New York: Thomas Y. Crowell Co., 1952. p. 5.

stocking and permitted him to work on the bunion, rubbing it directly with his hands.

Ten minutes later, Mr. MacMillan reported in his autobiography, the bunion had shrunk to almost normal size and the redness of infection also had almost gone.

"Thank you very much, sir," the housekeeper said. "I must get on with dinner. Perhaps if you don't mind, sir, we had better not mention this to the master. He might not like your coming to the kitchen this way."[6]

This was the beginning of a career in healing of which this American in England had had no anticipation whatsoever. Although he was religious even before the discovery of this gift, he became even more so afterward. But although he performed many healings, individually and sometimes in small groups, he never really became a mystic or religious recluse. Of himself he wrote in his autobiography, "But the Lord remains my Shepherd. Nor has my Teacher's promise failed. I have never been without spiritual teaching. Increasingly, I believe this promise to be true for everyone. My experience, if it is perhaps unusual in emphasis, is not unusual in essence. It is the story of every man. As brothers we all move forward laughing and frightened—proud and humbled—singing and tearful—held in the everlasting love of God."[7]

There have been many notable examples of men with this gift, both within and without the church. One of the greatest in the church was James Moore Hickson, a British healer whose American tour made a profound impression on Alfred Price as a youth and was a contributing factor to Dr. Price's decision later to start healing services at St. Stephen's in Philadelphia.

The charismatic healer, with an apparently special power in his hands, is a phenomenon well-known in this field. Many explanations of his "power" have been suggested. It has been called suggestion, hypnotism, hysteria, mind over matter. It has been called a projection of the faith of the individual, flowing from the patient to the healer and back to the patient through the overt action of his touch. It has also been called the power of God channeled through specially chosen individuals.

Several of these possibilities may be true at once. It may be suggestion, working with a real force in the healer, plus the faith

[6]*Ibid*. p. 11.
[7]*Ibid*. pp. 242-243.

of the healed. It may be that certain individuals are attuned to a level of the spiritual higher than most of us reach; it does appear that those most able in this field have an outgoing aura of warmth toward others, a sometimes Christ-like warmth.

Recently an interest in this force from a scientific point of view has developed in America and particularly in England, where a number of doctors have started to explore the dynamics of healing by touch. There have been instruments built of a highly sensitive character by which attempts are being made to measure the force in the hands of healers and "sensitives."

Mr. Worrall has participated in some of these; attempts were made to determine if electric current of any sort passed through his hands, or if they affected the needle of a compass. None of these experiments produced positive results of any sort with Mr. Worrall.

One suggested answer now much discussed is known as the "odic force."

The force of "od"—the term is said to stem from the mythological Scandinavian god Odin—was first named and examined by a scientist named Karl von Reichenbach in the first half of the nineteenth century.

Reichenbach was a remarkable individual—scientist, industrialist and millionaire. Son of a court librarian at Stuttgart, he traveled over Germany and France, he built iron works and steelworks, he discovered paraffin and creosote, built the first great charcoal works at Hansach and became an industrial prince.

At that time there was a great concern with mesmerism and with magnetism. As a student of natural science, Reichenbach came to believe that all matter was subject to the influence of a great cosmic power which he called "od."

Odic force, this scientist declared, permeated everything. In the hands of a healer this force would project itself in strong concentrated energy into the body of the sick person, driving out weakness and destroying sickness germs and bottling up the places in the body where the vital forces within the individual might be seeping out.

Such was the shape of his original theory of odic force; and he devoted much time and effort to his investigations, working with sick people and later with healthy people, exploring "od" and its potentialities. In his book on his researches into the dynamics of magnetism,[8] Reichenbach says that "odic force" irradiates the universe and everything in it, that it does not pertain to particular forms or special qualities of matter, but "dwells in matter and in and by itself."[9] He also states that this force manifests itself not only in contact but also at distances, sometimes great distances—as from the sun, the moon and the stars, and from all matter. He states that it is different from all hitherto known forces.

What may be the truth of odic force, what substance it may have, only the future can reveal. At the present time, leading physicians and technicians both in America and England, are investigating this subject, and many believe that those persons in and out of organized religion who have a healing touch are special channels for a kind of power we do not yet understand.

The distinguished British clergyman, Dr. Leslie Weatherhead, the religious healer and noted authority on this subject, declared in an article on odic force that inquiry into this field may be as important and epoch-making as was the exploration of the theories of nuclear physicists and the earthshaking energy of the atom.

---

[8] Karl von Reichenbach, Letters on Od and Magnetism. Trans. by F. D. O'Bryne. London: Hutchinson & Co. Ltd., 1926.

[9] Note that although he did not use the concept of God in terms of the Christian-Judaic world, he did name it after a pagan deity of neighboring Scandinavia.

15

Therapy of the Word

One force all religiously-oriented healers and healing services employ is the pre-eminent value of prayer and affirmation. There is no religion which does not recognize the therapy of prayer, spoken or unspoken.

In *The Varieties of Religious Experience,* William James says: "As regards prayers for the sick, if any medical fact can be considered to stand firm, it is that in certain environments prayer may contribute to recovery, and should be encouraged as a therapeutic measure."[1] Further on, he adds: "But petitional prayer is only one department of prayer; and if we take the word in the wider sense as meaning every kind of inward communion or conversation with the power recognized as divine, we can easily see that scientific criticism leaves it untouched."[2]

Prayer in this wider sense, Dr. James tells us, is the very heart and soul of religion.

It is also the very heart and soul of religious healing.

But there are many ways of praying, and many kinds of prayers. One prayer is a petition, repeated over and over; others are mental or oral affirmations of health, of well-being, of gratitude. There are prayers for ourselves and prayers for others, prayers spoken and prayers silent, prayers expressed in words, prayers expressed in the projection of an image: a healer "sees" the individual in his mind's eye, well and whole, wrapped in the protection of God. There is what is called "being in a state of prayer," having a prayerful attitude, which is not necessarily or usually an attitude

[1] William James, The Varieties of Religious Experience. New York: Longmans, Green and Company, 1902. p. 453.
[2] *Ibid.* pp. 453-454.

of petition to God as much as a physical, mental and emotional acceptance of His will. For those who have full and uncompromising faith, as the Reverend Bill Hunter put it, the need itself often becomes the prayer.

In Christian Science, and other denominations—where healing is basic—prayers are expressed most frequently as affirmations. An earlier chapter reported how a woman was healed of cancer, according to her story, by a single affirmation: "There is no power apart from God," which she repeated over and over, not as some witch doctor's chant, but as a religious experience; saying these words until their full meaning permeated her being and the power of that meaning and its affirmation and acceptance became a tremendous healing force in her body.

The objection may be raised that this is obvious suggestion and self-hypnosis; the answer lies in the fact that the fruits of prayer are often far in excess of what hypnosis or suggestion is capable of achieving without prayer. If any medical doctor had a technique for mesmerizing cancers out of the human body in a matter of minutes—as reportedly happened through affirmative prayer in the case referred to above—his practice would multiply.

Unity emphasizes affirmative prayers with the most precise application. In Unity's book of *Divine Remedies*, compiled by Theodosia DeWitt Schobert, we find specific affirmations to be used in many kinds of bodily afflictions. As an example for the healing of cuts, bruises or burns, birthmarks, scars, and the like, the following affirmation is suggested, after the individual has first centered his mind on realization of the omnipresence of Spirit, wholeness, health, peace and harmony:

"I am Spirit, the offspring of the living God. My body is spiritual and not material. My hand (or foot, or whatever part of the body it is that needs healing) *is spiritual manifestation. The life, substance, love, and intelligence of Spirit are always, everywhere present, and Spirit cannot sense error; therefore there can be no inharmony in my body.*

"The love and life of the Christ now flows freely into and through my entire organism, adjusting, harmonizing, healing, and restoring me to perfect manifest wholeness."[3]

The book gives affirmative prayers of this kind for many kinds of physical troubles. It is interesting to note that official medical

[3]Theodosia DeWitt Schobert, Divine Remedies. Lee's Summit, Mo.: Unity School of Christianity, 1923. p. 22.

terms for the disease are not given. The writer states in the fore-word: "It is good not to call inharmonies by any of the terms applied to them... To name a disease tends to give it a place in consciousness...."

But often prayer follows far simpler avenues. The Rev. Dr. John Heuss, rector of Trinity Church in New York City, in a booklet called *Our Christian Vocation,* reports the story of an elderly lady who had broken her leg three times and had been confined to her bed for a number of years.

"Much additional tragedy had come her way," the Rev. Dr. Heuss writes. "So great were her afflictions that her power to pray in utmost faith had gradually ebbed away. One day our conversation came around to miracles of healing. We talked about the healing that had happened at Lourdes in France. She said she wished she had such faith. On my next visit I found her out of bed and walking. She told me that after I had gone, she had decided to throw her whole faith on God and ask Him to make her able to walk again. She prayed and prayed. Exhausted, she had fallen asleep. In the midst of her sleep, she said she had heard a voice say, 'Rise, you are able to walk.' And from her bed she arose with the power of motion again restored. Since that day, I have never doubted that God can and does perform miracles of healing."[4]

A large portion of prayer, involuntary or otherwise, is petition. Automatically we turn to God in need, as a reflex action of the soul. But prayer must be more than petition, more than demanding or trying to cajole the Almighty into granting us some special gift. The Reverend Dr. Albert Day of the New Life Clinic declares that prayer should be a way of discovering what God wants for us and fulfilling His will. Alexis Carrel said that it "should be understood not as a mere mechanical recitation of formulas, but as a mystical absorption of consciousness in elevation, in the contemplation of a principle both permeating and transcending our world."[5]

In many instances a prayer may be expressed in words which do not seem to be a prayer at all.

[4] John Heuss, Our Christian Vocation. Greenwich, Conn.: Seabury Press, 1954. p. 10.

[5] Alexis Carrel, Man The Unknown. New York: Harper and Brothers, 1935. p. 147.

During World War II a sailor was rescued from a raft in mid-ocean weeks after his ship had been sunk. Reporters asked him many questions about his days and nights alone on the ocean, and how he rationed his limited supply of water and food on the raft, and speared fish occasionally, to keep alive. One of them asked him if he prayed. "No," the sailor answered. "I'd never prayed before. And I didn't think it was fair to begin out there."

I told this story to a Congregationalist minister who pointed out that the statement itself was, in one sense, a prayer, for it was a recognition of God's power, of his own previous lack of thought for God, of his unwillingness to make use of that power solely for selfish gain. "The temptation to ask God to save him must have been great," the pastor said. "Imagine those long hours alone out there; how many times he must have wanted to cry out to God to save him. But he had never prayed before and here he would be asking God for such a favor, it seemed, such a miracle, and he must have decided there were others who deserved such miracles more than he did, so he did not pray—for himself. But his attitude was a prayer."

One of the most effective modes of prayer in healing, according to Dr. Albert Day and Dr. Alfred Price of Philadelphia, is silent prayer, affirming the truth of Divine Power through meditation and contemplation. Ambrose Worrall also cites this kind of prayer.

What should one meditate upon, and through what thoughts?

In one of his booklets called *A Meditation on Health*, Dr. Price gives a series of affirmations for the individual to repeat, softly to himself:

"There is a Divine Power within me that permeates my entire being, that makes and keeps me perfectly whole."

"Restfully and peacefully I repose in the truth of the above words. I now relax and let go of nerves. I yield myself fully to the healing of Christ. His peace and love pervade my whole being. All tension is relieved. Slowly and quietly I repeat the words:

"There is a Divine Power within me that permeates my entire being, that makes and keeps me perfectly whole."

The pamphlet indicates that now there is silence for a moment. Then again the individual recites the prayer affirmation, "There is a Divine Power . . ."

And silence, and then again the prayer, and then again.

Later in this brochure Dr. Price gives another prayer:

"Into Thy hands I put myself, my soul, my body, my will, my desire—even for healing—my fears, my resentments, my ill-feelings, my ambitions. I want, dear Lord, to be what you want me to be—whole in soul and mind and body; that in my whole person I may glorify Thee, and show forth Your Wholeness. And now, O Lord, I see more clearly my own sins—my self-will, my ...(think what they are). All these, dear Lord, I confess. I let them go. Take them from me that I may be forgiven."

Ambrose Worrall says that meditation is "a continuous application of the mind to the consideration of religious or moral truth in order to promote personal wholeness, holiness and the love of all that is Divine." Contemplation he defines as "a state of rapt regard for things Divine." Repeated meditation brings us to the threshold of contemplation. Both meditation and contemplation are aspects of prayer. "They are steps that lead upwards from the plateau of vocal prayer," Mr. Worrall stated in a New Life Clinic sermon, later published as a booklet. "They are advanced forms of prayer which in its highest form is so simple that it is difficult to describe.

"Simple prayer," he continued, "has no words; no images; no ideas; the mind is pure; passive; non-selective; however, the consciousness is alert ... A watchful, listening vigilance is maintained with an expectancy to receive impressions not generated by oneself or the mental or physical stimuli that abound on every hand, but from the Supreme Intelligence that transmits only truth and knows what one needs to know."[6]

Important also in healing is the role of what is called "intercessory" prayer when we pray and petition not for ourselves but for others. Intercessory prayer, honestly made with no thought of personal gain by the one who prays, has a way of rebounding; this is the bread upon the waters of the universe. We see this in the story of the French communist who prayed for the boy at Lourdes—and was healed himself. There are many similar cases on record at Lourdes.

Religious writer Roland Gammon relates the story of a world-famous motion picture actress who was on a vacation in Rome when she received a wire from her sister in California. The actress had taken a personal interest in a seriously wounded war veteran in a Los Angeles veterans' hospital. The youth had become paralyzed from the waist down by a shrapnel burst. The wire from the sister informed the actress that the man had had an operation

[6]Ambrose Worrall, *Meditation and Contemplation*, Baltimore, Md., 1956. pp. 11-12.

and now doctors did not think he would live.

That night, the actress left the vacationing group she was with and flew to Lourdes. For two days she remained there, spending most of the time on her knees in the grotto, praying not merely that the veteran would live but also that he would conquer the despair and defeat and bitterness that had come to him after six years of lying paralyzed and helpless on a hospital bed.

All through the day and into the evening the screen star prayed, unknown and unrecognized and unanxious for recognition. Most of all, she prayed that he would learn to accept the will of God, and to try, with whatever strength was given to him, to accept and carry out His will, whatever might be the fate ahead.

When the actress arrived back in Hollywood two weeks later, she was met by her sister. The sister explained that when they had sent the radiogram, no one had expected the paralyzed veteran to pull through. Then, suddenly, he began to get better.

"You simply wouldn't recognize him now," the sister told the actress. "He's completely changed. He doesn't have to lie flat any more but sits up in a wheelchair and in a few weeks they say he'll be well enough to leave the hospital and move into a house of his own. You know—it's really a miracle."

It is undeniably true that many persons pray fervently and are not healed, that many of deep faith pray and are not made whole. And theologians now tell us that sickness is not ever the will of God but is caused by other negative and sin-absorbent conditions within us or our environment. But why does God not take the evil from the man who prays in faith?

Many answers may be found. There may be elements in the background of the individual which we do not know or understand, factors which are blocking the channels of help and healing. There may be environmental conditions, such as family hostility, which are setting up barriers. Freudians would say that the individual might be unconsciously clinging to the "will to die" or to remain sick in spite of his conscious prayer.

Variations on the possibilities are as endless, it appears, as individual personalities and situations themselves. Certainly we must accept the fact that we are mortal men reaching out to God and that we do not always understand and often we ask amiss, asking for what we desire, as if Heaven were a bargain counter where we pay our prayer and hurry off with our purchase.

A suggestion regarding the problem comes in Dr. Price's pamphlet on meditative prayer, in the prayer which asks God to help us curb our own selfish desires, even for healing. It is God's universe and we are His children and we pray to know more fully His will and to fulfill it.

On the eve of the Crucifixion, Jesus and His disciples were in Gethsemane, and Jesus said to them, "Sit ye here, while I go and pray yonder."

He took Peter, James and John with Him. Leaving them to keep watch, He went on a little further and fell to the ground and prayed: "O my Father, if it be possible, let this cup pass from me." Then he went on: "Nevertheless, not as I will, but as thou wilt."

This was the great example that the human Jesus gave us there in the garden. His prayer is the symbol of the simple normal desire of mankind to avoid pain and death.

He comes back and in very human terms upbraids Peter when He finds the three asleep whom He had brought with Him. "What," He says, "could ye not watch with me one hour?"

Then He leaves them again, and prays a second time: "O my Father, if this cup may not pass away from me, except I drink it, thy will be done."

He comes back and again finds them asleep. This time He says nothing but goes back and prays a third time, using the same words as before.

When He returns to His disciples the third time, He tells them that the hour is at hand when the Son of Man is betrayed into the hands of sinners.

Thus Jesus accepts, quietly and with dignity in this great symbolic series of events in the garden, the will of God, the suffering through which He will go for the sake of the sinners into whose hands He is betrayed.

This prayer in the garden is an example to us all. It says that we may pray for our seeming need, that the cup may pass from us, however small or great it may seem.

We may reach out to God from the human veil, within our human wants and prayers—and with an affirmation that spiritual truth remains unchanged and eternal.

But we do not know all things. And to all of our fervent petitions we must add, not with words but from the depths of our soul: "Not my will, but Thy will, be done."

16

<hr/>

Where Two or Three Are Gathered

Followers of spiritual healing turn to this phase of religion for many reasons. They are rich and poor; college graduates and illiterates; brilliant and clearheaded in one instance, neurotic or even psychotic in others. They represent every branch of modern religion, the orthodox, conservative and more liberal religions, and what many in spiritual healing circles call "our lunatic fringe."

Some turn to spiritual healing because they themselves are in need of cures and find no help in medicine, others because they find that they have a gift which they do not understand. They come because they are searching for an understanding of God's universe, because they are trying to find answers to hard questions about how the universe functions and what forces are operative in it.

They turn sometimes to spiritual healing (or what could be more properly called "faith healing" in this instance) through superstition, through ignorance and fear of medicine in some cases, particularly in isolated districts where medical care fails to provide for their needs. They come for adventure, because spiritual healing is still, after centuries, an area of exciting personal discovery.

Either they find what they want in the established orthodox faiths, or they turn from these to newer religions and sects. Occasionally, not finding what they seek, they form cults of their own and obtain their own coterie of followers.

There are hundreds of healing cults and sects in America, of every type, large and small, the commercial, the purely philosophical. Some are aimed at intellectuals and some at the ignorant, some are religious and meaningful, some blatantly pagan.

There are star-worshippers and tree-worshippers and nudists who talk of the healing fingers of the sun. There are those who claim the "gift of tongues" described in the Bible.[1] There are individuals who inspire great followings. There are snake-handlers who allow themselves to be bitten to prove the power of the Lord. (This was to carry out the biblical statement that they "shall take up serpents" and not be harmed.)[2]

There are groups employing mass hypnosis and mass emotional orgies for the exorcising of devils from the sick and "possessed." There are groups which practice weird nature rites. One is reported to have a practice of encircling a tree, holding hands, while the healer painstakingly deposits, one at a time, a hair from the head of each follower, on the limb of the tree.

There are also many groups, including some offshoots of the great denominations, which enjoy a recognized standing in the religious community.

But many healing sects, particularly in more remote areas, have fallen back on superstition and pagan practices. Tree-worship, for example, is an ancient primitive practice. In *The Golden Bough*, Sir James Frazer reported that in some areas of England they have a practice of passing a naked child through a cleft ash tree for the cure of rupture or rickets.[3] After the child is passed through the cleft,[4] the break in the tree is bound up tightly. If the tree heals, the child will also; if it does not heal, or if it dies, a similar fate, those who follow this ancient rite insist, awaits the child.

The practice is also employed, Frazer noted, in Germany, France, Denmark and Sweden, but here an oak is used instead of an ash.

Snake-handling and snake-worship is also a part of primitive folklore and pagan belief. Sir James reports also that in the Carolinas, the very area where America's snake-handling sects took root, the Indians of that area had great respect for the rattlesnakes and would never kill one because the Indian believed the soul of the snake which was killed would send other snakes to avenge its death.[5] From the dawning concepts of the force of religion in our

[1] Mark XVI:17.
[2] *Ibid*. XVI:18.
[3] Sir James George Frazer, The Golden Bough, New York: Macmillan, 1940. pp. 682-683.
[4] There are also reports that this must be done in the direction of the sun, or the whole thing fails.
[5] *Ibid*. pp. 519-520.

lives, the serpent has played an important symbolic role in the faith and myths of man.

Among smaller sects across the United States, evangelistic groups are the best known. We have already discussed the extraordinary ministry and vast following of Oral Roberts. It is not so well-known that Aimee Semple McPherson included healing as a part of her message. There are still thousands who follow her teachings and several hundred "Four-Square" Gospel churches throughout the country, devoted to her "Message for the World."

Only a few of the booming voices of the traveling evangelists, however, rise about the sawdust tumult to be heard by the world beyond the tents. Most are content to live a life of moving their tent and equipment and message from one city to the next, to preach and practice healing. Sometimes husbands and wives travel as evangelistic teams. Some attain such success that they engage large civic auditoriums and theaters for services. Their "advertising" in the local press may be rather startling:

"JESUS IS ALIVE," read one advertisement in large letters, and added as a follow-up, "Positive proof of this tonight and each evening next week 7:45."

Another advertisement reads: "Supernatural SIGNS and Phenomenal WONDERS follow this Man of God. Many have seen Jesus appear and stand by Rev.————————as he ministered. HEAR scores of local healing testimonies. YOU ALSO MAY RECEIVE HEALING."

Many healers belong to some of the Pentacostal groups, including the Pentacostal Holiness Church, of which Oral Roberts is a member. These groups, which began in Arkansas and later moved their headquarters to Springfield, Missouri, place their emphasis on a fundamentalist concept. They believe that they have returned to the original church of Jesus, that they have the "pentacostal gifts" of tongues and healing.

Originating mainly in the West and Southwest in the last decades of the nineteenth century, they reflected a frontier world of religion and a primitive return to the early church and its impassioned fervor. Shouting as the Holy Spirit sweeps through them, speaking in strange voices with the gifts of tongues, congregations in these early times were lifted to an emotional pitch of unleashed religious fervor.

This was religion of the new wilderness—wild and shouting and unrestrained. And their leaders preached that to those who received the anointment of God, the gifts of the Holy Spirit were theirs, including that of healing.

There are other churches, particularly in the South, which, although not widely known beyond their own districts, place their main emphasis on religious healing. Many are quite conservative and long-established. Such, for instance, is the denomination known as the Freewill Baptist, with headquarters in Nashville, Tennessee. Founded in 1727, this religion, among other fundamentalist rituals, practices spiritual healing through anointment of the sick with oil. The Pilgrim Holiness Church is another well-established "healing faith," with some fifty thousand members. It is an offshoot of Methodism. In Kentucky there is a sect which call itself the Holiness Church, whose members claim to heal any disease on earth by prayer and faith.

Looking at the most important of the groups, one is struck by the similarities of ideas. Certain basic facts recur again and again.

One catches echoes of Christian Science and Unity in the New Thought Movement which began in the 1890s in Boston. Many of these ideas had developed in Massachusetts in earlier decades through the Transcendentalists, led by Ralph Waldo Emerson, Henry David Thoreau, Phineas Quimby, and others. At a generalized conference in 1917, the New Thought creed was drawn up officially: "The essence of the New Thought is Truth and each individual must be loyal to the Truth." But, the creed adds, he must be loyal to it as he understands it. "The windows of his soul must be kept open at each moment," it goes on, "for the higher light, and his mind must be always hospitable to each new inspiration...

"We affirm the Good...

"We affirm Health...

"We affirm the divine supply...

"We affirm the teaching of Christ that the kingdom of Heaven is within us...

"We affirm the New Thought of God as Universal Love, Life, Truth and Joy..."[6]

In reporting on this creed, Gaius Glenn Atkins, in his book, *Modern Religious Cults and Movements,* quotes a saying that New

[6]Gaius Glenn Atkins, Modern Religious Cults and Movements. New York: Fleming H. Revell, 1923. p. 228.

Thought is "an attitude of mind, not a cult."[7] The two men who did most to launch this movement or attitude of mind, in any case, were Warren Felt Evans, a student of Quimby's, and Julius Dresser, also a student of Quimby's, and a friend of Mary Baker Eddy's. As their movement grew, considerable dissension developed and other groups sprang up with similar new ideas—among them a western group known as Divine Science, another called the Church of Advanced Thought and the Institute of Advanced Thought. All of these had the same general principle but varied in details. They affirmed the power of ideas, of love and good which transcended from material origins to the realm of pure Universal Spirit. All of them had faith in the healing powers of these abstract concepts, and the ability of these ideas to drive out what they considered the illusion and the lie of evil.

Foremost leader of the New Thought group in modern times is Dr. Ernest Holmes who started Religious Science and founded the magazine *Science of Mind.* With a church in Los Angeles, California, Dr. Holmes' work in therapy has become known throughout the world. The method of treatment applied is one of affirmation and invocation of the Divine Spirit whose Presence drives out negative "symptoms" brought on by failure to recognize or use the Divine Power within each of us.

In Religious Science, each minister is given full freedom in his own church. Each church operates as an individual entity; the minister sets his own service and raises his own finances. It is, in effect, a loose confederation rather than a tight-knit centralized organization. This fits the pattern and ideas of the New Thought movement, which is characterized by individualism; each person is in effect regarded as an individual power outlet of the universal force of God.

A number of these groups including Unity, The Church of Truth, Divine Science, and Religious Science, belong to the International New Thought Alliance, known as INTA, and regarded as a kind of National Council of Churches for the metaphysical group.

Dr. Erwin Seale, head of the Church of the Truth in New York City, teaches the non-creativeness of matter, not its non-existence. "It is not the germ which makes us sick; it is the thing within us which enables the germ to break through our spiritual defenses," he says. "The true creative force is spiritual and when that spirit

[7]*Ibid.* p. 210.

is not blocked out by wrong ideas, wrong emotions, wrong approaches to our problems, it is our great fortress against all harm.''

Dr. Seale's technique in healing and in "treating" is a dualistic kind of prayer, in which he begins by denying the existence of the evil as a reality and then affirms health and the successful working out of the difficulty. This alternating current of denial and affirmation continues, he explains, until in his own consciousness he is aware only of the affirmation. His part of the treatment is then accomplished.

Dr. Seale, who has had a number of healings in his own practice, teaches that sickness, germs, disease and disaster strike at us when we block the channels of "Divine Law and Order" which he considers to be "the will of God." God's will is for health, for joy, for success and for triumph, not for despair, not for heartbreak, not for trouble, not for misery. These forces have no power over us, no creative power to harm us, unless we let them by blocking the channels to the God-force within us.

In all New Thought concepts, the fundamental idea is that the rich, rewarding life is there for the taking, for the realization, for the understanding. Dr. Raymond Barker of the First Church of Religious Science in New York told me it was like "having a thousand-dollar bill closed up in some book and forgotten."

"The thousand-dollar bill is there but if you don't know about it how can you use it? It is of no benefit because you are not aware of it. We must recognize the universal within ourselves and once we recognize it, we must direct that force to good objectives."

In one of his pamphlets, Dr. Barker sums up much of New Thought in one paragraph of affirmation: "There is an impelling force for good. It is God. It is in all, through all and equally distributed in every person. Its main characteristics are intelligence and love. It is inspiration and warmth, but It is also mechanical law. There is an overshadowing Presence that is always with you. It is the primary, loving, creative action of life. You are always in It. It is always in you. It is always working for your good. It is always desiring the best for you. God wants you to be happy, healthy and to have love and self-expression."[8]

Some individuals merged these ideas with other more orthodox spiritual concepts. One of the most outstanding of leaders in spiritual growth and healing was the late Glenn Clark, founder of the

[8]Raymond Charles Barker, Spirit, Soul and Body. New York: Published by the Author, 1955. p. 5.

group of camps known as the "Camps Farthest Out."

A man of robust build, Glenn Clark was born in Des Moines, Iowa, in 1882, was a star athlete and scholar in college, and later became an athletic director at a college in St. Paul, Minnesota. He remained there until 1944, when he resigned to devote all his time to the spiritual development of his fellow men.

Mr. Clark worked for some time, at the start of his career, helping to build athletic programs for both the YMCA and the YWCA. He found that in many camps prayer and religious life in general had become routine rather than what he declared should be a "vital, living relationship with Christ."

In the early years of the century, he founded the first Camp Farthest Out at Lake Koronis, Minnesota. In these camps his aim was to develop what he called "athletes of the soul." Here, and in groups of individuals who clustered around him during winter seasons, he brought forth his concepts of religion and of religious healing. He believed and taught that bad thoughts and bad emotions bring bad health, although the worst invalids are not necessarily the worst sinners because he taught also that "illness is a sign of spiritual sensitivity."

Many persons found that his approach proved successful in their own cases, and called him a true healer. A Presbyterian elder, Mr. Clark told his followers that prayer did not heal in itself but produced a state of consciousness within the individual, an awareness and receptivity, which made divine healing possible.

One unusual facet of his belief was that he felt that there was no requirement that the sick individual pray or even have religious faith, provided someone around this person or close to this person is in what he called "a state of prayer."

One of the groups he launched is the United Prayer Tower in St. Paul. Mr. Clark's purpose was to found a "communion of praying people who have no doubts about the power of prayer to bring forth the perfection of God in all human affairs."[9] This prayer group, while still comparatively small, reaches people of many denominations, particularly in the midwest and northwestern states. One of the meditations used by this group reads:

"Dear Father:

"Let me be so peaceful that nothing can disturb my serenity . . .

"Let me think only the best, work only for the best, and expect

[9]The United Prayer Tower. St. Paul, Minn.: The Macalester Park Publishing Co., n.d. p. 2.

nothing but the best in return . . .

"Let me wear a happy countenance at all times and have a real smile for every one I meet . . .

"Let me be too big for worry, too kind for anger, too courageous for fear and too contented to permit trouble to take possession of me . . .

"Let me live in the faith that the Lord is on my side as long as I am true to the best that is in me. . . ."[10]

Glenn Clark and his followers—and similar groups and individuals—fall into a special category of those seeking to merge spiritual concepts into daily living and with the world of nature. It is a Christian faith blended with an almost Eastern sense of peace and power plus a strictly occidental practicality.

In his booklet, *The Divine Plan,* Mr. Clark says that there is a special Plan for each of us, and it includes health and happiness and success. He says if we fail in any of these it is because we have not permitted Divinity to act through us. Whatever comes into our life that is negative is not a part of this "God-created plan" but a distortion caused by our failure to harmonize ourselves with the Plan as God made it.

The plan for each of us, he states, is "wrapped in the folds of our Being, even as the oak is wrapped in the acorn . . ."[11]

Throughout the teachings of these healers and preachers one finds the same theme: that man is the expression of God's law and of God's will.

Dr. Albert E. Cliffe, Canadian biochemist who left industry to become a lay reader in the Episcopal Church, says: "Forget the old ideas you were taught ages ago of a God of wrath, a God who sent you a sickness to punish you, and demanded an eye for an eye and a tooth for a tooth. Jesus told us His Father was a God of love. He is all love, and when you show love to any person, or to an animal, you are expressing God. Our main reason for being on this earth is to express God. . . . When you are dominated by criticism or resentment or temper, you cannot express God, and you are breaking His laws; and when you break any law you have to pay the price for the breaking of that law."[12]

[10]*Ibid.* p. 11.

[11]Glenn Clark, The Divine Plan. St. Paul, Minn.: Macalester Park Publishing Co., 1953. p. 1.

[12]Dr. Albert E. Cliffe, Let Go and Let God, Englewood Cliffs, N. J.: Prentice-Hall, 1951. p. 40.

* * *

It is impossible, of course, to give more than a sample of the groups and sects and individuals concerned with them in spiritual healing. There is hardly a community in America or in the civilized world which does not have its own healers, of whose power many in the community are ready to testify. Some have strange names and some sound quite like average people. Some perform publicly, some in private sessions. Some base their teachings and techniques on religion, some on the power of mind, some on hypnotism, some on spiritualism and psychic phenomena, some on ancient and primitive techniques.

Obviously some groups are more spiritually based than others. Often the smaller sects are like side streets to God—they twist and turn unexpectedly, sometimes leading into even more obscure byways and occasionally to dead-end streets.

But some of the twisting byways lead ultimately to wide sun-splashed boulevards of faith. And for some individuals, tormented by doubts and weaknesses, conflicts and confusions, or merely by the need of personal adventure and discovery, these side paths may offer the only way.

Some individuals do not fit any category. One is a man I would like to consider—at least briefly—apart from the others. I do not attempt to explain him, for I have no explanation.

17

Edgar Cayce: The Miracle Man

Edgar Cayce was a religious man. He was a Presbyterian and a Sunday school teacher. On the surface he seemed like an average person. He was a book salesman and a life insurance salesman and a photographer. He came from an average American family. It was his inner, other life which made Edgar Cayce different in so many ways from other men.

There are many miraculous personalities in the records of paranormal healing. There is the grotto of Lourdes and the visions of Bernadette; there is Fatima and the visions of the children who saw "The Lady" there; there are the healings of Brother André of Montreal and Dr. Price of Philadelphia and Ambrose Worrall, the businessman-mystic of Baltimore.

Edgar Cayce claimed no power in his touch, employed no laying on of hands, nor did he employ prayer in his healing, as such. He healed by diagnosing illness while in a trance, although he had no knowledge of medicine and did not even remember what he was saying.

He gave readings, in this trance state, in more than twenty thousand cases involving all known types of diseases.

In more than 70 per cent of the cases, he was not only absolutely accurate in his diagnosis but his prescription was also correct and successful. A great many people came to believe in him and his works. Many of his followers were physicians and men of science.

Except in terms of reincarnation or special psychic power, explanations for Edgar Cayce's achievements have not been found.

The following are the facts as known:

Edgar Cayce was born not far from Hopkinsville, Kentucky, in 1877. His father was a justice of the peace. His grandfather was known as a water "dowser" who could find where to dig for water.

In school he was not interested in his studies. But he was deeply impressed by religion as a child and read the Bible closely and told people he wanted to be a medical missionary when he grew up.

There were many incidents in his childhood, visions, strange powers. To the objective observer, they combined elements of spiritualism, religion and fantasy. In some instances, they appeared to combine a photographic memory with "second sight," developed as he grew older. In other ways he was quite average. He worked in a bookstore and had a sweetheart whom he eventually married.

Long before all this—when he was twenty-one—he developed laryngitis and lost his voice. He could speak only in a whisper. Many physicians were consulted and could not agree on the diagnosis or the possible cure.

One day a New York hypnotist came to Hopkinsville. Since everything else had failed, the young man was encouraged to try to get his throat cured by hypnotism, at that time a new American fad. Several physicians and college professors began to be interested in the experiments with Edgar Cayce. Under hypnosis, he could speak. But posthypnotic suggestion failed; when he came out of the hypnosis he could not speak. From New York, one physician sent word that Edgar might find his own cure under hypnosis, inasmuch as he appeared to "take charge" in his hypnotic state.

In Hopkinsville was a man named Al Layne, who had studied hypnotism. Mr. Layne came to Edgar and suggested that they work together. Edgar informed Mr. Layne in his hollow whisper that in all the other instances, although he had seemed to go into hypnotic state under the suggestion of others, it had actually been accomplished by his own efforts. He had put himself into a trance state.

His suggestion to Al Layne was that perhaps, in this condition, he might be able to find his own trouble. Mr. Layne agreed, and Edgar put himself into the self-hypnotised condition. Then, seemingly asleep, he began to speak clearly, describing his own condition as if he were talking of a third person, explaining what the trouble was and that it could be cured by increasing the circulation to the affected area. This could be done by suggestion, Edgar said. Al Layne carried out this order by "suggesting" that the circulation of blood would increase in that area. The area around the throat, according to his report, became red. Somewhat later, Edgar awakened. He was able to talk, normally, just as he had talked in hypnotic state.

If he could help himself, Mr. Layne suggested, perhaps he could help others. Edgar Cayce was both pleased at this idea and frightened. Finally he agreed to try it with Mr. Layne, who was an osteopath by profession. A number of people were helped without knowing that it was Edgar Cayce who discovered what was wrong with them while in a self-induced hypnotic trance.

Mr. Cayce did not want to make a business of this, however. Nor was he ever mercenary about his efforts; most of his life he was forced to strain to pay household expenses for himself, his wife and his son, Hugh Lynn Cayce.

Yet reports of this ability spread and he was unable to avoid helping people because it was something that had to be used only for helping humanity. He found his strength and his answers in the Bible. He was carrying on a Christian work in his healing, by his own unique method.

In one case, involving a four-year-old girl who was having convulsions fifteen to twenty times a day, doctors had been unable to help the child. It was said that her mental and physical condition had developed following an attack of grippe at the age of two. Edgar Cayce, in his trance, said that the earlier disease had produced a lesion at the base of the spine and suggested osteopathic treatment by Al Layne. Each time the treatments were given, Mr. Cayce went into a trance and told Mr. Layne what he should do.

By the third treatment, the child's mind had developed to a point where she was beginning to speak—which she had not done before—and the convulsions had ceased entirely.

From that time on, the child grew normally.

Through much of his early career Edgar Cayce lived by working in a bookstore and as a photographer and carrying on his other "work" without payment on the side. Ultimately, hundreds of people were coming to him and he was giving two readings a day; outside work was simply not possible.

It was then, with the help of friends who believed in him, that he was able to start his foundation, devoted to scientific and psychical research. Headquarters were located in Virginia Beach, where the work of the society has been carried on by his son, Hugh Lynn Cayce, since his death in 1945, at the age of sixty-seven.

All of Edgar Cayce's more than twenty thousand readings have been carefully written down and indexed and have been examined by students and clergymen and writers. These readings were all

given by Mr. Cayce in his trance state. Hundreds of reliable investigators have examined the facts of these readings and testified
to their correctness. Many persons and patients were present during
the trance "readings" in which Edgar Cayce, with no previous
knowledge of the patient's condition, would describe what was
wrong with that person and how the person might be helped. Often
he would provide a suggestion of what kind of medicine should
be used and what doctor to contact. In some cases, the medicines
were unknown by doctors; in one, it was found that the medicine
prescribed was still in the process of manufacture and had not yet
been publicly announced. In others it was found that the medicines
were obscure and had not been heard of by pharmacists in many
years or were completely unknown to them and required further
instruction as to manufacture.

Hugh Lynn Cayce apparently inherited none of his father's
diagnostic gifts, but carries on this work through the Association
For Research and Enlightenment, sponsoring lectures and study
groups in the field of psychic research. The Association, under
the younger Cayce's direction, has also continued a valuable study,
indexing and processing of the thousands of "readings."

Theories about Edgar Cayce are many, but complete explanations are difficult.

A writer is obligated to seek first-hand impressions, however.
I talked, for example, to one well-known New York osteopath,
Dr. Frank P. Dobbins of Staten Island, to whom the elder Cayce
sent several hundred cases.

Some months after he had started his successful practice in New
York, Dr. Dobbins moved to Staten Island in 1931. Shortly after
this move, a woman and girl came to his office. The woman said
that the little girl had serious trouble with her hip. She said they
had a "reading" from Mr. Cayce.

Dr. Dobbins did not know what she meant by a reading and
had no knowledge of Mr. Cayce. Nor did he know how Mr. Cayce
had known about him.

The diagnosis in the reading, he said, was correct and was
reinforced by X-rays. He was able to treat the child and to help
her to an extent. From that time on, Edgar Cayce sent cases to
him, and over many years Dr. Dobbins came to know Mr. Cayce
and respect him.

In his personal evaluation of Edgar Cayce, Dr. Dobbins said
he was a warm man, genuinely religious, who talked with a hill-
billy southern drawl and who wanted to help humanity and cared

little for monetary gain. In many cases, he said, the "readings" were generalizations and not specific and precise diagnoses. Most of them were right, although it would not be correct, he stated, to say that 90 per cent were right. "But I will tell you this," Dr. Dobbins said. "I never saw anything in the readings that could do a patient harm, and many things could be and were beneficial."

This is one evaluation, from an objective point of view, by a man of science and healing, based on handling several hundred patients sent to him by Mr. Cayce through the trance readings.

But Dr. Dobbins' honest and forthright appraisal, on the basis of these several hundred cases sent to him, does not explain either how Edgar Cayce was able to make correct diagnoses at all, in a trance state, frequently after medicine had failed to find what was wrong, or how in Virginia Beach, Va., he could tell the woman and child to find Dr. Dobbins, who had moved to Staten Island so recently that his name was not even listed in the phone book, and they had to get the address from the telephone operator.

These are areas apparently beyond the scope of our present medical knowledge.

18

"We Find No Evidence..."

A special committee of the British Medical Association, assigned, in 1953, to gather evidence for the Archbishop's Commission on Divine Healing, prepared a formal memorandum on the subject following three years of investigations. Among the reports selected for inclusion in the appendices of this memorandum, out of the mass of material received by the committee, were the following from licensed and presumably reputable British physicians:

"An elderly lady had two strokes within about ten days and was given up as hopeless with a diagnosis of hemiplegia due to cerebral haemorrhage. Dr.——[1] expressed the opinion that this was probably a thrombosis. The patient lost her speech and her limbs were paralyzed. A healing service was held and, within days, the patient was about again, and now thirteen years later, at the age of eighty-three, this patient is still walking to church twice every Sunday."[2]

Another report from another physician was cited as follows:

"A patient with cancer of cervix uteri. Seen by Prof. of Gynaecology who confirmed the diagnosis and pronounced the case inoperable as it was too extensive. After prayer was started, the pain and the smell quickly went; the cancer itself disappeared in two months. No recurrence. Patient died eight years later from pneumonia."[3]

Still another report, from another doctor, declared:

---

[1] The name presumedly was included in the original report to the committee, but was omitted from the memorandum.

[2] Divine Healing and Cooperation Between Doctors and Clergy. London: British Medical Association, 1956. p. 34.

[3] *Ibid.* p. 38.

"A single woman, aged 29, living abroad. The patient was ill off and on from February, 1954, until September, 1954, with amoebiasis. Symptoms were fever off and on, attacks of diarrhoea, abdominal pain, and a bout of jaundice (in March) lasting six weeks. (? amoebic in origin ? virus hepatitis.) Amoebae were detected in the stools in April. During the course of her illness she was treated with quinine, plasmoquine, chloroquine, camoquine, milibis, and aureomycin, (not a full course). In August she had niraquire, emetine (gr. 8½) and enteroviofrom (ii t.d.s. for 20 days), but her temperature, which had been continuously elevated for 8 weeks, did not subside, and her pain continued. Stool tests were not available at this time. At this stage she was prepared for Divine Healing by the Laying on of Hands, and on September 5th a service was held in her room. Physically there was no dramatic change, but her mental attitude to her illness changed, and whereas she had previously been very despondent, she was now open to receive God's blessing. A week after the service, her temperature was completely normal and remained so, at least until early December.[4] In mid-September 4 stool tests were negative."[5]

Despite these statements by physicians, included in the appendices to its memorandum, the special committee of the British Medical Association declared as its own considered conclusion in that same memorandum:

"As far then as our observation and investigation have gone, *we have seen no evidence that there is any special type of illness cured solely by spiritual healing which cannot be cured by medical methods which do not involve such claims*. The cases claimed as cures of a miraculous nature present no features of a unique and unexpected character outside the knowledge of any experienced physician or psychiatrist."[6]

Further, they declare, "To summarize, *we can find no evidence that there is any type of illness cured by 'spiritual healing' alone which could not have been cured by medical treatment which necessarily includes consideration of environmental factors* . . . We can find no evidence that organic diseases are cured solely by such means. The evidence suggests that many such cases claimed to be cured are likely to be either instances of wrong diagnosis,

[4] Presumedly meaning latest report on her condition.
[5] *Ibid.* p. 37.
[6] *Ibid.* italics as in report. p. 13.

wrong prognosis, remission, or possibly of spontaneous cure.''[7]

This report, published in England in 1956, was a sudden and explosive public attack upon religious healing and healers. In England, where this type of healing had attained greater standing and popular support than in the United States, it came with tremendous impact.

It is a curious memorandum in many respects. In phrasings it has all the mannerisms of the "old school tie." On occasion the memorandum achieves an almost frightening stuffiness: "The Committee was convinced from the information given to it, and many doctors believe that prayer may be of value to patients, whether recovery takes place or not.''[8]

Perhaps the most important contribution of this memorandum, however, lies not so much in its individual conclusions or contradictions, as in what it symbolizes: the underlying and continuing area of disagreement between the medical world and the religious world. Throughout the report the doctors are with one hand accepting religion and urging co-operation, while at the same time insisting that any healing claimed by religion can be explained in terms of spontaneous cure or medical error.

It cannot be denied that many claims of religious healers are overstated and questionable, and challengeable on scientific grounds. This does not, however, give a scientific body making a supposedly scientific investigation of a serious subject the right itself to indulge in nonscientific guesses and contradictory statements.

Let us look for a moment at the situation in Britain which led up to this memorandum:

England and Scotland, in the years following World War II, experienced an unparalleled revival of interest in religious healing and in certain charismatic healers who have become leading forces in British religious healing.

It is possible that some of this revival was the result of a subtle post-war hysteria, an aftermath of protracted but well concealed terror. It is possible that many in Britain, quite unemotionally, wanted to plod forward to the truth of this subject. It is true that there has been a sizable revival of interest in psychic phenomena

[7]*Ibid.* italics as in report. p. 15.
[8]*Ibid.* p. 21.

in Britain and that some religious healers are also involved in spiritualism.

All of these elements played some part. In 1944, the Church of England established the Church Council on Healing whereby leaders of many healing associations and groups—such as the Guild of St. Raphael, the Friends Spiritual Healing Fellowship and a number of others—combined efforts in the development of this work.

Throughout England and Scotland, in these associations and in individual churches, religious healing became a subject of intense interest. In the compact world of England, Scotland and Wales, there were dozens of men and women healers—some of them working through the churches, particularly the Presbyterian and Methodist churches, in Scotland and England, some of them conducting individual healing "missions."[9] This interest became so great, and the volume of reported evidence regarding spiritual healing began piling so high, that the Archbishop of Canterbury appointed a special commission in 1953 to investigate Divine Healing on a broad basis under direction of clergymen, educators and physicians. The British Medical Association's memorandum was a part of this work. In Scotland, a similar commission was established. Religious healing services were being held in more than one hundred Presbyterian churches throughout Scotland.

Among the outstanding figures in England at this time were men who were almost unknown to the general public in America but whose names had become familiar in almost every British home. Harry Edwards was one. (It was said that Harry Edwards got more mail than Sir Winston Churchill when the former Prime Minister was at the peak of his popularity.) Alex Holmes was another. Dr. John Millard was a third. And Dr. Leslie Weatherhead was a fourth. These four men might well be called a cross section of the revival in Britain.

Dr. Weatherhead represents conservatism, deep faith, unwillingness to seek an easy answer or accept a facile explanation to fit his earlier opinions. His book, *Psychology, Religion and Healing*, remains a classic history in this field, a scholarly work going deep into the meanings of healings in Christian and pagan worlds. At the City Temple in London, Dr. Weatherhead himself has worked in religious healing for many years. Dr. Weatherhead's techniques are based on the idea of working with instruments

---

[9]Somewhat comparable to evangelistic crusades in the United States.

available, medicine, psychiatry, pastoral counseling, the sacraments, prayer and the use of charismatic healers. He has had many healings at the City Temple, where he is minister.

"It makes nonsense of Christ's healing ministry," this Methodist minister wrote on one occasion, "to say that religion and health are never connected. I want to suggest that there must be spiritual energies which have greater sway over the body and the mind than anything which science has brought within her tabulations and formulae."

Dr. Weatherhead has had, through his writings and sermons as much as through his actual healings, a profound effect on the thinking of the most serious-minded groups involved in spiritual healing. When he was visiting the United States in 1954, he attended one of the Spiritual Healing Seminars held at Wainwright House in New York City, in which psychiatrists, nurses, professors of psychiatry and psychology and prominent laymen participated.

Dr. Weatherhead's startling and original brand of theological thought about healing was brought into focus by one question asked him by the group: "What are we to answer when physical healing does not come?"

In the whole area of spiritual therapy, there is no more difficult question. We have already seen—in our explorations here of various religions and religious healers—many answers to it. Some equivocate as to who or what is to blame, the individual or his environment or his approach. Some blame man, some blame the devil, some still think of sickness as the just punishment of God.

Dr. Weatherhead says that sickness is never God's will for us, and that we should always strive to be well, because sickness is always evil.

But he adds that if the cure does not come, we should not surrender ourselves to despair but to the best of our abilities under whatever circumstances prevail, we should try to wrest good from the evil.

"God can use evil for our blessedness as powerfully as he can use good. I don't say for our happiness but for our blessedness," he stated at the Wainwright conference.

"When we contemplate physical illness which goes on in spite of the doctors, the surgeons, the psychologists, the healers, the hypnotists—having tried all the ways we are still carrying this burden of evil, illness—I think it always is a part of the kingdom of evil. Jesus regarded it as such, and so did Paul. Paul said, 'The messenger of Satan sent to buffet me.' ''[10]

In Dr. Weatherhead's view, we must look at physical healing through bifocal glasses; we should strive to get well through treatment "of any kind on any plane, spiritual, mental or physical," but we should at the same time accept what we must and still strive and not "lie down and resign.'"[11]

Our attitude, he insists, must still be that we will seek physical health. "This is the perfect will of God and I will try for that in every means open to me. Then I can give God a fitter body. But I will remember that God's excuse for the long rope he gives the devil is that he holds the end of the rope himself; or in other words, that God can use evil as potently for my ultimate welfare as he can use good. So I will accept this and I will so react to it that I will win gain out of it.

"God and I in cooperation can do this just as Jesus did with the Cross. Christ met it, he wrested victory out of evil. This symbol of evil has become the symbol of triumph and victory.'"[12]

Of the many "healing ministers" who gained followings of millions in England and Scotland in the decade of the 1950s, the two most outstanding figures were Harry Edwards and his pupil, the Reverend Alex Holmes. Mr. Holmes' ministry of healing at Cavendish Chapel, All Saints Church, in Manchester, is somewhat like that of Dr. Price of Philadelphia; he employs the laying on of hands, his service is stripped of emotionalism, he works with small groups at the altar and through individual private pastoral counseling.

Hundreds gather in his church for his healing services, coming from all over England, Scotland and the European Continent. The prayers of his congregations combine with his own in his healing technique.

In addition to his own healing, the Rev. Mr. Holmes has spent considerable time in training other ministers of various denominations in the methods and attitudes which seem most successful in practicing the healing ministry.

Harry Edwards is a healer and a spiritualist. He is a deeply religious man and believes firmly in Christian theology in healing.

[10]Spiritual Healing Seminar, March 25-26, 1954. Rye, N. Y.: Wainwright House Publications. pp. 72-73.

[11]*Ibid.* p. 73.

[12]*Ibid.* p. 74.

His gift of healing has produced an array of reported cures; thousands of followers claim that he is the most extraordinary healer of our age. He is also a center of controversy.

When he appeared before the British Medical Association hearings with his evidence, the committee listened, asked questions, investigated on its own, and made findings. When the Archbishop's Commission on Divine Healing accepted the report of the Medical Association and seemingly stood behind these findings, Mr. Edwards, determined to get his side across to the public, published the evidence he had presented and the medical committee's reactions.

One of the cases he cited was that of an eight-year-old boy who was suffering from leukemia.[13] The detailed report on this case outlined the stages through which this boy passed. His case was diagnosed as chronic myeloid leucosis—leukemia—and his condition, according to Mr. Edwards' statement, was called hopeless. H. F. Barker, a friend of the boy's father, suggested that they try spiritual healing. The father wrote to Harry Edwards, at Mr. Barker's suggestion, and asked for "absent treatment" for his son.

Harry Edwards began his prayerful treatments on December 19, 1952.

The records show that the "hopeless case" began to get better from that date on, Mr. Edwards says.

Doctors began noting the fact that the boy's blood count was showing an improvement and a month later deep X-ray treatment was begun. (Mr. Edwards made a strong point of the fact that the boy had started on the road to recovery before any X-ray treatments had been attempted.)

Following January 20, the X-ray treatment halted. But the boy continued to get better. In March he was back in school; his condition was practically normal at this time. On March 20 his condition was absolutely normal. It continued so with one slight relapse at which time the father asked for Mr. Edwards to help. The relapse was quickly "overcome."

The boy continued to stay well. His father reported that he played football, ate like a horse, loved to climb trees and seemed to be the picture of normality.

On September 24, 1954, the parents of this boy took him for his quarterly checkup. One of the physicians called the father into

[13]Harry Edwards, The Truth About Spiritual Healing. London: Spiritualist Press, 1956. p. 42 ff.

his office alone. In a letter to Mr. Edwards the father stated:

"The object was to inform me that the period of remission was now reckoned to be running out. Dr. Williams, head of the deep X-ray department, repeated the warning, saying there was no certainty that Graham would react to the deep X-rays in the same way. Naturally I questioned: 'Why the warning? Had they seen some signs?' But the answer was, 'No, the boy is perfectly fit and normal at the moment.'

"I was told quite bluntly that there is no medical record of recovery from this dreaded blood disease. One or two exceptional cases of three to five years' remission following deep X-ray treatment were known, and even one unaccountable case of 23 years' immunity, but it always returns. They said that we could think Graham was in the exceptional class if we got safely to three years' immunity, but on medical experience they would expect a relapse after two years, and after that his little life might not last more than six months."

In 1955 there was a higher white cell blood count but no corresponding anemia symptoms were noted. A blood specialist, Dr. Bodley Scott, was consulted. His statement was that as long as the physical and clinical condition required no remedial action, the increase could be ignored.

The boy continued well and happy.

The medical committee's report on this case was rather terse: "The third case of leukemia is still under medical treatment and continues to show signs of active disease, such as enlargement of the spleen and a characteristic blood picture."

Harry Edwards, in this as in other cases he presented, was disturbed at the findings of the committee, not so much by what they said as by what they left out, since their omissions did not allow an accurate picture of the situation to be given.

"These findings," he pointed out, "do not comment on Graham's recovery from certain death. It does not refer to the fact that Graham is now four years older and is therefore in the exceptional class. It ignores the statement by Dr. Bodley Scott that the discrepancy in the blood count can now be ignored. It presents the opinion that the enlarged spleen is indicative of the disease, when it is common knowledge that once a spleen has enlarged due to the diseases that affect it, it does not resume its normal size, and this need cause no impediment to continued perfect health. The findings do not mention that in his four years of recovery Graham is fit and well.

"It is submitted that the medical findings are intended to mislead, they have ignored the facts as stated . . .

"It is now over four years since the doctors said Graham would die. He is now in the 'exceptional class.' We cannot foresee the future, but the question that the doctors must face and try to explain is, 'Why did Graham recover in 1952 when the considered opinion of eminent doctors was that this was impossible?'"[14]

Edwards in his arguments was presenting his own case and it would be less than human nature if he did not marshal the facts to present the strongest possible position. However, if the child is or was at the time of the report in a state of full recovery, after physicians had said he would die, as Edwards declares—and we have certainly no reason whatsoever to doubt his facts—the question arises: Why did the committee omit them? Certainly the inclusion of these facts in their comment on "the third case of leukemia" would have altered the reaction of average individuals. One can hardly imagine that the committee deliberately omitted them simply to *prevent* the public from putting too much credence in this spiritual healing business. That was certainly not its assignment from the Archbishop of Canterbury.

Such a body of eminent physician as made up this British committee could hardly be accused on non-objectivity or unscientific bias. Yet the fact is that many of their statements betray a vagueness they themselves would not accept as scientific and a seeming acceptance of personal opinions and evaluations in which examination of the facts played little or no part. Speaking of the doctors who replied to their questionnaires, they made the following comments: "The bulk of the replies were from believers in Divine healing. Replies were presented in diffuse terms and conclusions could not be drawn from them. The fact that many doctors and others believed in the efficacy of Divine healing was worthy of note. Many of the examples of healing given were invalidated because witnesses did not distinguish between partial and complete healing. The word *healing* was used in a different sense and thus confused the issue. It must be borne in mind that the majority of the doctors who replied believed in prayer and so were naturally prejudiced in its favor."

This statement raises a number of perplexing questions. If so many men of medical science in Britain believe in Divine healing, is this not a situation of extraordinary significance, rather than

[14]*Ibid*. pp. 49-50.

merely a fact "worthy of note"? Are the people of Britain and
Europe and America aware that a considerable number of registered and practicing British doctors are believers in spiritual healing? Again, in their "invalidation" of cases that were not
"complete healings" was the committee possibly throwing out
cases where substantial help was given, as in the case of the
leukemia boy who, whatever symptoms remained, was alive instead of dead? Again in the statement that doctors who believed
in prayer naturally were prejudiced in favor of it, are they not
drawing a wholly unscientific, undocumented and actually un-
provable conclusion regarding the scientific objectivity of these
registered physicians? Are they saying that because a doctor believes in prayer, he cannot give an objective scientific report on
all healing techniques employed on his own patients or on patients
whose treatment he has observed? Would they question a physician's reports regarding aureomycin, merely because the doctor
happened to believe in this drug?

The objectivity of this medical committee's memorandum was
not strengthened by the declaration a little further on: "In drawing
up this Report, the committee did not rely solely on the views
expressed by those who appeared before it or submitted written
statements, but drew to a considerable extent on the cumulative
experience of its members."[15]

Only one physician's statement is included in the report itself,
a summary of a statement by a Dr. Cuthbert Dukes on the subject
of spontaneous recovery. Dr. Dukes is dubious about religious
cures of a spontaneous nature and states at one point: "In the few
cases that might be looked on as miracles one would need to know
whether to attribute them to the intervention of a supernatural
Power or to the action of natural laws as yet undiscovered."[16]

Under this dictum, no healing could be properly called the result
of divine intervention of any kind, since—short of an outright
warranty from Heaven itself—there would always be the possibility of finding a natural law to explain it at some future date.

Above the summarization of this letter from Dr. Dukes, is a
note that his statement is "endorsed" by the committee.

In a footnote, the committee goes somewhat afield to comment
on the healings at Lourdes, mentioning with praise the thoroughness of the scientific investigations of the "alleged cures" by the

[15]*Divine Healing and Cooperation Between Doctors and Clergy.* p. 16.
[16]*Ibid.* p. 19.

Bureau des Constatations Medicales, and pointing out that the number of miracles actually attested and registered over the years has been exceedingly small, not even one a year, and that "every attempt is made to emphasize the spiritual value of the pilgrimage rather than such healings as may be claimed."[17]

The committee in this instance does not give any evaluation, however, of those few "miracles" which they themselves declare have been given complete scientific investigation, and are attested and registered. Since they go to such lengths to point out the quantitative lack of miracles at Lourdes, would it not be objective for them also to mention the quality of those miracles that are accepted, in terms of evidence and facts and proofs?

It is entirely possible that everything claimed and stated by the British Medical Report is true.

The author is obligated to present what facts he finds, and to permit the reader to form his own opinions based on those facts.

I have given this detailed analysis of the report not because I wish to stack the cards for spiritual healing. There are still many dubious areas in this kind of healing, many answers we do not have and can only search for, many claims that cannot be proven, many cases in the shadowy world of psychosomatics.

But the findings I have reported in this book, and the cases reported and cited by the committee in its own report, sent in by reputable British physicians licensed to practice medicine under British law and the rules of the British Medical Association, indicate that there are healings under circumstances which defy normal explanations in terms of our present physical knowledge.

This area of healing may well be brought one day into sharper focus in terms of physical medicine and psychiatric knowledge. But at present the answers are unknown in scientific terms. It is important, moreover, for mankind that we do come to understand it. This can be done only with true and courageous scientific objectivity.

One almost pictures the committee as a group at bay, beleaguered by the clergymen and doctors who believe in prayer; desperately trying to find a way out and finally coming up with two brilliant italicized sentences which say exactly the opposite of what they seem to imply.

They say that the committee came upon no evidence of any

[17]*Ibid.* p. 10.

cure by spiritual healing alone that could not be accomplished equally by a competent doctor or modern psychiatrist.

The statement might seem to indicate that no evidence of spiritual healing was found.

In actual fact the statement says plainly that there *were* spiritual healings, of a kind comparable to the healing one might obtain from any physician or modern psychiatrist.

Then were these healings accomplished by prayer, by laying on of hands or other religious ministrations, as the evidence the committee itself presents does seem to indicate?

Is the committee saying that spiritual healing is unimportant because you can always get a doctor to do the same job?

Moreover, if—as they charge—there are doctors in Britain so prejudiced in favor of prayer that their testimony is prejudiced, are not these same doctors likely to reach prejudiced decisions that may possibly involve the life or death of patients?

If what the committee says is true, should they not have the courage to denounce these doctors publicly, and demand that their right to practice be withdrawn?

But if they are not saying that these doctors are unreliable, should they not also make that perfectly clear?

These men of the committee are doctors too, eminent physicians. They are scientists and men trained and honor-bound to search objectively for truth.

They owe the people of Britain and of the world, in this reporter's opinion, honest and unequivocal answers.

19

Jewish Healing Practices

"Heal us, O Lord, and we shall be healed"; the Jew is taught to say in his daily prayers, "save us and we shall be saved; for thou art our praise. Grant a perfect healing to all our wounds; for thou, almighty King, art a faithful and merciful Physician. Blessed art thou, O Lord, who healest the sick of thy people Israel."[1]

The prayer of petition for favors and for healing has always been a part of Jewish belief from the earliest days of Judaism. In the Pentateuch we find the story of Miriam, the sister of Moses, when she was smitten with leprosy and granted healing after Moses cried, "Heal her now, O God, I beseech thee."[2] There was also the healing of Naaman, the Syrian Army captain who was likewise afflicted with leprosy.

Later, in the eighteenth century came the Hasidic movement and the so-called "healing rabbis" or "miracle rabbis" who might be called a Hebrew counterpart of the "healing priests" who first came into prominence centuries earlier.

For the Jews, as for Christians, the problem of healing by any means, spiritual or physical, always held in it areas of dispute. A few early Jewish leaders, as already noted, were opposed to all attempts at healing as a thwarting of God's punishment. At the same time, the sacred writings themselves set up remarkably effective sanitary laws, and physicians and apothecaries did practice in Palestinian cities, regardless of an occasional disapproving rabbi.

Throughout the early Christian centuries when physicians were sometimes looked upon with high disfavor by church authorities—

[1]Dr. Joseph H. Hertz, The Authorized Daily Prayer Book. New York: Bloch Publishing Company, 1948. p. 141.
[2]Numbers XII:10-15.

and in some places barred by official edict—Jewish physicians did much in the development of medical science. Jewish doctors played leading roles in the development of medical knowledge at the schools of Salerno and Montpellier. One of the greatest of Jewish physicians was the twelfth-century Spanish rabbi, doctor and philosopher, Maimonides, a man of great wisdom and learning whose teachings left their mark on both Jewish and Christian thought.

Within some areas of Jewish thought, today as in ancient days, sickness is still in general accepted as a sign of punishment from God, although it may not be in specific cases. But the Jew is at the same time enjoined to go to his physician and it is also entirely proper for him to pray for God's forgiveness and healing.

In Jewish orthodox services, when there is sickness in the congregation, a relative or friend will be given the opportunity to ask for special prayers for healing, and indeed the entire congregation will also beseech God for healing.

Thus there is not in modern times, and never has been, any mainstream of Jewish thought which denies spiritual healing a full and proper role in Jewish ritual and belief. Indeed, according to rabbis to whom I talked, there are many extraordinary cases of healings effected through the prayers of faithful Jews.

The Hasidic movement, however, in which healing has played so large a part, began in the eighteenth century. It took its name from a movement of the fourth century, B.C., which was started as a reaction to those Jews who turned to pagan and particularly to Hellenistic practices, culminating in the order of Antiochus IV that all Jews must eat swine and make sacrifices to Greek gods. This brought on the revolt of the Maccabees which the earlier Hasidim supported.

The latter-day Hasidic movement developed out of the pitiable condition of most of the Jews in Europe, particularly Central Europe, by the end of the seventeenth century. Much of European Jewry was poor, illiterate and therefore unlearned and often unacquainted with the laws of their own religion.

Efforts had been made over the centuries to revitalize Judaism in these bleak centuries of dispersal and oppression. One of these was the Cabalistic movement, a system of mystic thought blending neoplatonic ideas with Jewish beliefs. There were spiritual values in this movement, whose origins were said to date back to the seventh century A.D., but it degenerated into a system of secret words and interpretations of the sacred books and its value was lost in a maze of code words and names and double meanings.

Modern Hasidism came to meet the plight of the European Jews. It sought to help lift up the lives and hopes of impoverished Jewry of Poland and other central European nations. In part also it was a reaction to the over-legalistic theology of the Talmudists. The poorer Jew, without learning, was in no position to participate in the rituals.

Then came the new leader of the poor in Poland and the Ukraine, Israel Baal-Schem-Tov, a central figure of many legends and re-portedly gifted with unusual powers. He is said to have healed many sick. He preached a doctrine of love and joy which was open to all, rich and poor, prince or rabbi or serf. He preached that Jews did not need to be well-dressed or well-educated or have high places in the synagogues to reach heaven: God is our Father and all can pray to Him in whatever words that come from the mind and the heart, however simple they may be, and He will hear them.

This was a radical new doctrine. It was an evangelistic thing that Baal-Schem-Tov brought to the masses. Scholars and rabbis were now joined by a new class of worshippers in a true sense—the plain people. They could participate, if not by reading and reciting the rituals, at least through joy. They could dance and sing. The Hasidic movement had in it the evangelic note, exu-berance, ecstasy, the excitement of salvation. Those who opposed this new joyful Judaism were called the Misnagdim, or Opponents.

There were also in Hasidism overtones of the miraculous. Baal-Schem-Tov became the subject of stories of miracles and healings. And in the Hasidic movement other later leaders were said to have extraordinary powers; the Zaddik, or leader, was supposed to have attained a degree of perfection so complete that they served as mediators between Heaven and earth.

The Zaddik was above mere ordinary men because of a higher spiritual attainment and a greater humility before God. It was believed that he had great curative powers, and many Zaddik rabbis were said to have performed marvelous acts of healing. So much was this so that some of the Zaddikim did not remain in the realm of the spiritual only. They attained positions of worldly power and wealth; many persons offered gifts to them for help.

Gradually the Zaddikim fell away from their lofty position, although many were and still are held as holy men by their fol-lowers.

The Hasidic movement with its spiritual force would not die.

It flourished, particularly in Europe, until Hitler and his crema-
tories destroyed many of the Hasidic leaders. Even so, the movement continues. Throughout America today there are many Hasidic
synagogues; the most important Hasidic revival has been in Brooklyn, N.Y.

With its overtones of poetry and mysticism, miracles and happiness and healing love, Hasidism provided an unusually affirmative, joyful approach to religion. This paralleled the development
in Christianity of Christian Science in the mid-nineteenth century.
In Judaism and Christianity alike, there was a renewed breath of
life in religion, a challenge to all older orthodox ideas in every
faith; religion could not allow itself to be mired in joylessness and
lamentation, in rules and ritual only; it had to be a thing of happiness. This was what the new metaphysical ideas—both Christian
and Jewish—held out, and persons of many faiths found the message appealing.

There is, moreover, nothing in any branch of Judaism—Orthodox, Conservative, or Reform—opposed *per se* to spiritual healing. But in the 1920s, some Jews began to turn to Christian
Science, others to the more dramatic rituals of Catholicism or the
intellectualism of special groups like Unity or New Thought.

Other Jews were alarmed by this trend, and saw no reason why
their own religion could not offer the spiritual healing for those
of Jewish faith who sought it. Did not they have the Healing Word
of God as their heritage?

Out of this a movement called Jewish Science was born.

As in the Christian metaphysical movements, there was a period
of considerable uncertainty as to what shape these new ideas would
take. One group, known as Jewish Science, Inc., was founded in
New York in December, 1924, by Rabbi Clifton Harry Levy.
While thoroughly optimistic in its faith, this movement was not
too much concerned with spiritual healing and tended to regard it
as "miracle working."

But even earlier, in 1922, another movement had been formed
under the name of the Society of Jewish Science, and it became
popularly called Jewish Science by its followers. Founded by the
late Rabbi Morris Lichtenstein, a graduate of the Hebrew Union
College of Cincinnati, who had received his earlier Talmudic training in the great European Yeshivahs, it was carried on by his wife,
Tehilla Lichtenstein. A descendant of five hundred years of un-

broken rabbinical lineage, she is the first woman to occupy a Jewish pulpit in this country.

Because of its emphasis on healing, as well as on other important phases of Jewish life and faith, Jewish Science attracted followers from among all wings of Jewry throughout the land, and also deterred many from leaving the Jewish fold. Within a comparatively short space of years, although still young and growing, the Society of Jewish Science became the healing movement of Judaism.

It is in no way separated from Judaism, however, and does not ask its members to leave their individual synagogues, although it does have its own meeting places and synagogues within New York City and Long Island, and its literature reaches followers in all parts of the United States.

Still a new force, it stresses the fact that it is Jewish; it is an appeal to the Jewish people to recognize that they have "within the faith of their fathers, all the spiritual goals that they are seeking, and that they need not . . . turn to religious practices which are foreign to their souls . . ." So declares one of their pamphlets.

The movement believes in and practices healing, through prayer, of both bodily and mental illnesses. Unlike Christian Science, however, it does not deny the existence of matter, of illness or of evil. Nor does it deny the value or efficacy of medical science.

"We could not shut our eyes, even if we wanted to," Tehilla Lichtenstein wrote in a statement on this point, "to the fact that medicine has practically conquered the once deadly maladies of diphtheria and smallpox and typhoid and numerous others. . . . We know that illnesses which once laid whole cities low, such as that of the black plague which almost destroyed London, and others which took away mothers and infants at birth, are now unknown even by name. We know the great human salvage for which surgery is responsible. We know the increased health, vigor, and stature of the young folks of this generation as the result of medical research into nutrition and vitamins and the principles of good living.

"Knowing all this, and facing it without bias or prejudiced antagonism, how can we be other than grateful for the ministrations of medicine, wherever and whenever they are conducive to restored health and more healthful living? . . . God is the Healer, the only Healer, but there are ministering hands which help to bring His healing about . . .

"Whether that healing process in man is evoked into action

through the ministrations of medicine, or whether it is reached through religious channels, or whether it comes into action of itself in response to the needs of the body that is ill, it is always a divine process, as expressive of God's goodness and God's love and God's presence as the very life that is within us.

"In Jewish Science we know that healing can be and has, again and again and again, been brought about through religious principles of healing. Particularly where medicine has declared itself as yet unable to cope with a particular condition, has religion proved itself of the greatest potency. But this does not mean that where medicine had found the way, we wilfully refuse to take it. There is no antagonism between Jewish Science and medicine; there are many ways to reach God's goodness."

Among the official fundamentals of this movement, as outlined by its founder, are the following:

"The Jewish faith is the only faith we acknowledge. Jewish Science is the application of the Jewish faith to the practices of life.

"We believe wholeheartedly in the efficacy of prayer. We believe that no prayer, when properly offered, goes unanswered.

"We shall endeavor every day of our lives to keep serene, to check all tendencies to violence and anger . . .

"We shall strive to be cheerful every day of our lives. The Talmud says that the Divine Presence departs from one who is in gloom. It is God's design that man should find joy and cheer in his existence on this earth.

"We shall seek to cultivate an attitude of love and goodwill towards everyone. We shall make no room in our hearts for hatred or bitterness. The world was created on a plan of divine love, and to admit thoughts of hatred or malice is to violate the plan of God.

"We shall cultivate a disposition to contentment, envying no one, and praising God for the good He has already bestowed upon us. Contentment is the greatest friend of happiness; envy, its greatest enemy.

"We shall make conscious effort to banish worry and fear from our lives. We regard these as the two greatest enemies of mankind and give them no place in our consciousness.

"We shall trust in God's goodness in every circumstance of our life.

"We believe that death is an elevation to eternal life, and not a cessation of existence.

"We believe that God is the Source of Health and the Restorer of Health."[3]

These are the principles of the Jewish Science movement. Apart from specific references to the Jewish faith, they are principles to which any person with belief in the Universal God could subscribe.

[3]Tehilla Lichtenstein, What To Tell Your Friends About Jewish Science. New York: Society of Jewish Science, 1951.

20

Danger Signals

A young woman suffering from diabetes visited a faith healer and was so impressed that when she returned to her home she refused, in spite of the warnings of the healer and members of her family, to continue her insulin.

She was certain that the healer had cured her of diabetes and to prove it refused to take medicine ordered by her physician.

This young woman died as a direct result of this act.

The healer in this instance was completely absolved from any blame, as the young woman had refused to take her insulin shots of her own free will. It was the girl's own zeal, her own desire to prove to herself that she had been healed miraculously, without a medical checkup of any kind, that proved fatal in this case.

The needless death of this woman is not cited as any proof that spiritual healing—when put to the acid test—is a failure.

It is cited as reaffirmation and reiteration of an obvious but vitally important truth: in this field of spiritual healing we are dealing in areas of uncharted depths and mortal peril.

For the safety of ourselves, our families, and those around us, we cannot blindly walk into any danger without full understanding and awareness of what we are doing.

Jesus is constantly warning, throughout His ministry, that His followers must stand on guard to know the false from the true. "Beware of false prophets," He tells the multitude in the Sermon on the Mount, "which come to you in sheep's clothing but inwardly they are ravening wolves."[1]

Again and again in the Bible we are told to stand on guard against the fortune tellers and diviners and sorcerers. It is equally important that we heed these warnings in our own day.

[1] Matthew VII:15.

Here, from the author's findings, are danger signals against which anyone venturing into this area, should be on guard:

1. The unknown or only slightly-known "cult" or cult leader whose practices seem to be far afield from religion. There is a vast array of sex cults, swindlers, confidence workers, and plain psychotics who operate in unheard-of groups with high-sounding names and purposes.

2. Faith healers who employ hysteria as a technique, stirring up the emotions of those seeking healing.

Healing in the name of God is not a medicine show. There is too much likelihood of disaster in which a human being collapses, like the little girl who dropped her crutches and walked.

William Laurence, Pulitzer Prize-winning science editor of the New York Times, tells of seeing a lieutenant in war time carry an iron safe up four decks to the main deck during a submarine scare. When the all-clear was sounded, it took four men to carry it back. "It was no miracle," Laurence pointed out, "it was adrenaline and hysteria."

One sign of the man of God is that he has compassion for all who come to him. He wants above all to make sure that nothing happens to harm these people, and does not take needless and reckless chances. Virtually every recognized church works directly with doctors and medical science. Christian Science is, of course, an exception, because of their special beliefs about the unreality of sickness.

3. Beware of healers who appear willing to use their gifts for harm to others in any way—financially, physically, or spiritually.

No man who heals in the name of God or Christ can employ evil or invoke evil, and if he does so—or promises to—he can only be a fraud. Resentment, hatred, wishing or working evil, can never be any part of the love of God or of Christ or of His teachings.

4. Be particularly careful of the "healer" who has products to sell (except perhaps a few moderately priced pamphlets or books); who has political axes to grind for one party or another; or who has business deals to suggest.

5. Be careful of the healer who appears to have no association in his teaching or preaching with an organized faith.

A psychiatrist at one of the largest mental hospitals in the United States told me, "A true spiritual healing could come only out of a truly religious experience. The healer whose concern is for the surface of the patient and his selfish desire to be more comfortable, without any concern with deeper causes or meanings, can do no

better at best than help the individual get rid of one symptom—
for which he will shortly develop another.''

6. The healer who treats an obvious psychotic who is hallu-
cinating, on the basis of accepting those hallucinations as valid
experience.

Priests, ministers, and rabbis can be of tremendous value in
helping psychiatrists in the treatment of psychotics of all types.
But great harm can be done when a healer attempts to cure these
cases without previous investigation of the facts in the case and
discussion with the physician involved.

Dr. Price, in Philadelphia, has had a number of such patients
whom he has helped and for whom in some cases he served as a
channel of healing. These people were usually sent to him by a
psychiatrist when the latter had done all he could, or the cases
were ''screened'' through physicians before spiritual healing was
tried.

The healer who attempts these cures without such previous case
investigation may do great injury to the individual.

7. The healer who takes personal credit for healing.

Spiritual healing has to be from God, and healers can be no
more than His channels, a role which the most honest and sincere
accept with humility and gratitude.

A spiritual gift is to be used, and it may be discussed, analyzed,
advertised. But certainly it is not to be bartered on the billboards
along with the soap and beer.

8. The healer who refuses to co-operate with the patient's
minister or physician.

If an individual healer begins to ''sell'' some story about losing
or weakening his healing power, should he talk with other clergymen, or with the doctor—this is a serious sign of danger.

There is no reason why a man truly concerned with healing
need be afraid of meeting members of these other disciplines. It
may be that he fears his claims may be exposed by these other
men.

9. Beware the healer who obviously preys on gullibility.

The cases already reported on in this book indicate that while
there are a number of extraordinary happenings, verified miracles
are not to be had at a dime a dozen.

If the healer seems to draw too long a bow, one must ask this
question: Is he telling the truth, or what he believes to be true, or
is he exaggerating or fabricating the entire thing?

This does not mean that a man who has achieved something he

considers of outstanding importance should not report the facts. It means that serious claims to miracles should certainly be examined, with candor and thoroughness, by those in search of truth.

10. Beware of "miracle workers" who perform feats that are closer to black magic than spiritual healing. There are many who spin yarns of witchcraft, and similar hocus-pocus. These things are not a part of true religion or religious healing.

There is a great deal at stake in these healers and their claims. There is the health and happiness and faith of many individuals.

There is an advance—or a retreat—in our understanding of the universe and of God's purpose for us on this earth.

There is the safety and well-being of our families and our selves.

There is the integrity of our own minds and hearts and souls, in our acceptances or rejection of the claims of these individuals.

There is the obligation we owe to society, to our fellow men, and to the laws of God.

21

The Anointing Spirit

We have examined thus far the healing of physical ailments in association with prayer and spiritual ministrations.

There are many among the public, and among physicians and other scientists, who doubt that such healings are possible.

Many physicians sincerely fear that any discussion of spiritual healing may tempt people to forsake medicine and neglect medical care.

Some doctors with whom I spoke appear to accept prayer and the work of hospital chaplains only from the psychological point of view.

When I questioned them about the possibility of healing by God, some of them took on an odd expression, a mixture of surprise and bewilderment. One physician told me, "Yes, we see these cases after the faith healers or spiritual leaders or whatever you call them get through wrecking the patients."

The writer heard another point of view from another physician, a surgeon.

It concerned an infant with an abscess in the brain who was in critical condition.

The surgeon was asked by the parents if he could help with prayer. They were aware of his deeply religious nature. The physician responded by calling together a small prayer group with whom he was associated.

Step by step, this surgeon outlined the operation that might be required, describing it in detail to the group, until they could picture in their minds the brain of this child.

"Now," he urged them, "picture Jesus going into this hospital and going into the room and touching the child. Hold the image of Jesus in your mind, touching this child."

They did as the surgeon asked, their heads bowed in silent prayer.

The following morning, the report came that the infant's fever had dropped sharply and indications were that there would be no need for an operation.

The prognosis continued favorable. Within a few days, the infant was apparently normal in all respects. There was no return of the abscess.

The child's fever had started to fall at the exact hour when the group met in prayer.

Such healing techniques are not scientific in any sense whatever.

But many have experienced the anointing of the Holy Spirit in prayer, and have felt its power, according to their own statements.

And many have experienced physical healing after calling upon this Power, for themselves, or for someone else, as in the case of the infant and the prayer group.

It is easy for laymen or scientists to find explanations that *might* fit for this case or for others.

It is always easy to denounce or reject the supernatural. Even the painstaking care given a certified "miracle at Lourdes" can be raked over the coals of doubt.

But it seems to this reporter that the facts presented cannot be lightly shrugged away. One physical healing might be, perhaps, or another; but not all of them, in all of these differing faiths. And if even one of them is inexplicable, then it is vital for all of us to find out every detail we can about this healing force.

This is the challenge in the revival of spiritual healing, for science and medicine, and laymen and clergy.

It is a challenge that involves our own universe, our world and ourselves.

BOOK TWO

═══════════════════════════

Healing the Mind

22

Our Name Is Legion

In the day of Christ they were called the "possessed of demons."

Today psychiatrists admit that there are indeed demons: the demons of hate and revenge and resentment and greed and guilt and fear; the high-pressure demonology of modern competition and stress and conflict, the keeping up with the Joneses, the unremitting pace of modern living, the plague of demons following in the wake of financial difficulties and family problems and the maladjustments of our overwrought era.

Our hospitals, the offices of our psychiatrists, ministers, priests and rabbis, our clinics of all kinds, are crowded with a stream of the lonely and frightened—a great army of the unloved and unloving. They seek help not for physical illness and, in most cases, not for advanced emotional or mental illness. But many have within them the sperm-cells of the demons, emotional conflicts and stress and problems they cannot resolve or control or destroy.

One of the outstanding experts in pastoral counseling, Dr. Carrol A. Wise, for many years chaplain in Worcester State Hospital in Massachusetts, draws in his book *Psychiatry and the Bible*, an important parallel between the days of Jesus and modern times:

"The Bible recognized good and evil spirits. Indeed, many sick persons were said to be possessed by an evil or unclean spirit or by a demon. Jesus is said to have cast out evil spirits and the disciples were given power to cast out unclean spirits and to heal diseases. It is evident from reading these sections of the Gospels that Jesus was here dealing with persons suffering from what today we would call neurosis and psychosis, persons who were 'out of their mind,' as we say; persons in whom destructive energies have overcome creative energies, whose life and energies are not organized and directed towards satisfying goals. The approach which

219

Jesus made to these persons was one of deep understanding and love, and it is evident from our psychological knowledge today that any who would help the mentally ill must be persons of deep understanding and love."[1]

It is interesting to note that the qualities which Jesus preached and practiced two thousand years ago have become front-line weapons today in the battle to save the "possessed" of our own age.

In what kind of amalgam of modern living are these ancient demons incubated?

One area is family animosity, the resentments and jealousies and conflicts within the basic social unit of our society.

Part of this comes from the number of broken homes, from the children raised with half-brothers and half-sisters, from the tremendous difficulties of personal adjustments within the family under modern conditions, morals and values.

I attended a strange birthday gathering once with my wife. It was given for a young husband. Present were the husband and his wife and his parents and several other relatives and ourselves. In the nursery an infant daughter of the young couple slept peacefully. The husband had a position that held high promise for the future and paid sufficiently to meet all the bills and leave a little besides. The wife had a small trust fund.. They and the parents and other relatives appeared in average good health physically.

One would have said that these people gathered at a happy occasion.

It wasn't. Throughout the evening, the resentments in this family flashed and lunged like swordplay. The parents resented the wife and did not accept her; whatever she liked they disliked, and whatever idea she put forward they cried down. What seemed most significant was that they argued about nothing of significance for the most part.

There was no open explosion. These were well-educated, well-brought-up people. But the bitterness, jealousy, and hate that my wife and I found there left us cold and greatly disturbed.

There was no reason, no need for any of it. These people, on analysis, had everything to look forward to; their lives held promise and hope. Everyone in the group should have been filled with

[1]Carroll A. Wise, Psychiatry and the Bible. New York: Harper and Brothers, 1956. p. 25.

a sense of joy at their prospects for the future. Instead they were trapped in a gilded cage crowded with a host of home-made demons.

Another important force in our modern demonology is guilt. Guilt crawls in through many unguessed and unnoticed crevices, past and present. It may have a basis in fact or in no fact at all. It may be a product of over-protective or perfectionist parents. It may be a reaction to a too-strict home, or a too-demanding theological upbringing, a too-frequent use of corrective measures in the very young, the rejection of a child, actively or emotionally or psychologically, so that the child grows up believing he is guilty of some crime.

Guilt manifests itself in diverse ways. Psychiatrists say that prostitutes, for example, are led into this field because they want to degrade themselves, to bring punishment upon themselves. The same is true of many young boys who commit senseless acts of vandalism, or rob stores when they have no need for money. The background in many of these cases reveals deep guilt feelings.

There are the demons of fear, of insecurity, of sheer physical fright, the cumulative effects of repeated traumatic experiences, loss of loved ones, the breaking up of homes, beatings and violence.

In a very real sense these things take possession of us.

They may not be demons with horns and tails, they may not speak in strange tongues, they may not be personal in the sense in which the Middle Ages thought of them as personal.

There are people who believe in devils in this personal sense as individual demons, even in our own day. There are many churches in which, if necessary and requested, exorcism is practiced. Rituals are performed. The demons are commanded to leave.

Perhaps such rituals and ideas may be accepted in a symbolic sense. The faith of the individual in the fact that his hate, his resentment, his guilt or whatever it is has been driven out, has been purged by Divine command through a minister or priest, could well result in getting rid of the baneful effect, of the negative emotions, in a truly spiritual purification, quite apart from superstition or demonology.

But in general the church today takes a much more modernized view. Psychiatry has given to the demons new interpretations and new shapes. They emerge from the black hell of fear and confusion and loneliness and rejection and selfishness and all the rest of their names, which are—beyond all question—legion.

The doctor and the preacher, each in his way, each with his special techniques, plays a role in leading these demons out of their victims, in leaving the victims free to live and to express the will of God in their lives.

In many instances an individual's difficulty may arise from a misinterpretation of religious meaning and truth and teaching, perhaps going back into earliest childhood. The idea of a God of punishment and revenge, for instance—the direct opposite of the teaching of Christ—is often instilled into the very young and memories of childish sins remain to haunt them throughout their years. Or the individual may rebel against this teaching and thereupon take on himself new guilt feelings he does not understand. Misinterpreted religion has been a cause of many of the demons real religion ultimately is called upon to help exorcise.

This is only one reason why spiritual healing in the area of the mind must be approached by the minister or priest or rabbi with loving concern—and caution. Faced with a parishioner with a broken leg, the clergyman calls the doctor and asks the congregation to pray. Faced with a broken mind and spirit, the minister may sometimes think he knows the answers because the problem on its surface looks simple. The demon may seem so close to the surface; get rid of this hate or that fear and all will be well. But psychiatry has learned that the surface demon is often only a shadow, and the real demon lies deep, well concealed in the recesses of the mind. Deeper therapy, by persons trained in this work, is required.

If the problem does have its roots in the twisted understanding or misinterpretation of religious ideas, then spiritual ideas may well be wasted until these beclouding misinterpretations are cleared away.

A. Graham Iken, in her distinguished book *New Concepts of Healing*, states the problem in an extremely effective analysis:[2] "There are cases where the very words 'God' and 'religion' have to be left out, since the patient's contact with them has been such a perversion of religion. . . . The psychotherapist has in such cases to rebuild . . . before the spiritual nature can function freely, whereas the spiritual healer tends to reinforce the weakness by the direct application of the religious appeal *which will go along the wrong channels previously developed . . .*

[2] A. Graham Iken, New Concepts of Healing. New York: Association Press, 1956. p. 25.

"It is not enough today for the religious-minded to say, 'We have the spirit and God is working through us,' and to ignore his work through psychiatrists and psychotherapists.

". . . It is no good sitting down in front of bad drains and praying about them: we have to get up and clean them out if we wish to check epidemics spread through faulty sanitation. So, if the drains of personality are blocked, if we have failed to learn how to dispose of the emotional rubbish, the psychotherapist gets down to the unpleasant job of cleaning them out, meeting as he does so the accumulation of the sins and vices of untold generations, which have been subterraneously blocking the free flow of spirit.

"It is most important that spiritual healing movements within the churches should avail themselves of such knowledge as even now is available, or instead of being free channels for God to work through, they will block the way by thinking they do God service along lines that take us further from reality instead of bringing us into closer touch with it."[3]

There are growing evidences of the awareness of the truth in these statements by both religious leaders and psychiatrists.

Striving to co-ordinate religion and psychiatry for the betterment of man is the Marble Collegiate Church's American Foundation of Religion and Psychiatry in New York City, founded by the Rev. Dr. Norman Vincent Peale. On the staff of the clinic are psychiatrists and clergymen. Among them is the chief psychiatrist, Dr. Smiley Blanton, and the "brother team" of minister Clinton J. Kew and psychologist Clifton E. Kew. Methods employed by the Kews and others on the clinic staff include group psychotherapy, psychoanalysis, individual counseling and spiritual therapy.

Dr. Clinton Kew has another battlefield against the demons through a "team therapy" program known as the "Foundation For Better Living" in which members of many disciplines—clergymen, psychiatrists, psychologists, attorneys and educators—join together in forum and workshop groups in which the latest findings regarding mental health are presented. Members of these forums also work to aid those beset with fear or loneliness or being unwanted, or whatever twisted shape their demon takes.

In 1956, in New York City the National Academy of Religion and Mental Health was founded. Its first president was Kenneth E. Appel, president of the Joint Commission on Mental Illness

[3] *Ibid.* pp. 27-28.

and Health, professor of psychiatry at the University of Pennsylvania and past president of the American Psychiatric Association. Clergymen of Roman Catholic, Jewish and Protestant faiths were on the board.

Through this group a number of research programs into the relationship between religion and mental health have been launched.

There are many other similar developments in which psychiatry and religion are joining forces. Divinity schools and seminaries now teach the basic rudiments of psychotherapy and its techniques, along with grounding in the techniques of pastoral counseling.

A new area of teamwork is developing, not only in physical healing but also in mental and emotional.

But in this new teamwork, what is the specific role of spiritual healing and how can its use be most effective for the multitude seeking for rescue from these demons?

23

A Cul De Sac Called Hate

Spiritual healing is at work constantly in problems of tensions and conflicts assailing the mind and the emotions. It is often unrecognized as spiritual healing because this entire area of need is still a world unexplored.

Many of the mental problems of our time cannot be diagnosed clinically as psychotic or neurotic or psychosomatic, and yet they are of such nature that help is required. We do not run to a doctor or hospital every time we have a cut or bruise or a cold in the head. But if we are wise we treat it. We do not leave the wound to fester. The same should be true of mental and emotional wounds. First aid is often indicated.

The spiritual healers are found not merely in our church clinics, but in many fields of religious and social effort. They may be volunteers on some front line of a "less chance" area. They may be Boy Scout leaders. They may be social workers. They may be teachers and college professors.

One of the writer's close friends is an Episcopalian priest, Father Drury Patchell, whose entire life is devoted to helping boys in the courts; his days and nights are spent helping boys who get into trouble in New York City's worst areas; his vacations are spent visiting reformatories throughout the state and talking personally with some of the boys who were sent away by the courts, and in helping to plan for their futures when they are released.

This is spiritual healing: behind all of his help there is the driving and abiding sense of love—religious love with its healing force. Once a week, during the season, Father Pat takes some of his boys to the opera. "Because it's something different for them," he says. "And it's part of the beauty of God's world instead of all the ugliness. And you see, no one can ever use the opera to them as a way of saying that there is a world beyond their reach, something they must resent and hate. All the beauty and goodness is theirs to share. Properly, under proper rules."

Healing of mind and emotions is found in many places and under varying circumstances. "For I was hungered," Jesus says, "and ye gave me meat: I was thirsty, and ye gave me drink. I was a stranger, and ye took me in:

"Naked, and ye clothed me: I was sick, and ye visited me: I was in prison, and ye came unto me."

And, He said, when the righteous shall ask when they did these things unto Him, the King shall answer, "Inasmuch as ye have done it unto one of the least of these my brethren ye have done it unto me."[1]

And of all the evils assailing those who are naked and thirsty, hungry, imprisoned, none is more corrosive or destructive than the virus of hate.

In a penitentiary in Western Canada, an inmate sat down to write a letter to his wife. Always before, his letters had been the one outlet for his venom, his rage against a society that had mistreated him and rejected him.

Today it was different. For some weeks he had been attending a "school" in the prison, classes in public speaking and how to get along with people. It was part of a program launched by the late Dale Carnegie, run by volunteer instructors from the outside.

Some of the talks the men gave in this class searched out the speaker's innermost thoughts. They stood up and talked to the class of fellow inmates about hidden dreams and hopes; openly and frankly they talked, the way many of them had never talked before to fellow prisoners, about what they liked and disliked most, their greatest success and their greatest mistake.

Some of it was amusing, some of it serious. One man said he was learning to ask instead of demand. Another said he had found out that you couldn't have any friends until you learned to be one yourself. Another said his greatest mistake was answering the front door at three A.M., when he should have been running out the back.

The inmate about to write his wife had listened and taken part and talked about himself, too, and his mistakes. And he had come to think about some of the principles taught in this course. Try to profit from your losses. Never try to get even with your enemies.

[1]Matthew XXV:35-40.

Give honest and sincere appreciation.

He wanted to try out the principle of honest and sincere appreciation in his letter. After much thought, he wrote:

"I wonder if you realize how much I appreciate the marvelous care you are taking of our two daughters. The girls are very fortunate to have a mother who thinks so much of their welfare and happiness. I, too, am fortunate to have a wife who can tackle a job so courageously. I wish I could say in person, 'Mary, well done . . . ' "

He was startled to discover how sincerely he meant the words after he put them down.

A few days later he had an answer from his wife:

"Tonight I arrived home terribly discouraged from a most harrowing day at work," she wrote. "I was wondering if it was all worthwhile. Your letter had arrived but I didn't open it right away for I thought it was the usual kind.

"I read it after I had tucked the children into bed and finished my housework. Oh, darling, what a Godsend that letter was! It was wonderful to know that someone cared and felt my work worthwhile . . . "

One of the great students of human emotions, Professor Pitirim A. Sorokin, founder of the Harvard Research Center in Creative Altruism, declared in his book *The Ways and Power of Love:*

"Hate begets hate, violence engenders violence, hypocrisy is answered by hypocrisy, war generates war and love creates love.

"Unselfish love has enormous creative and therapeutic potentialities, far greater than most people think. Love is a life-giving force, necessary for physical, mental and moral health.

"Altruistic persons live longer than egotistic individuals.

"Children deprived of love tend to become vitally, morally, and socially defective.

"Love is the most powerful antidote against criminal, morbid, and suicidal tendencies, against hate, fear, and psychoneurosis.

"It is an indispensable condition for deep and lasting happiness.

"It is goodness and freedom at their loftiest.

"It is the finest and most powerful educational force for the ennoblement of humanity."[2]

Professor Sorokin was talking out of experience and investigation. Three and a half decades before he wrote those lines, he

[2]Pitirim A. Sorokin, The Ways and Power of Love. Boston: Beacon Press, 1954. p. vii.

had been through the hell of Russian Communist revolution; he had been hunted, imprisoned, condemned to be shot, pardoned but kept in prison to live through horror and pain. In the midst of this, he wrote in his diary: "Cruelty, hatred, violence, and injustice never can and never will be able to create a mental, moral or material millennium. The only way toward it is the royal road of all-giving creative love, not only preached but constantly practiced."

Years later, after establishing the research center at Harvard, he was able to establish proof of his concepts of love and hate through empirical tests and studies.

His statement—like the letters between the prisoner and his wife—reveal how closely teachings of religion, psychiatry and modern sociology merge in regard to love and hate, whether considered in terms of the individual or of society itself.

The late Dale Carnegie started many free courses, under the direction of highly trained instructors, in penitentiaries in the United States and Canada.

These were classes of hate-eradication. They have helped and are helping to rehabilitate men in many prisons who were given up as hopeless. Students in these classes are not ordinary businessmen learning the fundamentals of after-dinner speaking. They are thieves, rapists, murderers. One of the murderers was a man they called Rocks. He had been in solitary confinement for some weeks after he first arrived in prison because of his violent outbursts of rage. Finally he was beaten down to a silent, glowering creature of hate.

Somehow, this man got himself into one of the Dale Carnegie classes. Through the first session or two—although all the others in the class made their opening speeches in the normal class procedures—all he did was to stare emptily, hardly seeming to realize or care what was going on.

Gradually a change began. He spoke up, asked a question. The perpetual scowl on his face was not quite so antagonistic.

One day the class instructor told him he had to make his speech. This was the moment. He found himself standing up before the group. For the first time he felt he could talk to these others without fear of ridicule or resentment. He had heard *them* talk about their mistakes, the meanest prank they ever played, their most exciting moment, their most embarrassing.

When he began to speak, the facts of his own life spilled out in a rush of words. The death of his father and mother, and after that an assortment of institutions and reform schools. But what was important, as he told all this, was that now, for the first time, he could tell it as if all had happened to somebody else.

Fourteen weeks later, as they do in all Dale Carnegie courses, wherever they may be held, there was a graduation dinner. There was a special menu with soup and steak and after-dinner mints, an invocation and a solo, speeches by the warden and the chief keeper and distinguished guests from the outside. There was also a commencement book with brief sketches of the graduates and predictions for their future success.

Among those who won special prizes for their ability in impromptu speaking was the lifer they called Rocks. The topic of the speech on which this prisoner won: "Learning to Meet The World."

C. I. Blackwood, president of Blackwood College, a business school in Oklahoma City, and one of the leading figures in this program to aid prisoners, made a checkup on statistics regarding one hundred eighty convict-graduates of these courses, released from one prison—El Reno Reformatory—over a two-year period.

By prison averages, seventy-two of these men, or approximately forty per cent, should have been arrested or returned for violations in the two-year period, reformatory records indicated.

But of the one hundred eighty, only twelve, or slightly more than seven per cent, had been arrested for violations or returned to the reformatory.

To anyone who has seen or worked with these men and youths before they are reached by help—in precinct houses and jails and courtrooms and on the streets and in the club-room hangouts—these courses are a symbol of what can be done in human salvage.

For in these places of trouble, hatred reaches extremity. It smolders below the surface. In the anti-social gangs one finds fear, and just beyond fear, hatred. I sat one night with a group of boys and girls fourteen to sixteen years old, all of whom lived in a gang-ridden area, and we talked. These youngsters had not yet been hardened, they had not yet been trapped.

Yet already the forces were at work. "To be safe you have to have pieces," one said. By "pieces" he meant weapons—knives, guns, home-made pistols, bits of broken glass to scrape across the face of the "enemy." Who were the enemies? The boys who lived on the next street. Or the street beyond that.

"You have to be strong," they told me. "Because if you're

not strong and you don't have pieces, then the other guys say you are soft, and they come and beat you up. Or a fight starts, you push one of their girls into an open hydrant or they push one of yours. Anything.''

They talked about it quite calmly. This was the way of life they had learned. It was the only way to survive in the jungle they had not created but in which they had to live.

These boys did not want to hate or to be hated. They were still only on the edges; another year or two and they would be more grown up and more a part of it.

Recently there had been a homicide in the district and police had arrested a number of youths, picking them up at random for questioning. I spoke of the case. "I hear they arrested about twenty-five boys that night," I said.

A change came in their faces; an almost chemical change, sudden and frightening.

"Not twenty-five," one boy corrected me. "Twenty-seven."

"They took them to that third-floor rear and beat a lot of them up and some of them had to go to the hospital."

"And none of them had anything to do with it; it was some other fellow, they picked him up the next day. Them others didn't know anything about it. But they beat them just the same."

There are many ways to hate.

There are those who hate themselves and their friends and rivals and their parents. Dr. Smiley Blanton in *Love Or Perish*, gives as one way to happiness the rule that we must forgive our parents for things that make us hate them, the injustices—real and imagined—which linger in our subconscious.[3] Do we all hate our parents then? Certainly not—if we employ the spiritual force of forgiveness for any resentment we may feel, conscious or unconscious, against them. And thus in adult years we are liberated by this forgiveness from guilt or need for self-punishment to pay for our resentment or rebellion against our parents.

Sometimes the corrosive force of hate is social and political and racial. The "hate groups" actively peddling their "lines"—sometimes in the very name of Christian love—have been often exposed and denounced. They continue active, however, and their work

[3] Dr. Smiley Blanton, Love or Perish. New York: Simon & Schuster, 1956. p. 205.

is abetted by individuals who, often without realizing the implications, repeat their vintage lies.

How do we deal with hate, in terms of spiritual healing? "We must treat it," one Presbyterian minister told me, "in terms of Divine love. We cannot hate the haters and hope to heal them. This is the most difficult part of the teaching of Our Lord. It is easy to love our friends; loving our enemies, truly loving them, forgiving them and loving them, this is the victory of victories."

But is it not a one-sided victory—to love our enemy? The reply I received was this, "Yes, it is one-sided. For it is the victory of God, of the Holy Spirit. And can the hatred in the heart of your enemy survive—in such a victory? How can we believe that it does—and believe in Christ?"

Among the destructive outcroppings of this virus is self-hate, self-deprecation, self-punishment—the prostitute who sells herself to punish herself, the delinquent sending himself to jail.

In psychological terms, hate is a definable quality, an aggressive need to inflict pain or other hurt upon something or someone else. On occasion, there may be ambivalent feelings of both love and hate for the same individual at the same moment.

In spiritual terms, hate is the absence of love. Where there is love automatically you destroy hate and its possible effects. The hateful demon disappears. This is the love that reaches out beyond the physical sense of the word, to the metaphysical.

Hate may win battles, but never victories.

In Philadelphia a woman was extremely ill. An operation was required. Physicians had very little hope of saving her life. The woman, mother of two children, was deeply religious. The husband was not; to him it was all just words, mumbo-jumbo.

On the day before the operation, the physicians told the husband they did not think his wife could survive. Somehow the wife seemed to know this, although no one told her. That night she could not sleep. One of the night nurses came to sit beside her and cheer her.

The nurse was a member of the prayer group at St. Stephen's Church. She had taken night duty at the hospital so that she could help in her spare moments, when most of the patients slept, by praying silently for those most in need.

The woman patient was afraid. Obviously she had a premonition that she would not survive the operation. The nurse had prayed that the woman would speak of her fears, since hospital rules forbade the nurse from volunteering spiritual counsel or prayer. But when the woman did speak, the nurse tried to ease her fears somewhat and finally said, ''I'm going to write something on a piece of paper. I'm not really supposed to do this, so tear this up after you've read it over.''

She began to write words from the Psalms: ''Wait on the Lord: be of good courage, and he shall strengthen thine heart: wait, I said, on the Lord.''[4] Then she wrote a verse from the hymn ''How Firm A Foundation.''

The woman read the lines and placed the paper by her bed. She seemed relaxed for the first time in some hours, and she went to sleep.

The woman did not survive the operation. She did not regain consciousness. She was pronounced dead in the operating room after many hours of fruitless effort to save her.

When they opened her clenched hand, they found in it the piece of paper with those lines the nurse had written. When the husband went through his wife's effects at the hospital he found among them this scrap of paper. He asked the nurse about it and learned the story.

One might have expected a man who did not believe anyway in prayer and its worth, to have been particularly bitter in that moment. Here were prayers and the words, and what good had they done?

This was not his reaction. The man who had not believed saw new meanings. It was not that the prayers hadn't worked. It was that someone, some stranger, had cared about his wife, and her fears on that last night, had bothered to write these things down for her on a piece of paper, to give her strength and courage.

It would have been easy for this man to hate—to hate the religion and the prayer his wife had clung to, because it had not saved her; to hate all religion and prayer because it had failed to save her.

But he could not hate the open manifestation of Divine love neatly written out on that bit of paper his wife had carried with her.

As a result of that bit of paper, the man instead of finding increased embitterment, found a refuge in the church to which he turned and in which he reared his two children.

[4]Psalms XXVII:14.

It is a victory not in terms of a physical healing but of spiritual salvage. It is a case where spiritual love reaching out—instead of the blighting hand of hate—was able to give meaning and faith for the future.

24

Seven-Eyed Monster

There is a special demonology in jealousy; there is action and counteraction, devil begetting devil, phantom outlooming phantom, one corridor of doubt leading on to the next. This is an emotion capable of creating hellish torment out of nothingness, a torment which can be heightened into exquisite torture by a mere gesture or word or laugh. The truly jealous need no Iago to plant false clues as in Shakespeare's *Othello*; the jealous read clues in every gesture, they make their own interpretations, not to fit the facts but to fit their own obsessions and fears.

The destructive demons of this emotion perform their demolition regardless of whether or not there is the slightest justification for their existence. Hundreds of marriages and families and homes have been broken up not for faithlessness but for lack of faith, hundreds of jobs have been lost, careers smashed, businesses ruined, even nations destroyed. Where there is actual cause for the jealousy, the evil it brings may be even worse. The jealous lover is perhaps a fool; the partner who taunts him may goad him into tragedy.

A woman who divorced her husband and married another man went with the new husband to the very barroom where the first husband was trying to drown his sorrows in whisky sours.

The first husband could not stand it when he saw them together. Later that day he obtained a gun, searched out the couple and killed the man. Then he quietly surrendered to the police.

In a case reported by Dr. Boris Sokoloff in his book *Jealousy*, a forty-seven-year-old woman, in a near delirium of jealous rage, got into the family car to hunt her husband down, trapped him in a dead-end alley in a small town in New Jersey and crushed the cowering man to death against an open cellar door at the end of the alley. "I loved him deeply," she told arresting officers.

"Jealousy," psychologist Alfred Adler, points out, "has a thousand shapes." In one of his lectures at the People's Institute in Vienna, he said: "It may be recognized in mistrust and in the preparation of ambushes for others, in the critical measurement of one's fellows, and in the constant fear of being neglected. Just which of these manifestations comes to the fore is dependent entirely upon the previous preparation for social life. One form of jealousy expresses itself in self-destruction, another expresses itself in energetic obstinacy. Spoiling the sport of others, senseless opposition, the restriction of another's freedom, and his subsequent subjugation, are some of the protean shapes of this character trait.

"Giving the other fellow a set of rules for his conduct is one favorite trick of jealousy. It is this characteristic psychic pattern along which an individual moves, when he attempts to foist certain laws of love upon his mate, when he builds a wall around his loved one, or prescribes where he should look, what he should do, and how he should think."[1]

In its extreme, jealousy leads only to destruction, to the broken marriage, to broken lives, to mental institutions, to crimes of violence and their punishment; it is the emotion of ruin.

Yet it is a universal emotion; it laps at the edges of every being, man and woman, child, animal.

The jealous love is not the love taught by religion; it is as far from the love of God as heaven is from hell. It is counterfeit love, possessive and destructive.

In New York, a woman began a divorce action against her husband. The charge was to be adultery. For weeks, silently, grimly, she had been gathering the evidence, through detectives hired to follow her husband. The facts were incontrovertible; he was meeting another woman regularly. Several times he went to the woman's apartment.

The wife knew that she had been over-worried and nagging; she had asked too many questions every time he came in; she had made too many rules about when and where he could go out and when he had to report in. If he failed to report, she was always half-convinced he was with some other woman.

Now with positive proof, she returned to the home of her par-

[1] Alfred Adler, Understanding Human Nature, (trans. W. Beran Wolfe). New York: Greenberg, 1927. p. 223.

ents. Her father, who had never liked the husband, told her she had done the only possible thing. "If he's done this once, he will again," the father said.

The mother was not that sure about the situation, even when the daughter told her the husband would be served with papers in the morning. She made the daughter go with her to the church and afterward they went to the rectory and talked this matter over with their pastor.

After he heard the story, the minister asked the wife, "Does your husband know about the detectives?"

"No."

"Do you know who the woman is?"

"They have her name. She lives alone in that apartment house."

"Do you love your husband?"

"Very much. That's why this is so terrible. Even though I suspected things, I never really believed them, not in my heart. I knew they couldn't be true."

"So you sent out detectives to prove you were wrong?"

"Yes. But I wasn't."

At this point she broke into convulsive sobbing. She loved her husband, and wanted him back, and realized that she had driven him from her with her jealousy and her demands and her "rules" and her reproofs when he was only five minutes late coming home.

The minister urged her not to file any papers but to wait until he had made his own private investigation. The following day the minister talked to the husband and learned the man had become furious at his wife's groundless suspicions and taken up with the other woman largely out of spite.

The minister and the husband had a long discussion of this problem. The following day he informed the wife that her husband wanted the marriage to be saved. "But you almost lost him," he told her. "This other woman is a charming creature, I understand, and she never made demands and was never jealous of you at all. That's why he liked her so much."

"And if I forgive him—and take him back?"

"He says he won't see her again. You have to believe him completely and accept him at his word. That is the love you promised him. And if you betray that love by distrust, what has he left to be faithful to?"

As the wife tried to grasp what part her own role played in driving her husband away, the pastor added, "And don't expect him to ask forgiveness and don't demand it and don't ever mention this again to him or discuss it. I told that to your husband, too. Tear up the old doubts and give your marriage an even break. No questions. Nothing. Just love. And your faith.''

Jealousy was in this case the product of basic insecurity and the healing words of a minister saved the marriage.

Perhaps the most important avenue for combating the destructiveness of this emotion—in terms of spiritual healing—is an understanding of what we mean by love; not adolescent infatuation or mere physical or chemical attraction, but the love of two people who agree in terms of mature thought and meaning to share their lives together.

This is a love that must have a spark of divinity in it. It is in part at least a non-physical love. It is in part religious love and selfless love.

At Unity they try to avoid words of dark connotations. I did not find ''jealousy'' mentioned by name in the considerable quantity of Unity literature and teachings I examined. I did find the word ''love.'' It was used in many ways, reaching out in different ways as a force of healing within the Unity concept.

''Love gives; it frees; it is a universal spirit.

''When we love most truly, we are most unselfish. Our love is big in proportion to its inclusiveness.

''It is small as we narrow it to some person or to some thing. Discovery of this impersonal, universal love does not destroy our human love, the love that makes marriage happy. Rather it fulfills the old love and is the way to happiness.

''. . . What we fight to get we must fight to keep. What comes to us by love is ours by divine right. It is held by invisible bonds, stronger than any outside power. . . .

''Love wins because it seeks not its own.''[2]

It is this fact that is of supreme importance. Love is not love which crushes and destroys and demands and imprisons.

''The great message of love,'' one preacher told me, ''was given to us on the Cross. Jesus was faced with no mere imagined wrong or hurt. He was nailed to those boards and His life blood flowed out in His agony.

''Yet He forgave and He loved, and prayed to God to forgive those who did this to Him. This was the symbol of what He was, this was the first sign on the Cross of His triumph.''

[2]Ernest C. Wilson, The Great Physician. Lee's Summit, Mo.: Unity School of Christianity, 1953. p. 114.

Writing of this in his book *The Story of Jesus,* another minister, the Reverend Theodore Parker Ferris, states of this aspect of the Crucifixion: ". . . It is not the definition of love that counts. It is the demonstration of it. To go out and forgive the unforgiveable and love the unlovable means more than all the definitions and understandings of love that you or I or anybody else will ever entertain.

"It is almost impossible for us," he continues, "to believe that Jesus could have loved those people. I do not believe that we should have loved them, even at our best. . . . Such love is not in man except as he reveals the love of God. Only God could love like that."[3]

But this is the challenge of our lives, according to the teachings of all churches and faiths: To seek the love of God in our lives, in our business, in our careers, in our homes and in our families.

We can at least seek to emulate it within our own limitations.

For this is a healing love, it is of God, and it drives before it monsters like jealousy and hate and fear and sweeps them out like clouds before a fresh clean breeze.

[3]Theodore Parker Ferris, The Story of Jesus. New York: Oxford University Press, 1953. p. 98.

25

We the Guilty

The visitor was a well-dressed man who seemed in excellent health. The pastor asked him what was wrong. The man said he had pains in the heart and serious depression.

"What does the doctor say?"

"He says there's nothing wrong with me."

"Congratulations."

"But doctors don't know. I know more about it than they do."

The pastor discovered this man devoted most of his waking time to concern over his pains and his depression, he followed all the newest medical developments and was the first to try any new medication or tonic he could buy in the drug store.

Prodding brought out that earlier in his life he had been involved in an emotional situation in which he had acted, as he saw it, badly. Guilt clung in his mind and was definitely involved in his imagined heart condition.

There was no real guilt; he had committed no crime. He had said things in anger he would not have said otherwise, and thereby he had hurt someone he loved.

But the guilt clung on. Even after a number of sessions the pastor could not convince this man that God did not want to punish him, or let him be punished, all these years, for so trivial a sin. Finally, the minister decided that in this instance he needed the outward symbol of forgiveness.

Merely saying it, merely telling him he was forgiven, was not enough. The guilt had to be washed off spiritually or the man would live on with his imaginary pain and depression. A kind of spiritual shock treatment was indicated.

At the next meeting the pastor appeared in the church vestments he wears only for high services of unusual significance—his most ornate vestments, and around his neck a richly embroidered stole.

241

The man of guilt walked into the church and up to the altar, where the minister asked the man to kneel, and he put his hands upon the man and prayed, reassuring him that God had long ago forgiven him and that he need not feel guilt any longer for there was none.

In the large church, with no other human there except these two, the pastor's words reverberated across the empty pews. "As a priest of the church of the living Christ." he intoned, "I proclaim that God has forgiven you."

For some moments the man remained bowed at the altar. When he arose the look on his face told the story. He was smiling, radiant. God had forgiven him; now he was sure.

From that instant, the pain also was miraculously gone.

The tramp of the guilty echoes across the world—in temples, mosques, synagogues and cathedrals, in the offices of psychiatrists, surgeons and general practitioners. Needlessly we shoulder guilt that is not ours—race guilt, national guilt, religious guilt, theological guilt, guilt for things long past and over and repented of, as in the case of the man with his heart pains. Guilt, often deep and unrecognized by the sufferer, has become one of the great plagues of a civilization that has eliminated hundreds of other diseases assailing mankind.

There is guilt that is justified and can only be eliminated by removing the real cause, by paying whatever price society may demand; guilt in terms of crime, of violence, of injury; there is the guilt of injury done to others in business, in our family or social life. For many of these society has its fixed penalties. For others, the individual must make his own amends.

It is not real guilt only that causes the great army of sufferers who today wait in doctors' offices and ministers' front halls for a chance to tell their stories, to drag it all out and see what can be done. Much guilt is rooted in unreality, in what is called "neurotic anxiety." One Manhattan mother tormented and almost destroyed herself because she had had children, and she was a member of the Negro race. It was a sin to have brought Negro children into the world; wonderful, lovable youngsters, who would have to suffer all the indignities of a minority. That the children were happy and glad to have been born and growing up into full and productive lives did not change her sense of personal guilt. She had transferred to herself the full responsibility for all the evils of segregation.

The pastor who worked with her and helped her most explained,

"You have to understand that these young people aren't your personal property. They are also the children of God. And their burden—their cross—is also their opportunity. You should help them make the most of that rather than sit around wishing they had never been born into such a wicked world, and taking blame upon yourself."

Our guilt comes from many sources, it has elements of tribal memories. Sometimes it attempts to transfer itself to others; often it is a nameless generalized guilt, a compendium of guilt gathered in small batches through our lives.

An interesting manifestation of "group guilt" is the attempt of one generation to hand guilt over the next. During the 1920s, the United States passed the fantastic prohibition experiment, violated at every turn and behind every door. Almost everyone had his personal bootlegger—and the underworld grew into a multi-billion dollar business. People drank bathtub gin and needle beer—and the editorials denounced "flaming youth" for its lack of moral fiber.

In the 1950s, an adult generation which found itself involved in world tensions and hatreds, in revolutions and social upheavals on every continent, in inflation, corruption of police and law, overcrowded schools and underprivileged teachers, and in reliance on a stockpile of massive retaliation as the only defense we have or know against a ruthless enemy, placed the blame for its rising number of delinquents squarely upon the children themselves.

I talked with one woman of some standing in social service work who declared unequivocally, "What the younger generation needs, those who get into trouble with the law, is more punishment. They must be made to have respect and the way to do that is to let them know they can't get away with anything. The old-fashioned whip is the answer."

One could explore all the various aspects of this and argue pro and con. Father Edward Flanagan, founder of Boys Town, believed in discipline and punishment up to a point, but not punishment in terms of bodily pain. He said pain punishment operates through fear and is successful only until the boy meets something else he fears more; for instance, gang leaders on the street corner. Father Flanagan's reliance was on love, particularly on giving the boy knowledge of the love of God. Imposition of a sense of guilt was not part of his technique.

Dr. Karl Stern, the psychiatrist, a Roman Catholic convert from the Jewish faith, describes a case of a man whom he first examined in a hotel room in Montreal.[1]

"He was in bed in a suite on the first floor, under the influence of alcohol and barbiturates, but still in a depressed and anxious mood. His state was so deplorable that I felt he might have to be hospitalized. When I mentioned this he became, like so many patients, even more anxious, but the reason he gave me was curious: he was afraid he might have to be hospitalized on one of the 'higher' floors of the hospital. By this he meant any floor above the third. For several years he had been suffering from a morbid fear of heights, so much so that he could not attend any business meetings in the usual tall office buildings without 'doping himself' with great amounts of sedatives.

"Even then he often had to leave the meeting in an inner state of panic after ten minutes, using any excuse which came to mind. During the war he had some important government function besides his business and at times he would be summoned on short notice to go somewhere by plane. It was often necessary for him to refuse. While his history was being taken he suddenly said, 'I am going to tell you something you ought perhaps to know. I've never told this to anybody before . . .' He had grown up in the north of England under very poor circumstances. His father had been a peddler. 'I used to get along well with my father, I think, but one day we had a most awful row, and I told him I wished he were dead. And the most extraordinary thing happened. That very day my father went out and never returned. He was drowned in the moors.' "[2]

Dr. Stern points out that part of the guilt of this man, a part of the self-conviction of his responsibility in his father's death, came also from his guilt about success. He was outstripping his father because his father had been a peddler and he was a successful man of business and government.

"It soon became apparent that his fear of heights was to be understood metaphorically. He had a rocket-like career, which put him 'high above' his father's position in life. But when he had reached the zenith, he became panic-stricken by height in the literal, spatial sense."[3]

[1] Karl Stern, The Third Revolution, A Study of Psychiatry and Religion. New York: Harcourt, Brace and Company, 1954. p. 190.

[2] *Ibid*. p. 192.

[3] *Ibid*. p. 192.

Only by giving the patient insight into the actual oneness of "metaphor and reality," Dr. Stern indicates, can the patient be made to understand the needlessness and purposelessness of his self-torture.

But Dr. Stern, while skilled in his psychiatric therapies, is also aware of a therapy beyond the physical and mental treatment. "There is to the faithful Christian," he insists, "an aspect of guilt and atonement which has not been touched. The therapy was effective. But we know that guilt and redemption have a supernatural aspect. That aspect has not been approached during the entire procedure. What the therapist has achieved at best is a primitive foreshadowing of something which lies beyond the psychological plane."[4]

Guilt both real and imagined strikes at human beings in many disguises. It may be mental illness or physical illness. It may be a combination. There is the case of the wife who was discovered at a rendezvous with her lover. At the moment of discovery she and the lover were in the midst of the soup course of their dinner. Thereafter this woman became violently ill whenever she tasted soup of any kind, although her husband forgave her and there was a full reconciliation.

Many "guilt symptoms" often go unrecognized by the sufferer, or his doctor or minister. "Unconscious guilt reactions," New York psychiatrist Dr. Peter Laqueur declared in one of his lectures, "are expressed frequently in psychoneurotic symbolic symptoms such as obsession, compulsion, phobia or conversion hysteria in which unconscious conflict is converted into bodily symptoms, blindness, deafness, inability to make sounds or to walk or to stand. Unconscious guilt is resolved by an analytical process in which the symbolic symptoms tend to disappear."

Much of the present effort of clergy and psychiatry is to minimize the effects of guilt on the individual and those around him. In February of 1955, at a forum held by the McAuley Psychiatric Clinic of St. Mary's Hospital in San Francisco—the first Roman Catholic hospital to establish a psychiatric clinic in the United States—a panel of leading psychiatrists and priests explored their attitudes toward guilt. In the exhaustive analysis it was ultimately agreed that the priest is concerned with the sin above all, and the psychiatrist above all with the guilty feelings. One of the psychi-

[4]*Ibid*. p. 304.

atrists declared that he saw his role not as making his patient non-guilty but in enabling the individual to straighten out his values and bases for judging.

Both groups, however, were concerned with the problem of freeing individuals from the *sense* of guilt. The priest does so by absolving them through confession. There are occasions, the priest pointed out, when even after absolution the patient continues to feel guilty. In such instances, the priest said, he considered it best to send the individual to a psychiatrist.

We see a combination of spiritual and physical forces working together, each in its own area, in the effort to alleviate this emotional burden.

Guilt can be as stubborn and difficult to eradicate as weeds along the road. A "healing pastor" tells of one woman who came to his services, prayer groups and counseling sessions for five years, plus visits to a psychiatrist, before she was able to comprehend the truth. When she realized that her mental and emotional problems were caused by something that happened when she was a little girl and for which she had been needlessly punishing herself all her life since, she was well again. But the case took five years of psychiatry and prayer.

There are many interpretations and misinterpretations of the doctrine of "original sin" and the fall of man and the depravity and guilt of man. Some churches teach that man is a fallen creature by his own very nature, but that by baptism he receives salvation. The collective guilt of mankind, however, cannot be and is not considered as individual guilt, even under the most stringent theological concept of what the fall of Adam and Eve symbolized.

Throughout history and through all stages of civilization, both group and individual guilt play a stellar role. Primitive peoples of the Pacific have their taboos, some of them utterly senseless; violations may bring on the punishment of the gods. In some African tribes, it is forbidden for a man to speak of his mother-in-law. In others guilt is involved in walking on the shadow of a chief or king. The gods grow angry if certain places are profaned, certain words spoken.

The rigmarole of guilt patterns and ideas is a bewildering complex of religious, social, ethical, and superstitious doctrine; from the early sacrifices in the Old Testament to modern concepts of penance and forgiveness, guilt and sin have also permeated every phase of the Christian-Judaic history and tradition. Step by step, however, it has been an unfolding of ideas, from the Garden of Eden to the teachings of Jesus and the disciples. It is a progress of our own understanding from the idea of a God of punishment to a God of forgiveness.

Madeleine S. and J. Lane Miller, in their remarkably complete *Bible Dictionary,* have a lengthy section on guilt in the biblical sense. One paragraph in particular seems to sum up the sin-and-guilt concept: "But every human being sooner or later incurs guilt before God. The very imperfections of his nature lead him to deliberate wrongdoing, and guilt necessarily goes with this. The history of sacrifice and of penance is the evidence of how wide-spread is the sense of guilt among mankind."[5]

Concepts of guilt and sin underwent many distortions through medieval centuries and the Renaissance down to modern times. It is difficult for us to believe today—but still is historically a fact—that many religious leaders condemned lightning rods and Benjamin Franklin for inventing them, because they thwarted God's will in punishing guilt. Many of the foremost developments in medicine and surgery were fought by both Roman Catholic and Protestant leaders as interfering with the "will of God."

These interpretations have undergone radical changes. Church interpreters of many faiths have retreated and retracted. They have done so because the interpretations themselves were wrong.

For God sent His Son to earth, we learn in the gospels, not to punish but to forgive; not to destroy, but to save.

What, then, is the role of guilt in the eyes of Christ, as He tells it to us through the records of the New Testament?

As a reporter I turned to a source of importance regarding spiritual healing: The Bible. What do we have reported in the words of Jesus as set down by His followers, about guilt?

In Matthew, Chapter IV, Verse 17: "From that time Jesus began to preach, and to say, Repent: for the kingdom of heaven is at hand."

Repent of our sins, our guilt. And the implication is that we will be forgiven, since it is stated that heaven is close at hand.

In Matthew, Chapter V, Verses 44 and 45: "But I say unto you, Love your enemies, bless them that curse you, do good to

[5]Madeleine S. and J. Lane Miller, Harper's Bible Dictionary. New York: Harper and Brothers, 1952. p. 238.

them that hate you, and pray for them which despitefully use you, and persecute you;

"That ye may be the children of your Father which is in heaven . . ."

We must not impose guilt on others by condemning them or accusing them of doing us evil.

In Matthew, Chapter XVIII, Verses 21 and 22: "Then came Peter to him, and said, Lord how often shall my brother sin against me, and I forgive him? till seven times?

"Jesus saith unto him, I say not unto thee, Until seven times: but, Until seventy times seven."

There must be no limit, then, to our forgiveness.

In Chapter XXI of the same gospel, Jesus goes to the temple and talks with the chief priests and elders, and they try to trap him into theological traps with their questions, but he puts them to rout.

Then Jesus tells them, "Verily I say unto you, That the publicans and the harlots go into the kingdom of God before you.

"For John came unto you in the way of righteousness, and ye believed him not; but the publicans and harlots believed him: and ye, when ye had seen it, repented not afterward, that ye might believe him."[6]

Publicans and harlots who repent and accept God are forgiven and will go to heaven sooner than learned scribes and elders of the church who do not repent and do not accept.

Guilt is forgiven if we repent in our hearts. But it is what we mean in our hearts that is important. It is not just the words and rituals.

"Woe unto you, scribes and Pharisees, hypocrites!" He cries out, "for ye devour widows' houses, and for a pretense make long prayer: therefore ye shall receive the greater damnation."[7]

Hypocrisy and cant and double-talk in the temple, taking money from the widows while praying long and loud, is guilt which will bring damnation.

"Woe unto you, scribes and Pharisees, hypocrites!" He cries out, "for ye pay tithe of mint and anise and cummin, and have omitted the weightier matters of the law, judgment, mercy and

[6] Matthew XXI:31-32.
[7] *Ibid.* XXIII:14.

faith: these ought ye to have done, and not to leave the others undone.''[8]

These smaller things are important, but the truly important things of religion and life are judgment and if guilt is found, mercy.

Throughout His gospel, these were His basic preachments: Love of God, love of our fellow man, love of our enemies, forgiveness of our enemies, repentance of our own mistakes, a willingness always to try again, seventy times seven times, and judgment with mercy.

In such a philosophy, there is hardly room for guilt to sit down.

This is what we find emphasized above all else in the recorded teachings of Christ.

[8]*Ibid.* XXIII:23.

26

They and Their Shadows

One day at a spiritual healing service in a church just outside of Philadelphia, Dr. Alfred Price acted as visiting pastor and healer. Among those who came forward for the laying on of hands were some of his own parishioners of St. Stephen's. Also present was a child about whom the pastor knew only that he was badly crippled from polio.

The child, not quite seven years old, sought to undo his braces so that he could kneel at the altar. Those kneeling beside the boy, also seeking cures, turned to help, three women and two men, fumbling nervously to help undo the straps.

One of those who helped was a woman who had been a psychotic, in and out of hospitals for a number of years. Another was a man with arthritis. The other three—a woman and two men—had less serious troubles, rheumatic conditions and sinus trouble.

All five who helped that child were cured that day.

The child was not. But these five, with all of whom Dr. Price had been working for some time in counseling as well as through prayer, apparently acquired spiritual force of unusual strength in the act of helping the boy to kneel.

Perhaps their healings could be called religiosomatic. For here, whatever shadows in their lives lay behind their illnesses, realization of religious meanings in each of the five who turned to help the boy with the braces apparently had its effect.

These five healings at the same time, which Dr. Price considers one of the most remarkable instances in his experience, involve cases which might not, in ordinary instances, fit into a spiritual healing category. Certainly at Lourdes they would have little chance of being termed miraculous. Yet they were healings, by spiritual means, of troubles long standing in the lives of each.

These were the shadows of fear and guilt and doubt and anxiety and other negative emotions which had erupted in physical symptoms.

The shadows do not always erupt physically. They may hover and fade in and out, so that the individual is never really sick and never really well. We see such people and know such people, those who hide, those who run. The girl afraid to marry, who withers until no one wants her. The man who distrusts banks and keeps his wealth in a shoebox that one day burns up in the closet.

In ancient centuries, these shadows were treated as demons. Spirits were supposed to invade us and leave at will so that man must have been, with some of these old-time notions, more like a revolving door than a human entity. We speak of a man today as being "in good spirits" in deference to those ideas that good and evil spirits kept moving in on the individual personality.

The early Christian philosopher known as Origen is quoted as saying of the dark spirits: "It is demons which produce famine, unfruitfulness, corruptions of the air, pestilences; they hover concealed in clouds in the lower atmosphere, and are attracted by the blood and incense which the heathen offer to them as gods."[1]

Throughout the Middle Ages such ideas not only were accepted but people lived and worked and acted in the firm belief that they personally were the targets of demons and witches and spells. Early allergies were considered the work of witches and devils. We say "God bless you" when someone sneezes—to keep the devil from slipping in to your body at that precarious moment, according to ancient authority. Every right thinking person knew that there were spells for giving people devils and spells for fending them off.

Today, under other names, the demons still ride. We are haunted, all of us, by shadows. None of us escapes them completely. They are shadows of fear, doubt and uncertainties, of frustration, of our own mistakes, of our misjudgments, of prejudice, of our own suddenly discovered limitations, of our insecurities, our anxieties, real or imagined.

Only rarely are they cases of a clinical nature in themselves. It is easy to diagnose hallucination. A shadow is more elusive.

Sometimes the shadows can be deadly. Yet even when they seem to triumph, other healing factors may be at work.

I interviewed a woman doctor who is a believer in healing of

---

[1] Andrew D. White, A History of The Warfare of Science with Theology in Christendom, Vol. II. New York: George Braziller, 1955. p. 27.

the total individual through medicine, psychiatric procedures if required, and spiritual treatment, primarily prayer.

One case she described was that of a middle-aged patient who had lived through a background of hate and poverty and had finally reached a point where she apparently wanted to die. The shadows closed in. The woman even revealed a dream which clearly had in it, the doctor said, symbols of the death wish.

She was ill and required an immediate operation. The doctor was aware from the patient's state of mind and half-articulated wish for death, that the chances for a successful operation were not good.

Nevertheless the doctor tried to save this woman's life. The physician sent the patient to the city hospital, where she had the care of several of the finest surgeons in the city.

First-day reports from the hospital said merely that the operation had been performed and the patient had survived. Later, the doctor visited the patient herself. The woman seemed changed, almost radiant.

"Doctor," she said, all her unhappiness gone from her voice, "I want to tell you that I've seen kindness and humanity and goodness down here in the hospital that I never knew existed. I've seen love that I never believed people could give you—from strangers, nurses, the doctors, the other patients.

"I want to tell you something. Being here and seeing this has been the most meaningful experience in my whole life."

The patient died the following day.

The woman doctor told me, "I believe she had to live long enough to learn that what she had seen and experienced before was not all of life. She had to live at least long enough to learn how wonderful and how full of the spirit of God's love human beings can be."

Some appear to be fated to make war on shadows—for themselves, or others, or for society.

When I was a correspondent in the Pacific theatre during World War II, I interviewed a Hollywood screen star named Lew Ayres. This young hero of the Dr. Kildare series had created a storm early in the war by insisting that his religious beliefs would not permit him to kill anyone in combat. Since the army would not assure him of assignment in a non-combatant post, he was classed as a conscientious objector.

In the midst of war the "conchie" is not looked on with great affection and for a star like Mr. Ayres to take such a step seemed like professional suicide.

After all the headlines and editorials denouncing him had had their hour, Lew Ayres quietly was shifted, with no announcement whatever, from conscientious objector into the army—attached to a forward area hospital.

I interviewed him in Hollandia, New Guinea, at an army hospital consisting of tents and wards unfloored and open to the elements in the midst of New Guinea's mud. He was weaving jungle greens, in the little office he had set up at the end of one of the tents. All through the interview we were interrupted by calls: Corporal Ayres was wanted by this lad or that; a man on crutches would drop in to ask a favor or thank him for something—a book, or a letter the actor had written home for the man.

Lew Ayres told me a little about his ideas, his desire not to be just another actor after the war, his hopes to work in the field of religion, perhaps making use of his knowledge of screen techniques in carrying these ideas out.

His own effort in the war he tried to dismiss. It was only when the men he had helped came in and began to tell me their side of the story that the full picture came clear. "Ask him about the night the ammo dump went up and the place was being splattered all night long with shrapnel and some of the injured guys were screaming murder," one of the men said.

Corporal Ayres didn't tell it, but I got the story. Men shivering in their beds, cripples crouching in holes while death was dropping out of the skies from the exploding ammunition.

In the midst of this, a man walked from tent to tent, bed to bed, chatting with these beleaguered patients. Nothing dramatic. Nothing put on. This was Lew Ayres, a real Dr. Kildare, doing a job few people knew about or understood.

When injured Japanese prisoners were brought in for first aid before being sent on to prison camps, Corporal Ayres gave them cigarettes and treated them as people. Some of the G.I.s in the hospital did not understand: sometimes they called Lew Ayres a dirty Jap-lover.

Lew didn't mind. Some day, he said, they would understand.

"But he's a stinking Jap, Lew."

"The war will be over some day," he'd tell them. "This man is your brother and he's a child of God."

It was not popular to say things like that in a hospital in Hollandia, in the middle of a war.

But Lew Ayres did. Ultimately he was to come back after the war and turn to the production of films of a special kind, seen by millions, telling the story of world religions, carrying out his pledge.

But back in the mud of New Guinea, and later in the Philippines, he made his first effort to drive out restless shadows of the war hate.

He did it in terms of aid for the injured, regardless of who they were, in terms of a cigarette and a light for a wounded enemy in the jungle heat.

This was his brother and also—as Lew said—the child of God.

27

Healers Anonymous

That Alcoholics Anonymous is, in fact, an organization devoted exclusively to spiritual healing is frequently overlooked. There are no crutches left on the walls of an A.A. meeting hall that are visible to the naked eye. There are no religious services or rituals as such, no laying on of hands or anointing.

Yet the first three steps of the Twelve Steps in A.A. bring in factors which are a process of transfer, from physical to spiritual concepts. Here are these first three steps as given in A.A. pamphlets:

Step One: We admitted that we were powerless over alcohol—that our lives had become unmanageable.

Step Two: We came to believe that a Power greater than ourselves could restore us to sanity.

Step Three: We made a decision to turn our will and our lives over to the care of God *as we understood Him.*

Thus the break comes with medical and psychiatric treatment. Medicine and psychiatry admit that alcoholism is a disease, or as some call it, the symptom of a deeper disease of mind or psyche. But medicine does not usually write prescriptions involving God.

On the other hand doctors and psychiatrists, concerned with helping people get well, and entirely pragmatic, willingly accept A.A. as a valuable tool in many cases, metaphysical concepts and all.

It is a paradoxical situation, unique in the history of modern medicine.

The story begins with a man the world knows only as Bill W.

A prominent dealer in stocks and bonds, Bill W. lived up to his last dollar and the last drop of whisky. He found himself on a toboggan ride to nowhere, losing friends, business, jobs, all but wrecking his home. One day in 1934, he was drinking alone in his kitchen when a friend dropped in, also a drunk. That day the friend looked healthy and happy. Bill offered him a drink. The friend said he wasn't having any; he'd gotten religion.

Bill W. looked up in shock. The friend stayed and talked while Bill drank gin and listened. Bill was no atheist. But this kind of talk—God on a personal basis—wasn't for him. Still here was his companion, insisting that God had done for him what he could not do for himself. This was a man who had lost everything but was now sober. When he saw that Bill recoiled from talk about God, the friend said, "You don't have to think of God in any terms. Choose your own conception of God."

Old thoughts of faith came to his mind. The idea of God began to slip back into his consciousness. He could get well, he could be healed of this thing most doctors called incurable alcoholism. It was only a matter of turning his life over to a Power beyond himself.

That was all he needed for the start. Because of his physical condition, after months of steady drinking, he was taken to a hospital. He did not want alcohol; he wanted to seek this new idea. His friend came to see him and they talked things over.

It was to be a new start, with a God-consciousness as its cornerstone. He would make a list of people he had hurt, he would try to right these wrongs to the best of his ability.

He went over all this with his reformed drinking companion. His friend talked about how he had himself begun. He had been about to be committed for drunkenness. Two men, members of the religious movement called the Oxford Group, pleaded his cause, urging the judge to give him a new chance to find himself through a simple religious approach of turning all his problems over to a greater Power than himself. The judge had given him this chance.

"It means destruction of your self-centeredness," the friend said. "You no longer concern yourself so much about yourself. You forget yourself. Then you don't need that drink to keep yourself going."

"These were revolutionary and drastic proposals," Bill W. was later to write, in *Alcoholics Anonymous*, the story of the movement, "but the moment I had fully accepted them the effect was electric. There was a sense of victory, followed by such a peace and serenity as I had never known. There was utter confidence. I felt lifted up, as though the great clean wind of a mountain top blew through and through. God comes to most men gradually, but His impact on me was sudden and profound . . ."[1]

In his first days, he was helped by a brilliant medical man, Dr. William Silkworth, who is regarded by A.A. people as almost "a medical saint." Later, in Akron, Ohio, he contacted another reformed alcoholic when he felt that his will to drink was weakening. This was a physician now known as Dr. Bob.

It was from this awareness that only alcoholics could help alcoholics to stay sober that the two began to work to build the worldwide organization of ex-drunks, healed by putting their faith in God.

The movement they started could not have been halted by any human beings; it grew too deeply out of human need. It required no proselyting beyond letting people know about it. There were no dues, there were no expenses; it was a voluntary thing and mostly the people who came to it had no money in any event. It is still financed by local contributions supporting individual groups. But by 1957, it numbered six thousand groups in the United States alone and hundreds more on every continent, and in isolated posts in the islands of the Pacific and elsewhere; far off tropic worlds of palm trees and enchantment and frustrated lives.

The people in these groups have learned that alcoholism is a progressive illness which cannot be cured but which can be arrested. The members are all alcoholics who frankly admit to being alcoholics. It is not something to hide in shame. They cannot take a drink, not a single drink; their physical bodies cannot stand alcohol, and one drop is enough to lead to full-fledged drunkenness. If they fall off they are helped back on. Sometimes this happens a number of times before the individual gropes his way to recovery. Alcoholics must always be on guard; some have slipped simply by eating candy that had rum or whisky inside, or a rum cake, or plum pudding with brandy sauce.

A.A. teaches that one must learn to live with liquor normally, just as a diabetic does not find it necessary to avoid the sight of sugar. Alcoholics in A.A. serve liquor themselves, in their homes—to their relatives and friends.

Indications are that there is a large area of self-centeredness at the root of the illness; an absorption with self and the inability of

[1] Alcoholics Anonymous. New York: Alcoholics Anonymous Publishing, Inc., 1955. p. 14.

that self, for real or fancied reasons, to meet the problems of the world. Thus, the retreat to the bottle. Some psychiatrists insist that alcoholism is a form of self-murder to avoid the challenge of life, its competitions and conflicts. It is, some doctors say, suicide in slow doses.

Bill W., founder of A.A., told me in an interview that the first essential for the success in A.A. is the "defeat of the ego in depth." Whatever the resentments or insecurities which led him to drink, A.A.'s founder explained, the alcoholic finds himself in an impossible situation because he is relying on himself, on his ego, and this is not enough to stop him from drinking.

"This is why in A.A. we ask the drinker to turn to God, not in the concept of any individual religion, but only as the drinker can understand that term. Since he has not the power himself to stop drinking, he has to find the power beyond him," Bill said.

"We have had some pretty wild and unexpected ideas develop out of that. One man told us all right, he would think of the radiator as God, because the radiator was performing its function, and that was more than he was doing. So it had a power beyond his own.

"We accepted that—as a start," the six-foot, silver-haired founder of A.A. informed me, with an easy, good-natured smile. "Later we were able to lift his spiritual horizons to a somewhat higher plane."

We sat at luncheon, and Bill talked. It seemed to me that in the quiet of his voice, the calm with which he listened, one felt a special kind of strength. "You have to believe in God every hour of every day," he said, "you have to realize that He is with us all the time; in every breath we breathe, there is God."

In operation, A.A. is a program of practicality. "Alcoholics Anonymous," according to the A.A. magazine, *Grapevine,* "is a fellowship of men and women who share their experience, strength, and hope with each other that they may solve their common problems and help others to recover from alcoholism. The only requirement for membership is an honest desire to stop drinking. A.A. has no dues or fees. It is not allied with any sect, denomination, politics, organization or institution; does not wish to engage in any controversy, neither endorses nor opposes any causes. Our primary purpose is to stay sober and help other alcoholics to achieve sobriety."

A.A. is perhaps the most unusual fellowship in the world. In addition to having no dues, it has no rules or regulations, no "musts," no constitution, no bylaws. One of the unwritten traditions is that anyone who is still a drinker and making enough disturbance to upset a meeting may be requested to leave. But he is always welcome back the moment he has sobered up again.

Only neophyte A.A.s say they will never have another drink. "Stay sober today," is a saying of the movement. "Take care of all the todays; the tomorrows will take care of themselves."

Group meetings are run under the general direction of the Association but are independent units in themselves. Money is raised by passing the hat at meetings to defray normal expenses. Voluntary contributions from these groups help to maintain the main office and its staff in New York. The A.A. Publishing Company, which prints A.A. books, pamphlets and other material, is a going concern which pays for itself. Any profits go into a special fund to be used in case of financial emergencies in the organization.

"The important consideration is that membership in A.A. is in no way contingent upon financial support of the fellowship," one of its leaflets points out. "Many A.A. groups have, in fact, placed strict limitations on the amount that can be contributed by any member. A.A. is entirely self-supporting and no outside contributions are accepted."

Where possible in the groups, responsibilities are carried on by elections, so that no one is burdened too greatly and service is rotated. There is usually a secretary, a treasurer, a program committee and a food committee. On a national and international level, there is the General Service Board of Alcoholics Anonymous (formerly the Alcoholic Foundation), which serves as custodian of "A.A. traditions" and assumes responsibility "for the integrity and service standards of A.A.'s General Service Headquarters in New York."

Delegates from various A.A. areas meet with headquarters staff and trustees of this board once a year. Unlike most annual meetings, this conference has no authority whatever to make rules or regulations for the fellowship. It meets as a consultative body empowered only to explore and recommend.

Recently formed as an associate group of the A.A. movement are the Al-Anon Family groups, composed of the wives and families of alcoholics, even when the latter are still drinking. Started in 1935, these groups had become officially accepted and numbered more than eight hundred by 1957. They are open to alcoholics' relatives or friends trying to discover how they can help the alcoholic and his needs, and the needs of others in the family.

Wives or husbands of still-drinking alcoholics often get the first glimmerings of understanding at these meetings as to why their mate is drinking, and how much of it is the result of what they themselves do. "I used to wonder why *my* prayers were never answered. Now I can see that they were completely selfish, that I was not ready, spiritually, for them to be answered. How could I expect to have answers to my prayers when I was filled with enmity, self-pity and resentment?"

This was not an alcoholic speaking, but the wife of an alcoholic. "I became aware of my own defects and what I could do to change them," she went on. "I 'let go and let God.' I substituted positive thoughts for negative ones—love for enmity, praise for criticism, forgiveness in place of resentment.

"Working the Family Group program on a twenty-four-hour basis, with daily time for prayer and meditation, gave me new confidence and faith...."[2]

In most of the world's great cities, there are frontline A.A. posts, manned by former alcoholics. Here the drunks stagger in or telephone for help. Here the skid row bums, the derelicts and prostitutes, drunks of all ages and condition, turn for help. About one in six is a woman.

At one of these posts in New York, I watched this unusual, unrecognized spiritual war. Outside, on the street, pedestrians went about their normal activities. Inside, in the front room, one might have thought it a typical business office.

Two women answered phones which jangled constantly. Conversations sounded almost casual. These workers are trained not to give the callers the feeling of guilt or undue excitement, or emotion. Often the caller is a drunk reaching out for help in a desperate moment when he has finally "touched bottom." The object is to get him to this outpost to begin the drying-out period—and the recovery.

Sometimes it will be a man or woman who has fallen off and who is trying to grope his way back. Then the object is usually to get in contact with someone from the group to which he belongs.

As recovered alcoholics, those who man the posts are prepared to handle anything that comes in. They themselves have been through it. In the back room at any hour there may be half a dozen

[2]The Al-Anon Family Groups. New York: Al-Anon Family Group Headquarters, Inc., 1955. pp. 85-86.

men in various stages of "drying out," grim and drawn-faced and
in agony.

Sometimes a man who has been off liquor only a few hours or
days will go into a convulsion. "Then we put a spoon in his mouth
and call an ambulance," one of the women in charge told me.
Occasionally they have to call the police to quell an incipient one-
man riot. Sometimes an irate wife shows up with a drunken husband, pushes him inside and vanishes. In one case a drunk went
into the men's room and slashed his wrists—not too badly, luckily,
because he missed the arteries. When he came out, one of the
women workers said, "Look at you, spilling blood all over the
place!" She explained that usually this kind of thing is a bid for
attention.

In the back room, I listened to their stories, the repetition of
troubles brought on by drinking, the slow recognition on their
part, as job and family and friends and money and health and
everything in their lives began to go, that something had to be
done or this sickness would kill them.

Some of those coming in recent years are much younger than
in the past.

I talked with a youth of twenty-two who had been an alcoholic
for more than a year. He had been involved in several drunken
automobile accidents, had lost his sweetheart and had come to
New York and spent his money drinking and finally was down to
his last fifteen cents. "Somehow, in my stupor," he said, "I
began to realize that I had to do something. I got to the phone
and called information and asked for the number of A.A.

"The girl at information was wonderful. She took a real interest.
She searched trying to find the A.A. place nearest to me. It took
a long time but she kept on until she got this place. Then she
listened in on the call and when it was over she came back on the
line and she said, 'Now you go right up there and I'll say a prayer
for you.'"

He smiled. "She asked me if I had any money and I said I had
five cents. So she returned the dime for the call to A.A. She
wanted to be sure I had carfare. You know, the fact that she said
she'd say a prayer helped me."

He said he'd given up alcohol. He hadn't had a drink in twenty-
four hours. It was just a start, he knew. But he was going to try
to make it.

"And I'll owe my thanks to God and A.A. and that telephone
operator."

28

Laboratory

Wainwright House, located at the water's edge in Rye, New York, is a slate-roofed, stone château of many chimneys. In its setting of lawns and shrubbery and gravel driveways and high, ivy-covered gateposts at the entrance, it looks much like some ancestral mansion in Normandy. Instead it is a laboratory—a strange and exciting laboratory of faith.

Here men and women from all parts of America and the world, from all spheres of life and its activities, come to examine and explore and learn. This is a research center of the ways and means of applying the Word of God in our lives, in our problems, in health, in business, in human relations. Courses are held here in new and still unfolding methods of bringing help to people in need. Five seminars on spiritual healing have been held here and more are to follow. Clergymen and doctors, psychiatrists and hospital chaplains and surgeons, physicists and radio technicians and chemists, educators and psychologists and parapsychologists have participated in these and other seminars.

In charge of this unique laboratory of faith is a group known as the Laymen's Movement for A Christian World, under the direction of its secretary, Weyman C. Huckabee. The movement comprises some fifteen hundred laymen of various faiths—Roman Catholic, Protestant and Jewish, from all parts of the United States, as well as from Canada, Europe, Japan and Latin America.

Behind this Laymen's Movement is the purpose of making Christian principles apply in the daily lives of its members, and through them in the lives of the people with whom they come in contact. Wainwright House, presented to them by Mrs. Philip K. Condict, in memory of her parents, Colonel and Mrs. J. Mayhew Wainwright, is the group's research and training center.

The spiritual healing seminars, and the invaluable transcribed reports of these investigations, are only part of the activities the Laymen's Movement is attempting to carry out here in this laboratory of religious exploration.

A second project is the training of laymen members in a new technique known as "non-directive counseling." This is a new opportunity, especially for talented laymen who have a gift for listening to other people's troubles.

Non-directive counseling is a kind of spiritual-psychotherapy, a blend of Carl Jung and faith, originally developed by Professor Carl Rogers of the University of Chicago and other psychologists. Fundamental in this method is the belief that every individual has within him the wellsprings of strength and insight to find his own answers.

Training sessions in this project are held regularly at Wainwright House, through weekend seminars. As the House is also a retreat and a center of prayer, this training is held in an atmosphere of religious belief.

But an uninformed outsider wandering into Wainwright might have difficulty comprehending what was happening during one of these training sessions. Here in the handsome rooms, he would find pairs of individuals off by themselves in corners, seated alone in rooms, quietly engrossed in themselves and their problems, one talking and the other listening.

For the purpose of training, some of the problems are made up, while others are real. The "invented" cases always have a sting in them, they strike close enough to stir emotions and reactions. The "problem" may be something about religion or ideas of family duty, or about corruption in government. The man talking is upset about corruption. He worries about what is happening to his country.

The "counselor" already has had sessions devoted to his own attitudes to help him understand himself and to develop humility. Then he develops the techniques of listening and understanding; the techniques of non-directing, of letting a man talk and giving him help without saying where he should go next. "Now, let me see if I understand you," the counselor says. "You say you get upset because of such-and-such a thing. Am I right?"

The man goes on. Step by step, without directing, without suggesting, without advising, without sign of approval or disapproval, the non-directive counselor allows the man to tell his story, to "bounce it off" the counselor and back to himself. Often counselors are tempted, as any person is when listening to another's troubles, to break in, to give advice. The rule at Wainwright for this temptation, is: "Clamp one hand firmly over your mouth and point with the other."

Donald R. Boyce, associate secretary in the Laymen's Movement in charge of this project, states: "We are trying to draw upon the resources of the individual within himself. The counselor becomes a kind of mirror, reflecting the man and his psyche."

These laymen counselors are not psychiatrists, or doctors, or even social workers. They are trying to help humans in trouble who are not mentally or emotionally sick enough for real psychiatrists, but who search for guidance.

This is a program of first aid for the soul. A husband and wife have separated and the man is bitter and hurting. He is not sick and yet he needs help and emotional support. If he keeps on in his bitterness he will need far more—he will be a case for the psychiatrist.

"Our program is designed to keep him out of trouble," Mr. Boyce said.

The theory behind this method is that 20 per cent of counseling is skill and 80 per cent is attitude. What Wainwright House has added is the idea of invoking, in addition, God's help.

"A man begins to tell you about his antagonism," one of the counselors told me. "You listen. He pours out his hate and his vitriolic feelings without realizing that that is what they are. You listen. You make a seemingly idle comment.

"He grows restive, trying to reach you. Some of his words indicate that he begins to be aware of this bitterness himself. He has lost a child and he cannot see why it should have happened. He had been trying to find someone to blame and to hate. Perhaps even to hate God.

"Then, as he talks, answers begin to come to him. This is the last part of the technique. Out of the spewed-up mass of emotions in this non-directional method, he draws out of himself his answers:

"'Do I understand you then—are you saying that you don't hate the universe as you thought you did? You've changed that part?'

"'That's right. I suppose I'm really beginning to admit that I hate myself for not having moved quicker in the sickness. Yet should I hate myself? Or isn't my real trouble that I do blame myself and that's just a way? I think . . .'"

The conference goes on until the man has poured out all that had to rush to the surface. Then a change begins to occur in the interview. This is the stage, one expert in the non-directive method told me, when bitterness dies like a flame without fuel, when the individual's insight shows him not only his real problem but its answer within his own terms of reference.

It is also, the counselors say, the most intense part of the program. Listening is a difficult art, even for the trained. It requires tremendous concentration; there is no pause for questions, there is no moment when the listener's mind may wander to any outside matter. It is a difficult thing even for a short time to listen with undivided attention, an absorbing thing.

"It is as if," one of the counselors put it, "you were to climb a high hill, the two of you. And at the very top, the meaning becomes clear, in the spread of sky and clouds and the world below. It is a religious experience at this stage and it involves both the individual talking and the person listening."

Counselors must be persons of emotional stability themselves, people who like to take on other people's problems. They must be of unquestioned character. They must like people—all people, and have a ready response to others. They must be prepared to make counseling an important mission in their lives. And they must treat it as a sacred and inviolable trust.

This religiously oriented psychological technique is in its early stages. As the program develops, the Laymen's Movement hopes to open other "laboratories" for training counselors in these techniques, in various sections of the country.

One Wainwright House seminar brought together forty scientists, theologians and philosophers to discuss what philosophy might replace mechanistic materialism in our modern age.

A scientist at this meeting stated that atoms must now be described as "a series of singularities haunting space."

Another declared that matter had become "nothing, moving very swiftly and without velocity."

A biochemist told the seminar that it was not enough for scientists simply to begin using words like "spirit" and "God."

"They also need help," this biochemist said, "in discovering real operational meanings in these ancient terms and concepts."

The Laymen's Movement and its unique laboratory of faith are pilot programs to bring the operational meanings of God and religion and of God's healing power to a world in action.

29

Interim Report

The evidence so far examined appears to lead to certain inescapable conclusions regarding the subject of religious healings. In sum, these can be listed as follows:

1. From the mass of reports from a variety of sources—including ministers of major religions, medical staffs of Roman Catholic shrines, priests, physicians, patients and eyewitnesses—the fact that there are healings of a paranormal character cannot be questioned.

2. That the reported healings are achieved by a variety of religious and spiritual techniques, beliefs and rituals is evident.

3. These techniques, rituals and beliefs have at least one element in common: prayer to God.

4. In spite of many reported healings, the percentage of reported failures is high and there is as yet meager understanding as to why in almost identical situations, one person gets well by these methods while another does not.

5. Many individuals turn to religious healing only after doctors have given up and sent them home to die. And some of these patients recover after spiritual ministrations.

6. Faith of the petitioner appears to play as important a part as the denomination or shrine or relic through which the healing is claimed.

7. But intercessory prayer by one individual on behalf of someone else appears particularly effective.

8. There are persons who seem to have the gift of healing, particularly through their touch.

9. Many churches and ministers are holding spiritual healing services.

10. Some seemingly miraculous healings may be the body mending itself by normal processes.

11. Some types of spiritual healing may be psychosomatic.

12. Some reported spiritual healing might be coincidence: a spontaneous cure or remission occurring through unknown but nevertheless physical means at the time of the spiritual ministration.

13. Some reported spiritual healings may actually be nothing but medical error in diagnosis.

14. Some reported healings are accomplished by hysteria and suggestion. These are usually not permanent.

15. Some reported spiritual healings are inexplicable by physical laws as we know them and, unless the facts presented are false, can only be described by reasonable men as supernatural.

16. The importance of the emotions in both sickness and healing has been established medically.

17. Love and kindred feelings—kindness, friendliness, compassion, forgiveness—are emotions that appear to lead in the direction of both health and happiness.

18. Hate, fear, envy, resentment and kindred feelings are emotions that appear to lead up to sickness, mental and physical.

19. This appears to be increasingly the teaching of psychiatry and medicine, in humanistic terms.

20. This was also a part of the teaching of Christ two thousand years ago, in terms of the human being, but also in terms of man's relationship to God.

21. This is the teaching of most religions today.

22. Most religious leaders today seem to agree that there is an inseparable relationship between religion and health.

23. In spite of the opposition of some doctors, there are others who believe in the efficacy of spiritual ministrations in medicine. Religion, medicine and psychiatry can and are working together, toward the achievement of what is called "total healing."

The definition of total healing is usually healing of the body, the mind and the soul.

But when we speak of healing of the soul, we leave other known therapies behind us. This is an area not frequently considered in medical textbooks. Psychiatrists and psychologists and psychoanalysts have their *psyches* and *ids* and *egos* and *superegos*, but "soul" is a word one hears rarely in scientific circles. There are no clinics of the soul, as such.

Then what do they mean when they speak of total healing of mind, body and soul? What is the third ingredient, where is it found, and how is it healed?

BOOK THREE

Healing the Soul

30

Half-Lost Souls

The reporter is hard pressed to find documentation relating to healing of the soul. Such material is scanty. When found, it is open to debate. Is it truly the soul of which the document speaks? The soul in terms of modern psychology has been given a dozen appellations and subdivisions. Yet in the integration of man in terms of wholeness and totality of health, it cannot be safely discarded, whatever symbol or terminology we use to describe it.

"Some years ago," Carroll Wise points out, "psychology bowed both God and the soul out of the universe. But it could not get along without an equivalent, so it used the symbol 'ego' or 'self.' Regardless of the symbol, religion should be primarily concerned with those conscious psychic processes which function toward integration and wholeness."[1]

Soul-sickness is perhaps the most difficult of all illness to diagnose or treat. There are no medicines to prescribe, no exercises or diets. It is perhaps the only illness in the world for which the patient himself must ultimately be his own physician. The patient and God.

An excellent and fully-detailed story of a man who was sick of soul is the early history of St. Paul. A young man preparing to be a rabbi—of good family, a Jew and a Roman citizen too, a skilled craftsman—Saul could look with scorn on the lowly, indecent, illegal sect called Christians.

He could hold the cloak of Stephen while the others stoned Stephen to death. He could drag Christians from the temples and from their homes and have them beaten and thrown into prison.

He did all of this in righteousness and pride. Everything he did

[1]Carroll A. Wise, Religion in Illness and Health. New York and London: Harper & Brothers, 1942. p. 168.

to these people only won him higher esteem. He was having his brother man beaten and imprisoned and slain, but to him it was right.

He set off to Damascus to ferret out more of these vermin Christians, as he saw them. And on the road in his vision Christ appeared to him, and said, "Saul, Saul, why persecutist thou me?"[2]

As a result of this experience, Saul changed in his soul. Saul became Paul and preached the word of Christ to Jew and Gentile.

This "case history" out of the New Testament provides us with data, details and implications entirely applicable to our own age, our own "half-lost souls." For the half-lost often do not appear to be lost at all. Frequently they appear to have everything, and it is only later that they or the world discover how little they had really.

Few in Jerusalem in the period before Saul's conversion, when he was having Christians whipped, would have considered him sick in body, mind or soul. He was doing something of which the great majority, as well as the government and religious authorities, approved. He was a benefactor by these actions. Furthermore, he was neither poor, nor ill, nor defeated, nor unhappy.

Saul would have fitted remarkably into modern society. A vigorous young man of good family background, he could have been found at our best cocktail parties, and very possibly ushering on Sunday in the most social church in town.

He would have been a part of the dominant group or political party in the community, foremost in denouncing the opposition, helping to ferret out the weaknesses and failures and shadowy places in the opposition's background.

Possibly he would have had a few well-wrought hatreds against Jews or Negroes or Italians or Irish or Roman Catholic or Chinese or Japanese or Buddhist or Protestant or whomever it happened to be acceptable to hate in that particular area.

At cocktail parties and other gatherings he would air his hatreds with full self-justification, not literally throwing stones at Stephen, but using instead well-polished phrases: "I'm as strong a believer in the church as anyone in this room. However, there are some types of . . ."

This is Saul before he saw Christ.

The rejection of God in our lives is the soul-sickness of man.

[2] Acts IX:4.

Stoning our neighbors to death for whatever high moral cause cannot be squared with the biblical injunction that we must love God with all our heart and soul, and our neighbor as ourselves.

Stoning our neighbor to death with words or ideas or hatred subtly spun; stoning our competitors or rivals or enemies to death with lies, distortions, half-truths; stoning our own loved ones, friends, parents, relatives, in-laws, wife or husband or child to death, with our jealousy, our indifference, our resentment, our unforgiveness—these too are rejections of God that bring on sickness of the soul.

But what do we mean by the soul? The reporter finds it difficult to obtain an objective definition. There are many definitions, from various points of view. To some, the soul is a visible substance. To many Protestant faiths, the soul is not a substance but a part of Spirit, existing in a totally different kind of existence that is of us and around us, but cannot be weighed or seen. To the "fundamentalists" the soul is a non-materialistic but sensate being, capable of enduring the agony of hell-fire or the wonder of heaven. To the Buddhist, the Yoga, the Hindu, the Arab bowing to Mecca in the East, the soul has differing descriptions and meaning.

Yet all agree on basic points of understanding, that the soul is that part of us closest to divinity; that part within us most like God; that part of us which hungers most for God, that reaches out to Him—often in spite of our physical bodies, intellects or emotional drives.

This much one can say objectively: If we assume the existence of soul as an entity in man, then it can only be that part of the human being which strives toward God.

Rejection of God may be intellectual or emotional, it may be partial or complete. One may decide that the universe made itself or that no one knows how or by whom it was made—and why should it be of any concern to us? There are some who say that God is the creation of the wealthy to appease the poor; that He is the product of ignorance to quiet the fears manufactured by the ignorance itself; or that He is the product of the unhappy and maladjusted to assuage their own misery.

There are as many ways of rejecting God as there are of understanding Him. The alcoholic who decided to believe that the radiator was God, because it was functioning and he was not, was not rejecting Deity or committing a profanity. He was reaching out for God, through alcoholic fumes, as far as he could understand in that condition and at that time.

We reject God when we disbelieve in Him, when we assume that we are gods, that we can know everything, that power rests in us, that we are the masters of the universe, we alone. We reject Him when we announce that only hypocrites worship Him, when we assail others who, for all their imperfections, reach out toward Him.

Few of us are free from having, in one way or another, participated in this rejection. But the soul that is sick is the one that strives in vain against the power of the intellect or emotional or prejudicial patterns to be allowed to turn toward its Maker. It is then the soul must wither almost to its death.

What then is the cure?

It cannot lie in outward symbols only, in going through the motions of religion for the sake of appearances with no inner meaning. It cannot lie in any form of deception of ourselves or of society. It cannot lie in surface rituals only. It cannot lie in rationalization of our actions, our hates, our prejudices.

It cannot lie in pretense. If a man's intellect tells him that there is no God, it does not aid him much to pretend that he believes, merely for social acceptability, for physical prosperity, and position. "For what shall it profit a man, if he shall gain the whole world, and lose his own soul?" Jesus asks.[3]

But the man who intellectually rejects God completely is not necessarily lost forever by the reason of his intellect. There is every indication from the records of human beings and their lives that God understands the strivings and struggles of the mortal mind to comprehend Him, and that in the groping itself is growth. Eventually, through the mind, the individual may see the nonsense in the idea of a spontaneous universe, created by nobody out of nothingness. All the evidence indicates that the elimination of God from scientific thinking ultimately leads to the reinstatement of God under some other name as the only means of explaining the inexplicable.

Honest doubt may well lead the individual to God sooner than a dishonest façade of faith. This the evidence indicates also.

Nor is the answer found in those who accept God but still believe that if outward rituals are observed—at Sunday service or mass or Holy Communion—then all religious requirements have been

---

[3]Mark VIII:36.

met and what happens the rest of the time is solely the business of the individual.

These are the hypocrites whom Christ warns again and again. His warnings indicate by their tone and application that there is some of this hypocrisy, small or great, in most of us. Insofar as it exists, our soul is indisposed.

Nor is cure found through indifference. The soul striving for God battles vainly against the imperturbability of the cocktail party agnostic. Indifference, the evidence indicates, is ranked among the greatest of sins. For we are here in a growing universe that is not our own, and not to care is to be an ungracious guest. But if it is not through ritual or strict attendance at Sunday service or strict adherence to rules—then wherein is cure?

From the records, it would appear to lie in our willingness to learn to listen to the promptings of the soul.

For if the soul does exist, most certainly it would be a source of our highest instincts and promptings. From this source would come our impulse to elemental truth and right and good. In this aspect of our being also would lie the special significance of meditation and contemplation. "Be still," the Bible tells us, "and know that I am God."[4]

One of the strangest stories I know concerns a country whose name and location shall be kept a secret.

This was a country of people who did not like cripples. They considered cripples a sign of shame and sin, and they hid them in back rooms, behind closed doors. No one ever spoke about such things.

But ten thousand miles away, a business executive of a major American corporation heard of this situation. Years before, he had taken an interest in cripples, paraplegics, youngsters without legs, the paralyzed and helpless.

He had hired quite a few handicapped people, given them jobs in some of his company's plants—difficult jobs, in machine shops, handling complicated apparatus. The men did well.

He helped them organize a wheelchair basketball team to compete with other paraplegic wheelchair teams. They went to the Paralympics held at Stoke-Mandeville, England, and played against other teams in wheelchairs and became wheelchair champions.

[4]Psalms XXXXII:10.

This man was disturbed about a nation where the people were ashamed of cripples. He sent several representatives to the country on business.

On the side they did a little proselyting. They helped to organize a few wheelchair basketball teams in that country. They helped to awaken the conscience of the leading citizens about this subject.

Finally, he and his cohorts organized a great public demonstration in a vast stadium of the capital city. The president of the country and his wife, other government officials and their wives, leaders of society and their wives, all were invited.

But the front rows were taken not by governmental leaders or the thousands of sport fans, but by cripples—hundreds of them, from homes and backrooms and institutions, from hopeless shadowy worlds out of sight.

The teams put on their game and afterward put on precision demonstrations and the people were bewildered to discover that cripples could shoot baskets from a wheelchair with all the skill of professional players.

It was the beginning of a new day for these cripples, and new understanding for these people.

This was a soul-sickness they had not recognized in themselves until an outsider had shown them a different way. But the prompting of the inner spirit must have been present long before.

Not all of us can hope for a vision on the road to Damascus or even for a business executive ten thousand miles away to help us locate our path.

But we can learn to listen to the promptings within, to recognize them and to have the courage to act on them in our lives.

To this reporter there can be no other meaning to the teaching of Christ that the kingdom of heaven is within us.

The wellsprings of the Eternal Good are within us, and they can be ours. We have only to learn to listen.

And listening and acting upon this inner voice we may not have heard before, we can become changed, we can be reborn in this new awareness.

It is only then that the half-lost finds it way. It is then that we begin to fulfill the command of Jesus: "Be ye therefore perfect, even as your Father which is in heaven is perfect."[5]

---

[5]Matthew V:48.

31

Roads

We have examined healing at Roman Catholic shrines, Episcopalian altars, Christian Science churches, healing through the spiritual power of Alcoholics Anonymous, through Jewish Science, the continuous prayer groups at Unity. We have looked at some of the evangelists and television healers.

There are others, too, of which we know, but which were beyond the scope of our work: Yoga and Buddhism, Mohammedans and Hindus, Taoists and Confucians and others. All of these also have their miracle workers and their miraculous healings to which they point, just as the followers of Asklepios pointed to the clay testimonials on the walls of the temples with the signed gratitude from the healed.

Are all of the roads valid then, and right?

One deduction at least appears irrefutable from the evidence of the centuries, including our own: Those religions and movements which appear most successful in healing results, and those individuals who appear most successful in healing, have certain characteristics in common, whatever differences exist in creed.

All have a recognition of a force beyond ourselves, a benevolent force to which we can turn.

All agree that the individual must first of all accept his own relationship to God, in all humility, his own powerlessness before God.

All share belief in the force of divine love.

The force of love was present wherever I turned in my investigations for this book. I found it sitting in the comfortable living room of Olga and Ambrose Worrall, waiting for a child to come whom Ambrose would try to help; I found it in Dr. Day; I found it listening to Dr. Price in the rectory of St. Stephen's Church in

Philadelphia; chatting with Dr. Large during a seminar at Wainwright House; talking over the long-distance telephone with Agnes Sanford.

I found it in a dozen places I visited: churches, synagogues, hospitals, shrines, offices, in talks with the people of Unity, or sitting across the luncheon table with a man called Bill W. and his assistant, who help direct Alcoholics Anonymous.

In history books and the source material, I catch also this note of love among the ancient healers even before the days of Christ. I feel certain that the Temple of Epidaurus was also a center of this force of love.

This sense of love—this compassion that is more than compassion—is found in our great physicians today, in our great psychiatrists, in the discoveries of our modern system of psychology, particularly in the case of Jung.

To this reporter, it would seem that all of these roads that have lasting truth and meaning in the healing of humanity, by whatever circuitous and difficult routes they travel, ultimately converge upon this force of divine love.

Whatever name we give it, whatever ancient ritual or modern prayer, or wordless meditation we employ to draw it into our lives, this is the great healing power of our universe.

32

The Faith Within You

"And in the fourth watch of the night, Jesus came unto them, walking on the sea."

The disciples saw him coming toward them as their ship was tossed in the storm, and they thought it was a spirit and they cried out in their fright. And Jesus told them to be of good cheer: "It is I; be not afraid."

Peter, probing in his righteousness, not wanting to be fooled by some vagrant spirit, said, "Lord, if it be thou, bid me come unto thee on the water."

And Jesus answered, "Come."

Peter tried. He got out of the boat and began to walk on the water, but suddenly he saw the wind and the waves and was afraid and cried out, "Lord, save me."

Jesus stretched out his hand, and caught Peter, but then he said to him, according to the gospel, "Oh, thou of little faith, wherefore didst thou doubt?"[1]

Jesus did not upbraid Peter for questioning to make sure that it was really Jesus walking on the water.

He chides Peter only when, knowing it is Jesus who has called to him, Peter starts to walk on the water and then sinks as his faith falters.

Few passages in the Bible reveal so completely the tremendous difficulties and demands implied and involved in the meaning and operation of faith. If it was so difficult for Peter—and there are many other instances when the faith of the disciples fell short—how much more difficult is it for those who live at an even greater distance from the Master?

For Peter and the others were with Him, and saw with their

[1]Matthew XIV:25-31.

own eyes the miracles which they recorded later in the Gospels and The Acts.

How many persons today who may or may not call themselves Christians, who may or may not go to an organized church, believe that Jesus visibly and actually walked upon the water? How many believe that it did happen—or that it could happen?

How many of any religion or non-religion—surrounded by the miracles of science—have faith in the miracles of God?

Faith is a fact which exist, grows, flourishes or withers not outside ourselves, but within us.

But is faith only a belief in the miraculous?

There are many definitions. A dictionary describes faith as "unquestioning belief . . . complete trust, confidence, or reliance."

St. Paul says in his epistle to the Hebrews, "Now faith is the substance of things hoped for, the evidence of things not seen."[2] A Roman Catholic definition declares: "Faith is the virtue by which we firmly believe all the truths God has revealed, on the word of God revealing them, who can neither deceive nor be deceived."[3] The British Methodist healer and theological writer, Leslie Weatherhead, gives his own definition of faith within the Christian church generally: "Christian faith is the response of the whole man, thinking, feeling and willing, to the impact of God in Christ, by which man comes into a conscious, personal relationship with God . . ."[4]

There are creeds and theologies which hold that faith is a matter of grace and cannot be commanded by us. It appears true that we cannot become truly faithful merely by wishing; we cannot truly believe in the "things unseen" merely by deciding to do so. When we have achieved faith, certainly, we have a gift from God.

But are we helpless to reach out for that faith ourselves, particularly those among us who want to believe but who greatly doubt, who do not easily accept miracles that seem to supersede the physical laws of God's universe?

Scholars of religion and faith, and all the great prophets of the world, have rejected dishonesty and hypocrisy, the acceptance of dogma which our reason and our mind tell us we do not really

---

[2]Hebrews XI:1.

[3]A Catechism of Christian Doctrine. Revised Edition of the Baltimore Catechism. No. 3. p. 89.

[4]Leslie D. Weatherhead, Psychology, Religion and Healing. p. 425.

accept. But the Bible tells us also that God is "the rewarder of those that diligently seek him."[5]

There is every evidence from the great prophets of God's compassion in the area of faith; there is an understanding of our groping, and a desire to help us when we seek.

Perhaps the most beautiful example of this is the story of the father who has a son who throws fits, and he brings the boy to Jesus. There in front of Jesus, the boy suddenly falls to the ground, wallowing and foaming.

Jesus asks the father, "How long is it ago since this came unto him?"

The man says that the son has been thus afflicted since a child. "If thou canst do anything," the father says to Jesus, "have compassion on us, and help us."

The father's faith is not too strong, obviously. But he is at the end of his rope and Jesus is a last resort.

With no anger at this attitude, Jesus nevertheless throws the conditional clause back at the man, "If thou canst believe, all things are possible to him that believeth."

Immediately the man is affected. This kind of reply searches out his own need. "And straightway," St. Mark records, "the father of the child cried out, and said with tears, Lord, I believe; help thou mine disbelief."[6]

Jesus then freed the son of his affliction.

We are told that the kingdom of God is within us. And we are told that God is the rewarder of those who diligently seek Him. And we are told that by faith all things are possible.

Thus we must seek faith within ourselves. We must not be afraid to probe ourselves, our motives, our conscience, our understanding, our needs. For faith is not mere wish, it is not a dream, it is not running from reality. It comes by a probing of ourselves and our innermost meanings.

This is the beginning of one of the great adventures of life.

It is a demanding mission. We may falter and fall back and retreat. We may surrender to the limitation of things known and seen. Or we may reach beyond the stars.

[5]Romans XI:6.
[6]Mark IX:20-29.

It is a sphere where only the individual can go.

It is the exploration of the Kingdom of God of which Jesus spoke.

It is where faith is found.

Appendix A

MAJOR SPIRITUAL HEALINGS DESCRIBED OR REFERRED TO IN THE BIBLE

OLD TESTAMENT

Abimelech and his wife and female slaves healed by the Lord at Gerar: *Genesis XX:17*.

God heals Miriam's leprosy after prayer by Moses at Hazeroth: *Numbers XII:10-15*.

The widow's son raised by Elijah at Zarephath: *I Kings XVII: 17-24*.

The son of the Shunammite woman is raised by Elisha at Shunem: *II Kings IV:32-37*.

Healing of Naaman of leprosy by washing seven times in River Jordan as commanded by Elisha: *II Kings V:10-14*.

Resurrection of dead man on Elisha's bones in Syria: *II Kings XIII:21*.

Healing of Hezekiah by prayer to God: *II Kings XX:1-11*.

NEW TESTAMENT

Healing of the nobleman's son at Capernaum in Galilee by Jesus: *John IV:46-53*.

Jesus heals all manner of sickness and disease among the people in Galilee: *Matthew IV:23*.

Healings by Jesus of divers diseases and torments and those possessed with devils, of lunatics and those with palsy, by Jesus, from Galilee, Syria, Decapolis, Jerusalem, Judea and from beyond the Jordan: *Matthew IV:24-25, Mark III:10, Luke IV:40, Luke VI:17-19*.

Healing of the leper by Jesus after He came down from the mountain, when leper declares, "Lord, If thou wilt, thou canst make me clean": *Matthew VIII:2-4, Mark I:40-42, Luke V:12-15*.

Healing the centurion's palsied servant by Jesus at Capernaum: *Matthew VIII:5-13, Luke VII:1-10*.

Healing of the demoniac by Jesus in the synagogue at Capernaum: *Mark I:23-27, Luke IV:33-35*.

Healing of Peter's mother-in-law, who was ill of a fever at Capernaum when Jesus touches her hand: *Matthew VIII:14-15, Mark I:30-31, Luke IV:38-39*.

Healing of the sick in Capernaum by Jesus: *Matthew VIII:16, Mark I:34*.

Raising of the widow's son by Jesus at Naim: *Luke VII:12-15*.

Healing of Mary called Magdalene by Jesus: *Luke VIII:2*.

Gergesenes demoniac healing by Jesus: *Matthew VIII:28-33, Mark V:1-13, Luke VIII:27-36*.

Healing of man sick with palsy by Jesus: *Matthew IX:2-7, Mark II:3-12, Luke V:18-25*.

Healing daughter of Jairus by Jesus after Jairus believes her dead: *Matthew IX:18, Mark V:22 and 35-43, Luke VIII:49-56*.

Healing the woman with the issue of blood by Jesus: *Matthew IX:20-22, Mark V:25-34, Luke VIII:43-48*.

Jesus, in his own country, can do no mighty work, but lays His hands upon a few sick folk, and heals them: *Mark VI:5*.

Healing of the two blind men when Jesus touches their eyes: *Matthew IX:27-30*.

Healing of a dumb man possessed of demons by Jesus: *Matthew IX:32-33*.

Sabbath healing of the man with a withered hand by Jesus in the synagogue: *Matthew XII:10-13, Mark III:1-5, Luke VI:6-10*.

Healing of a blind and dumb demoniac by Jesus so that he both sees and speaks: *Matthew XII:22, Luke XI:14*.

Jesus, moved with compassion for the multitude, heals their sick: *Matthew XIV:14, Luke IX:11*.

Healing of the possessed daughter of Syrophenician woman by Jesus in coastal region of Tyre and Sidon: *Matthew XV:22-28, Mark VII:24-30*.

Deaf man named Ephphatha with impediment in his speech healed by Jesus in the region of Decapolis: *Mark VII:31-35*.

Healing of a blind man by Jesus at Bethsaida: *Mark VIII:22-26*.

Jesus on mountain near Galilee heals the lame, blind, maimed and dumb as multitudes come unto him: *Matthew XV:30*.

Curing of the demoniac child by Jesus after the disciples had not been able to cure the boy: *Matthew XVII:14-18, Mark IX:17-27, Luke IX:38-42.*

Jesus heals great multitudes along coasts of Judea beyond Jordan: *Matthew XIX:2.*

Curing two blind men—one man possibly the blind Bartimaeus, son of Timaeus—at or near Jericho by Jesus: *Matthew XX:30-34, Mark X:46-52, Luke XVIII:35-43.*

Healing of the people throughout the towns by the disciples: *Luke IX:6.*

Healing in the synagogue by Jesus through laying on of hands of the woman who was bent over for eighteen years: *Luke XIII:11-13.*

Healing the man with dropsy by Jesus in the home of a ruler of the Pharisees: *Luke XIV:1-4.*

Cure of the ten lepers by Jesus in the region between Samaria and Galilee: *Luke XVII:11-19.*

Healing of a man ill for thirty-eight years by Jesus at Bethesda: *John V:1-15.*

Healing with clay and spittle of the man born blind by Jesus: *John IX:11.*

Raising of Lazarus of Bethany by Jesus: *John XI:1-44.*

Cure of the blind and the lame in the temple at Jerusalem by Jesus: *Matthew XXI:14.*

The ear of Malchus, servant of the high priest, healed by Jesus: *Luke XXII:50-51.*

The lame man at the Beautiful Temple gate cured by Peter and John: *Acts III:2-11.*

Healings of the people by Peter and the apostles: *Acts V:12-16.*

Paul's sight restored through Ananias in Damascus: *Acts IX:10-18.*

Aeneas cured of palsy by Peter at Lydda: *Acts IX:32-35.*

Dorcas raised to life by Peter at Joppa: *Acts IX:36-41.*

Healing by Peter of a man crippled from birth at Lystra: *Acts XIV:8-10.*

Paul at Philippi cures the maid with a spirit of divination: *Acts XVI: 16-18.*

Many miracles of healing performed by Paul at Ephesus through handkerchiefs and aprons that had touched him: *Acts XIX:11-12.*

Paul at Troas raises to life Eutychus: *Acts XX:9-12.*

The father of island chief Publius and others cured by Paul on barbarous island called Melita: *Acts XXVIII:7-10.*

Appendix B

THE RITUAL OF THE LAYING ON OF HANDS[1]

O Saviour of the world, who by Thy Cross and precious Blood hast redeemed us, Save us and help us, we humbly beseech Thee, O Lord.

Here shall be read the 91st Psalm (or a part of the same).

The Psalm shall close with the Gloria: Glory be to the Father, and to the Son: and to the Holy Ghost, etc.

Then shall follow The Lord's Prayer. "Our Father, Who art in heaven, etc."

Minister: O Lord, save Thy servant:

Response: Who putteth his trust in Thee.

Minister: Send him help from Thy holy place:

Response: And evermore mightily defend him.

Minister: Help us, O God of our salvation:

Response: And for the glory of Thy Name, deliver us, and be merciful unto us, for Thy Name's sake.

Minister: Lord, hear our prayer:

Response: And let our cry come unto Thee.

Minister: Let us pray.

O BLESSED REDEEMER, relieve, we beseech Thee, by Thy indwelling power, the distress of this Thy servant; release him from sin, and drive away all pain of soul and body, that being restored to soundness of health, he may offer Thee praise and thanksgiving; who livest and reignest with the Father and the Holy Ghost, one God, world without end. Amen.

Minister: I LAY MY HANDS upon thee, In the Name of the Father, and of the Son, and of the Holy Ghost; beseeching the

[1] From the Manual of Christian Healing, handbook of The Order of St. Luke The Physician, edited and arranged by its founder, Dr. John Gayner Banks.

mercy of our Lord Jesus Christ, that all thy pain and sickness being put to flight, the blessing of health may be restored unto thee. Amen.

(Alternative form)

Then an Intercessor, or some friend present, shall say:
God give a blessing to this work; and grant that this sick Person, on whom thou dost lay thy hands, may recover, through Jesus Christ our Lord.

(Silent Prayer)
Then the Minister, standing by the sick Person, shall lay both his hands upon the head of the same, saying the words:
IN THE NAME of God Most High, may release from thy pain be given thee, and thy health be restored according to His Will shown in Christ Jesus.

IN THE NAME of Jesus Christ, the Prince of Life, may new life quicken thy mortal body.

IN THE NAME of The Holy Spirit, mayest thou receive inward health, and the peace which passeth all understanding.

And the God of all Peace Himself sanctify you wholly; and may your whole spirit and soul and body be preserved entire, without blame, at the coming of our Lord Jesus Christ. Amen.

Let us pray. (Silent Prayer)

Minister: The Voice of joy and health is in the dwellings of the righteous.

Response: The right hand of the Lord bringeth mighty things to pass.

O ALMIGHTY LORD, and everlasting God, vouchsafe, we beseech Thee, to direct, sanctify and govern, both our hearts and bodies, in the ways of Thy laws, and in the works of Thy commandments; that through Thy most mighty protection, both here and ever, we may be preserved in body and soul; through our Lord and Saviour, Jesus Christ. Amen.

The Blessing—Unto God's gracious mercy and protection we commit thee. The Lord bless thee and keep thee. The Lord make His face to shine upon thee, and be gracious unto thee. The Lord lift up His countenance upon thee, and give thee peace, both now and evermore. **Amen.**

APPENDIX C

FIGURES AND PERCENTAGES OF CROSS-SECTION SURVEY BY NATIONAL COUNCIL OF CHURCHES ON SPIRITUAL HEALING CHURCHES IN UNITED STATES [1]

AREAS	Number Issued	Replies	Percentage replying	Unqualified "yes"	Qualified "yes"	Total "yes"	Percentage of those replying	Unqualified "no"	Qualified "no"	Total "no"	Percentage of those replying	Replies without "yes" or "no" answer
Atlanta	30	18	60	4	1	5	27.7	10	3	13	72.3	
Atlanta [2]	30	(No returns)										
Boston	40	27	67.5	7		7	26	15	5	20	74	
Chicago I [3]	40	11	25.5	2		2		9		9		
Chicago II	24	16	66.6	3	6	9		6	1	7		
Dallas	30	12	40	5		5	41.6	6	1	7	58.4	
Denver	40	23	57.5	10		10	43.4	8	5	13	56.6	
Duluth	30	16	53.3	3		3	18.7	11	2	13	81.3	
Durham	15	6	40	2	1	3	50	3		3	50	
Florida	40	18	45	6	1	7	39	10	1	11	61	
Houston [4]	40	(No returns)										
Los Angeles	40	16	40	5		5	31.3	7	4	11	68.7	
Madison	30	22	73.3	4		4	18.1	12	3	15	81.9	3
Minneapolis	30	17	56.6	2	1	3	17.6	12	2	14	82.4	
Montana	40	27	67.5	13		13	48.1	12	2	14	51.9	

Nashville	30	15	50	2	2	4	26.6	11		11	73.4	
New York	40	25	62.5	9	1	10	40	13	2	15	60	
Philadelphia	40	18	45	7	1	8	50	9	1	10	50	
Portland	30	18	60	9	1	10	55.5	5	2	7	38.8	1
Rural I [3]	40	22	55	4	1	5	22.5	16		16	72.7	1
St. Paul	40	22	55	14		14	63.6	5	3	8	36.4	
San Francisco	40	17	42.5	4		4	23.5	8	5	13	76.5	
Tacoma	50	23	46	4		4	17.4	17	2	19	82.6	
Toledo I [3]	50	9	18	4		4	44.4	5		5	55.6	
Toledo II	30	18	60	5	1	6	33.3	11	1	12	66.6	
Washington, D. C.	30	15	50	7	1	8	53.3	5	1	6	46.7	1
Rural II	23	23	100	3		3	13	20		20	87	
Utah	40	3	7.5	3		3	100					
Miscellaneous [5]		3		1		1		2		2		
Total	982	460	46.8	142	18	160	34.7	248	46	294	63.9	6

1 Adapted from the report of Professor Charles E. Braden (see Chapter 9).

2 Two sets of questionnaires were issued in Atlanta but no replies were available from the second set.

3 Two sets of questionnaires were issued in Chicago, Toledo and the rural area covered.

4 Replies from the questionnaires issued in Houston were not available.

5 These apparently were questionnaires returned by persons who had not been issued them originally but had obtained them from some other person who did not wish to complete a questionnaire.

Appendix D

SOME OF THE CHURCHES AND SHRINES WHICH HAVE SERVICES OR NOVENAS ASSOCIATED WITH HEALING

(This is the first list of its kind, covering all religious groups, ever compiled. It is obviously incomplete. The author would welcome any additional information which could be included in future editions of this book.)

PLACE	CHURCH	DENOMINATION
Auriesville, N.Y.	Shrine of the North American Martyrs	Roman Catholic[1]
Baltimore, Md.	Grace and St. Peter's Church	Episcopal
	Boundary Methodist Church	Methodist
	Mt. Washington Methodist Church	Methodist
Boston, Mass.	First Church of Christ, Scientist, Mother Church of Christian Science	Christian Science[2]
	Emmanuel Church	Episcopal

[1] It is impossible to list the thousands of Roman Catholic churches which have novenas under this or any other invocation, although Roman Catholic shrines and churches listed do have novenas.

[2] This church and all Christian Science churches, found in communities throughout the world, are devoted to Christian healing and teaching. Information can be obtained at any Christian Science church or reading room.

Bridgeport, Conn.	St. George's Church	Episcopal
Chicago, Ill.	Basilica of Our Lady of Sorrows, National Shrine of the Sorrowful Mother Novena	Roman Catholic
	Church of Universal Truth	Religious Science
	First Divine Science Church	Religious Science
	St. Dominic's Church—shrine to St. Peregrine (called the cancer Saint)	Roman Catholic
Cincinnati, Ohio	Universalist Church and City Temple	Federated
Coldwater, Mich.	St. Mark's Episcopal Church	Episcopal
Columbus, Ohio	United Christian Truth Center	
Denver, Colo.	Epiphany Episcopal Church	Episcopal
	First Church of Religious Science	Religious Science
	Our Lady of Lourdes (novena)	Roman Catholic
	Our Lady of Mt. Carmel (novena)	Roman Catholic
Dundee, Ill.	Dundee Methodist Church	Methodist
Elmhurst, Ill.	First Methodist Church	Methodist
Elmhurst, N.Y.	Congregation of Jewish Science	Jewish

Hartford, Wis.	Church of Mary, Help of Christians (Miracle Hill)	Roman Catholic
Iowa City, Iowa	First Methodist Church	Methodist
Kewanna, Indiana	Methodist Church	Methodist
Lee's Summit, Mo.	Unity School of Christianity	Unity[3]
Mamaroneck, N.Y.	Mamaroneck Methodist Church	Methodist
Montreal, Canada	St. Joseph's Oratory	Roman Catholic
New York City, N.Y.	Broadway Temple Methodist Church	Methodist
	Calvary Episcopal Church	Episcopal
	Church of the Healing Christ	Divine Science
	Church of the Heavenly Rest	Episcopal
	Church of the Truth	Religious Science
	Church of the Holy Cross (novena). This novena is that of the Miraculous Medal	Roman Catholic
	Church of St. Jean Baptiste (Relic of St. Anne)	Roman Catholic
	Congregation of Jewish Science	Jewish
	Fifth Avenue Presbyterian Church	Presbyterian

[3] All Unity centers conduct healing services. A complete list can be obtained from the United headquarters at Lee's Summit.

	The First Church of Religious Science	Religious Science
	Marble Collegiate Church	Dutch Reformed
	Mother Cabrini Chapel, Mother Cabrini High School	Roman Catholic
Norfolk, Va.	World Literacy Prayer Group-Ghent-Methodist Church	Methodist
Old Bethpage, N.Y.	Synagogue of Jewish Science	Jewish
Philadelphia, Pa.	St. Stephen's Church	Episcopal
Pittsburgh, Pa.	Ascension Church	Episcopal
	Calvary Church	Episcopal
	Good Shepherd Church	Episcopal
	North Presbyterian Church	Presbyterian
	St. Peter's Episcopal	Episcopal
	St. Peter's Evangelical and Reformed Church	Evangelical and Reformed[4]
Raleigh, N.C.	Christ Church	Episcopal
Soddy, Tenn.	Tennessee Mountain Rural Mission	Episcopal
South Bend, Ind.	Congregational Church	Congregational Christian[4]

[4]The Evangelical and Reformed Church and the Congregational Church recently effected a union and now are known as the United Church of Christ.

Washington, D.C.	Augustana Lutheran Church	Lutheran
	Ascension and St. Agnes Church	Episcopal
	Emmanuel (Anacostia) Church	Episcopal
	Church of the Healing Christ	Divine Science
	New Thought Center	New Thought
	First Congregational Church of Washington	Congregational Christian[4]
West Palm Beach, Fla.	Holy Trinity Church	Episcopal
	Church of the Holy Spirit	Episcopal

Readers in Great Britain may write to the National Federation of Spiritual Healers, 33 East Road, Goodmayes, Essex, for the addresses of healers in their locality.

Appendix E

BIBLIOGRAPHY

(Asterisk denotes pamphlet or booklet)

"A.A."* Alcoholics Anonymous Publishing, Inc. 1951.

*A.A. For the Woman.** New York: Alcoholics Anonymous Publishing, Inc., 1951.

Adler, Alfred, *Understanding Human Nature*, trans. W. Beran Wolfe. Garden City, New York: Garden City Publishing Company, Inc., 1927.

The Al-Anon Family Groups, *A Guide for The Families of Problem Drinkers*. New York: Al-Anon Family Group Headquarters, Inc., 1955.

Alcoholics Anonymous. New York: Alcoholics Anonymous Publishing, Inc., 1955.

Aradi, Zsolt, *The Book of Miracles*. New York: Farrar, Strauss and Cudahy, 1956.

Armstrong, William A., *Miracle Hill*. Milwaukee: Cramer, Aikens & Cramer, 1889.

Atkins, Gaius Glenn, *Modern Religions, Cults and Movements*. New York, Chicago: Fleming H. Revell, 1923.

Barker, Raymond Charles, *Spirit, Soul and Body*.* New York: Raymond Charles Barker, 1955.

————, *Treat Yourself to Life*. New York: Dodd, Mead & Company, 1956.

Barth, Karl, *Prayer*. Philadelphia: The Westminster Press, 1952.

Beard, Rebecca, *Everyman's Goal*. Wells, Vt.: Merrybrook Press, 1951.

————, *Everyman's Search*. Wells, Vt.: Merrybrook Press, 1950.

Berkeley, George, *A New Theory of Vision*. London, Toronto: J. M. Dent & Sons, Ltd.; New York: E. P. Dutton & Co., 1910.

Berry, Gerald L., *Religions of The World*. New York: Barnes & Noble, Inc., 1947.

Bernard, Henry, C.S.C., *What's What About Brother André*.* Montreal: Fides, n.d.

———, *What's What About Devotion to St. Joseph*.* Montreal: Fides, n.d.

Bill, "W.", *A.A. Tradition—How It Developed*.* New York: Alcoholics Anonymous Publishing, Inc., 1955.

———, *Alcoholism the Illness*.* New York: Alcoholics Anonymous Publishing, Inc., 1955.

Blanton, Smiley, M.D., *Love or Perish*. New York: Simon and Schuster, 1956.

Blessings From The Unity Household.* Lee's Summit, Mo.: Unity School of Christianity, n.d.

Blundell, Mrs. Francis, *Little Pilgrims To Our Lady of Lourdes*. New York: P. J. Kenedy & Sons, 1916.

Boggs, Wade H., Jr., *Faith Healing and The Christian Faith*. Richmond, Va.: John Knox Press, 1956.

Bristol, Claude M., *The Magic of Believing*. New York: Prentice-Hall, Inc., 1948.

Brother André and His Work on Mount Royal.* Montreal: Fides, 1955.

Burton, Katherine, *Brother André of Mount Royal*.* Notre Dame, Ind.: Ave Maria Press, 1952.

Carrel, Alexis, M.D., *Man, The Unknown*. New York, London: Harper and Brothers, 1935.

———, *Prayer Is Power*.* Cincinnati, Ohio: The Forward Movement Publications, n.d.

———, *Reflections on Life*. New York: Hawthorn Books, 1953.

A Catechism of Christian Doctrine, A Text for Secondary Schools and Colleges, No. 3. Paterson, N.J.: St. Anthony Guild Press, 1949.

Church Directory of the Sorrowful Mother Novena.* Chicago, Illinois: Novena National Shrine, May 1955.

Clark, Glenn, *The Divine Plan*.* Saint Paul, Minn.: Macalester Park Publishing Co., 1953.

Cliffe, Albert E., *Let Go And Let God*. Englewood Cliffs, N.J.: Prentice-Hall, Inc., 1951.

Cranston, Ruth, *The Miracle of Lourdes*. New York: McGraw-Hill, 1955.

Daniel-Rops, Henri, *Jesus and His Times*, trans. Ruby Miller. New York: E. P. Dutton & Co. Inc., 1954.

Dawley, Powel Mills, *Chapters in Church History,* (The Church's Teaching: Volume Two). Greenwich, Conn.: Seabury Press, 1952.

Dawson, George Gordon, *Healing: Pagan and Christian.* London: Society for Promoting Christian Knowledge, 1935.

Day, Albert Edward, *An Autobiography of Prayer.* New York: Harper & Brothers, 1952.

————, *Discipline and Discovery.* Baltimore, Md.: Disciplined Order of Christ, 1947.

Demarest, Donald & Coley Taylor, eds., *The Dark Virgin, The Book of Our Lady of Guadalupe.* New York: Coley Taylor, Inc., 1956.

de Saint-Pierre, Michel, *Bernadette and Lourdes,* trans. Edward Fitzgerald. Garden City, New York: Image Books, 1955.

*Divine Healing and Cooperation Between Doctors and Clergy.** London: British Medical Association, 1956.

Drake, Durant, *Invitation to Philosophy.* Boston: Houghton Mifflin Company, 1933.

Draper, Maurice L., *What Is Christ's Church?** Independence, Mo.: Herald Publishing House, n.d.

Dunbar, Flanders, *Mind and Body, Psychosomatic Medicine.* New York: Random House, 1947.

Dwyer, Walter W., *Spiritual Healing in the United States and Great Britain.** New York: Saphrograph Co., March, 1955.

Eddy, Mary Baker, *Retrospection and Introspection.* Boston: Published by The Trustees under the Will of Mary Baker G. Eddy, 1891, 1892.

————, *Rudimental Divine Science, No and Yes.* Boston: Published by The Trustees under the Will of Mary Baker G. Eddy, 1891, 1908.

————, *Science and Health with Key to the Scriptures.* Boston: Published by The Trustees under the Will of Mary Baker G. Eddy, 1875, 1903.

————, *Unity of Good and Two Sermons.* Boston: Published by The Trustees under the Will of Mary Baker G. Eddy, 1887, 1891, 1908.

Editors of Guideposts, *What Prayer Can Do.* New York: Doubleday and Company, 1953.

Edwards, Harry, *The Truth About Spiritual Healing.* London: Spiritualist Press, 1956.

Emerson, Ralph Waldo, *Essays* (First and Second Series). Boston, New York: Houghton Mifflin Company, 1865 and 1876.

Fellowship of St. Luke.* San Diego, California. St. Luke's Press, n.d.

Ferris, Theodore Parker, *The Story of Jesus*. New York: Oxford Press, 1953.

Fillmore, Charles, *Jesus Christ Heals*.* Lee's Summit, Mo.: Unity School of Christianity, 1952.

————, *A Six-Day Healing Practice*. Lee's Summit, Mo.: Unity School of Christianity, 1955.

Fillmore, Myrtle, *God Is My Health*.* Lee's Summit, Mo.: Unity School of Christianity, n.d.

Flower, B. O. *Christian Science as A Religious Belief and A Therapeutic Agent*. Boston: Twentieth Century Company, 1909.

Fox, Emmet, *The Yoga of Love*.* n.p., 1933.

Frazer, Sir James George, *The Golden Bough*. New York: The Macmillan Company, 1940.

Freeman, James Dillet, *The Story of Unity*.* Lee's Summit, Mo.: Unity School of Christianity, 1954.

Fremantle, Anne, *The Age of Belief*. New York: The New American Library of World Literature, Inc., 1955.

Gatlin, Dana, *The Great Helper*.* Lee's Summit, Mo.: Unity School of Christianity, n.d.

Germain, Walter M., *The Magic Power of Your Mind*. New York: Hawthorn Books, Inc., 1956.

Goldston, Iago, M.D., *Ministry and Medicine in Human Relations*. New York: International Universities Press, Inc., 1955.

Good St. Anne, Her Power and Dignity.* Clyde, Mo.: Benedictine Convent of Perpetual Adoration, n.d.

Gregory of Tours, *Selections from the Minor Works,* trans. William C. McDermott. Philadelphia: University of Pennsylvania Press, 1949.

Le Guide Du Pèlegrin.* Ste. Anne de Beaupré, Quebec: Basilique Sainte Anne, n.d.

Hamilton, Mary, *Incubation, or The Cure of Disease in Pagan Temples and Christian Churches*. London: Simpskin, Marshall, Hamilton, Kent & Co., 1906.

Harrison, R. K., *Health Begins In the Soul*.* Cincinnati, Ohio: Forward Movement Publications, n.d.

Hatch, Alden and Seamus Walshe, *Crown of Glory*. New York: Hawthorn Books, Inc., 1957.

Hertz, Joseph H., Dr., *The Authorized Daily Prayer Book*. New York: Bloch Publishing Company, 1948.

Heuss, John, *Our Christian Vocation.** Greenwich, Conn.: The Seabury Press, 1954.

History of Holy Hill.* Hubertus, Wisconsin: Discalced Carmelite Fathers, 1939.

Hocking, William Ernest, *Types of Philosophy.* New York: Charles Scribner's Sons, 1929.

Hoyt, Ethel P. S., *Spirit, A Study In the Relation of Religion to Health.* New York: E. P. Dutton & Company, 1921, 1928.

Hulbert, Jesse Lyman, D.D., *Hulbert's Story of the Bible.* Philadelphia, Toronto: The John C. Winston Company, 1952.

Hutschnecker, Arnold A., M.D., *The Will To Live.* Garden City, New York: Permabooks, 1954.

Ikin, A. Graham, *New Concepts of Healing.* New York: Association Press, 1956.

In Him Who Strengthens Me,* New York: Mother Cabrini High School, n.d.

James, William, *The Varieties of Religious Experience.* New York: The Modern Library, 1902.

————, *The Will To Believe.* London, New York, Toronto: Longmans, Green and Co., 1931.

Jayne, Walter Addison, *The Healing Gods of Ancient Civilizations.* New Haven: Yale University Press, 1925.

Kemp, Charles F., *Physicians of the Soul.* New York: Macmillan Co., 1947.

Kew, Clifton E. & Clinton J., *You Can Be Healed.* New York: Prentice-Hall, 1953.

Keyes, Frances Parkinson, *The Grace of Guadalupe.* New York: Julian Messner, Inc., 1941.

Lefebvre, Eugène, C. Sc. R., *Land of Miracles,** *Sainte Anne de Beaupré.* Ste. Anne de Beaupré, Quebec: St. Alphonsus Bookshop, 1951.

LeBec, E., Dr., *Medical Proof of the Miraculous,* trans. Dom. H. E. Izard. New York: P. J. Kenedy and Sons, 1923.

Levy, Rabbi Clifton Harby, *The Helpful Manual.* New York: The Center of Jewish Science, n.d.

————, *Judaism Applied to Life.* New York City: Jewish Science Advance Publishing Co., 1925.

Lewis, J. Louis, *The Mystery of Christian Healing.* Cincinnati, Ohio: Forward Movement Publications, n.d.

Lichtenstein, Morris, *Jewish Science and Health.* New York: Jewish Science Publishing Company, 1922.

Lichtenstein, Tehilla, *What To Tell Your Friends About Jewish*

*Science.** New York: Society of Jewish Science, 1951.

MacMillan, William J., *The Reluctant Healer*. New York: Thomas Y. Crowell Company, 1952.

Madden, Father Richard, O.D.C., *Men in Sandals*. Dublin: Clonmore & Reynolds, Ltd., 1956.

*Manual of Christian Healing.** Edited and arranged by Dr. John Gayner Banks. n.p., 1955.

Mars, Gerhardt, *The Interpretation of Life*. New York: D. Appleton and Company, 1908.

Millard, Joseph, *Edgar Cayce*. New York: Fawcett Publications, Inc., 1956.

Miller, DeWitt, *Reincarnation—the Whole Startling Story*. New York: Bantam Books, 1956.

*New Horizons of The Mind.** Parapsychology Foundation, Inc., New York, New York, n.d.

*Novena Prayers and Sketch of the Life of Saint Peregrine.** Compiled by Rev. John G. Bosco, O.S.M. Park Ridge, Ill.: Graphic House, 1954.

Novena Service, *Shrine of the Healing Presence.** Denver, Col.: Epiphany Episcopal Church.

O'Reilly, Right Rev. Bernard, *The Good Saint Anne and Her Shrine in the Church of Saint Jean Baptiste.** New York: Blessed Sacrament Fathers, n.d.

Overstreet, H. A., *The Enduring Quest*. New York: W. W. Norton & Company, Inc., 1931.

Palmer, Clara, *You Can Be Healed*. Lee's Summit, Mo.: Unity School of Christianity, 1953.

Paulsen, Friedrich, *Introduction to Philosophy*, trans. Frank Thilly. New York: Henry Holt and Company, 1895, 1930.

Peale, Norman Vincent, *The Power of Positive Thinking*. Englewood Cliffs, N.J.: Prentice-Hall, Inc., 1952.

———, *Stay Alive All Your Life*. Englewood Cliffs, N.J.: Prentice-Hall, Inc., 1957.

Powell, Lyman P., *Mary Baker Eddy*. New York: The Macmillan Company, 1930.

*The Order For The Ministration To The Sick,** Prayer Book Studies III. New York: The Church Pension Fund, 1951.

Price, The Rev. Alfred W., *A Meditation on Health.** Philadelphia, Pa.: n.p., n.d.

———, Healing—*The Gift of God.** Philadelphia, Pa.: n.p., n.d.

———, *Religion and Health.** Philadelphia, Pa., 1943.

———, *Spiritual Aids for Healing the Sick.** n.p., n.d.

Rhine, J. B., *New Frontiers of the Mind*. New York, Toronto: Farrar & Rinehart, 1937.

Roberts, Oral, *Best Sermons and Stories*. Tulsa, Oklahoma: Oral Roberts, 1956.

————, *Deliverance from Fear and from Sickness*. Tulsa, Oklahoma: Oral Roberts, 1954.

————, *If You Need Healing, Do These Things*. Tulsa, Oklahoma: Healing Waters, Inc., 1954.

————, *Life Story*. Garden City, New York: Country Life Press, 1952.

————, *The Fourth Man and Other Famous Sermons*. Tulsa, Oklahoma: Healing Waters, Inc., 1953.

————, and G. H. Montgomery, *God's Formula for Success and Prosperity*. Tulsa, Oklahoma: Oral Roberts, 1956.

Rodford, Edwin & Mona, *Encyclopaedia of Superstitions*. New York: Philosophical Library, 1949.

Roguet, A.M.O.P., *The Sacraments: Signs of Life*, trans. Carisbrooke Dominicans. London: Blackfriars Publications, 1954.

*Saint Frances Xavier Cabrini,** trans. The Missionary Sisters of The Sacred Heart. New York: Mother Cabrini High School, 1938.

Schobert, Theodosia DeWitt, *Divine Remedies*. Lee's Summit, Mo.: Unity School of Christianity, 1952.

Sharkey, Don, *After Bernadette*. Milwaukee, Wisconsin: Bruce Publishing Company, 1945.

Sokoloff, Boris, *The Achievement of Happiness*. New York: Simon and Schuster, 1935.

————, *Jealousy*. New York: Howell Soskin, 1947.

Sorokin, Pitirim A., The Ways and Power of Love. Boston: The Beacon Press, 1954.

Southard, Dr. C. O., *Truth Ideas of An M.D.** Lee's Summit, Mo.: Unity School of Christianity, 1954.

Stern, Karl, *The Third Revolution*. New York: Harcourt Brace and Company, 1954.

————, *The Pillar of Fire*. New York: Harcourt, Brace and Company, 1951.

The Third Legacy Manual of A.A. World Service. New York: Alcoholics Anonymous Publishing, Inc., 1955.

Turner, Elizabeth Sand, *What Unity Teaches.** Lee's Summit, Mo.: Unity School of Christianity, n.d.

Twelve Steps and Twelve Traditions. Alcoholics Anonymous Publishing Inc., 1952, 1953.

The Unity Treasure Chest, compiled by Lowell Fillmore. New York: Hawthorn Books, 1956.

Van Pelt, Dr. S. J., *Hypnotism and The Power Within.* New York: Fawcett Publications, 1956.

*A Visit to Saint Joseph's Oratory.** Montreal: Fides, 1955.

Ward, C. M., *What Are They Saying About Divine Healing?** Springfield, Mass.: Assemblies of God, 1956.

————, *What The Bible Says About Public Divine Healing Services.** Springfield, Mass.: Assemblies of God, 1955.

Werfel, Franz, *The Song of Bernadette,* trans. Ludwig Lewisohn. New York: Viking Press, 1942.

West, Georgiana Tree, *Healing Power Almighty,** New York City: Unity Center of Practical Christianity, 1955.

————, *Miracle Working Prayer.** New York City: Unity Center of Practical Christianity, 1951.

Wilson, Ernest C., *The Great Physician.* Lee's Summit, Mo.: Unity School of Christianity, 1953.

Weatherhead, Leslie D., *Psychology, Religion and Healing.* New York, Nashville: Abingdon Press, 1951.

White, Andrew D., *A History of the Warfare of Science with Theology in Christendom.* New York: George Braziller, 1955.

Wilbur, Sibyl, *The Life of Mary Baker Eddy.* Boston, Mass.: The Christian Science Publishing Society, 1907.

Wise, Carroll A., *Psychiatry and The Bible.* New York: Harper and Brothers, 1956.

————, *Religion in Illness and Health.* New York & London: Harper and Brothers, 1942.

Worrall, Ambrose Alexander, *Essay On Prayer.** Baltimore, Md.: A. Hoen & Co., 1952.

————, *Meditation and Contemplation.** Talk given at New Life Clinic. Baltimore, Md.: n.p., 1956.

————, *The Gift of Healing.** Baltimore, Md.: n.p., 1955.

Worrall, Olga, *How To Start A Healing Service.* Chicago, Ill.: Inner Creations, 1957.

*Young People and A.A.** New York: Alcoholics Anonymous Publishing, Inc., 1953.

Index

ROBERT H. SCHULLER

INSPIRES YOU!

Millions of people have learned the way to success in business, interpersonal relations, and every other aspect of life by following Robert H. Schuller's inspiring messages. You too can take charge by applying his principles to your own life!

__MOVE AHEAD WITH POSSIBILITY THINKING	0-515-08984-2/$3.95
__PEACE OF MIND THROUGH POSSIBILITY THINKING	0-515-08985-0/$3.50
__SELF-LOVE	0-515-08986-9/$3.95
__SELF-ESTEEM	0-515-08912-5/$3.95
__LIVING POWERFULLY ONE DAY AT A TIME	0-515-08443-3/$3.95
__LIVING POSITIVELY ONE DAY AT A TIME	0-515-09608-3/$4.50

For Visa , MasterCard and American Express orders ($10 minimum) call: 1-800-631-8571

FOR MAIL ORDERS: CHECK BOOK(S). FILL OUT COUPON. SEND TO:

BERKLEY PUBLISHING GROUP
390 Murray Hill Pkwy., Dept. B
East Rutherford, NJ 07073

NAME_____

ADDRESS _____

CITY_____

STATE_____ZIP_____

PLEASE ALLOW 6 WEEKS FOR DELIVERY.
PRICES ARE SUBJECT TO CHANGE WITHOUT NOTICE.

POSTAGE AND HANDLING:
$1.00 for one book, 25¢ for each additional. Do not exceed $3.50.

BOOK TOTAL	$ ____
POSTAGE & HANDLING	$ ____
APPLICABLE SALES TAX (CA, NJ, NY, PA)	$ ____
TOTAL AMOUNT DUE	$ ____

PAYABLE IN US FUNDS.
(No cash orders accepted.)

267

STORIES OF ENCOURAGEMENT AND FAITH

__ASHES TO GOLD Patti Roberts

0-515-08976-1/$3.50
The heartbreaking true story of Patti Roberts' life with the son of
Oral Roberts—and how she rebuilt her life and restored her faith
after their "perfect" marriage failed.

__THE CROSS AND THE SWITCHBLADE
David Wilkerson

0-515-09025-5/$3.50
New York's most desperate ghettos had little hope—until a young
country preacher arrived, and began preaching a message of
renewal, miracles, and God's love.

__ALL THINGS ARE POSSIBLE THROUGH
PRAYER Charles L. Allen

0-515-08808-0/$3.95
A practical guide to effective prayer that shows how you can
change your life through faith.

For Visa, MasterCard and American Express
orders ($10 minimum) call: 1-800-631-8571

Check book(s). Fill out coupon. Send to:
BERKLEY PUBLISHING GROUP
390 Murray Hill Pkwy., Dept. B
East Rutherford, NJ 07073

NAME_____

ADDRESS_____

CITY_____

STATE_____ ZIP_____

PLEASE ALLOW 6 WEEKS FOR DELIVERY.
PRICES ARE SUBJECT TO CHANGE
WITHOUT NOTICE.

POSTAGE AND HANDLING:
$1.00 for one book, 25¢ for each ad-
ditional. Do not exceed $3.50.

BOOK TOTAL $ _____

POSTAGE & HANDLING $ _____

APPLICABLE SALES TAX $ _____
(CA, NJ, NY, PA)

TOTAL AMOUNT DUE $ _____

PAYABLE IN US FUNDS.
(No cash orders accepted.)